Machine Learning Security with Azure

Best practices for assessing, securing, and monitoring
Azure Machine Learning workloads

Georgia Kalyva

BIRMINGHAM—MUMBAI

Machine Learning Security with Azure

Group Product Manager: Niranjan Naikwadi
Publishing Product Manager: Tejashwini R
Book Project Manager: Kirti Pisat
Senior Editor: Tiksha Abhimanyu Lad
Copy Editor: Safis Editing
Project Coordinator: Shambhavi Mishra
Proofreader: Safis Editing
Indexer: Hemangini Bari
Production Designer: Ponraj Dhandapani
DevRel Marketing Coordinator: Vinishka Kalra

First published: December 2023

Production reference: 1291123

Published by Packt Publishing Ltd.
Grosvenor House
11 St Paul's Square
Birmingham
B3 1RB, UK.

ISBN 978-1-80512-048-3

www.packtpub.com

To my mother, Maria, and my father, Michael, for their sacrifices and their unwavering love and care.
To my partner, George, for being my inspiration and support through every challenge.

– Georgia Kalyva

Foreword

I have known and collaborated with Georgia Kalyva for 15 years, starting from her involvement in the technology communities, when she was a university student. Georgia showcased an amazing set of skills during her work as a developer combined with a truly magnificent way of delivering technical presentations in a great number of events. She led many initiatives and also proved herself by winning the Microsoft Imagine Cup national title as a college freshman.

Her improvement in not only in her technical skills but also in her presentations and public relations made her a person of reference, initially in the Greek IT market and later on the global community. During her professional years, she managed to get to a managerial position quickly, and her involvement with new technologies made her the go-to person. She had no problem jumping into issues and projects that were out of her comfort zone; thus she managed to get experience in infrastructure, architecture and cybersecurity. Her passion for Artificial Intelligence motivated her to create an amazing blog, to share her knowledge with other people, to speak about Artificial Intelligence in numerous tech events and thus to become a Microsoft MVP in Artificial Intelligence. She continued by becoming a Microsoft Technical Trainer and she also started teaching about the technologies she is so passionate about.

By reading *Machine Learning Security with Azure*, you will learn best practices on implementing security in your machine learning implementation, and you will also get the experience and knowledge of the tools that can be used, which Georgia not only delivered them during her trainings, but also implemented in many production customer scenarios. After you complete Georgia's book, you will have a very good understanding of the core features, frameworks and solutions you can use to secure your machine learning environment. Georgia managed to point out all the features and options that Azure provides you, not only from a developer's perspective but also from a security engineer's side. *Machine Learning Security with Azure* will be your own security baseline walkthrough that you can follow to build secure machine learning solutions.

-George Kavvalakis

CEO and founder of Blacktrack Consulting, Azure Solutions and Security Architect, Top 100 Leaders in Global Healthcare awardee, Outstanding Leadership awardee x2, and Visionaries awardee.

Contributors

About the authors

Georgia Kalyva is a technical trainer at Microsoft. She is recognized as a Microsoft AI MVP, is a Microsoft Certified Trainer, and is an international speaker with more than 10 years of experience in Microsoft Cloud, AI, and developer technologies. Her career covers several areas, ranging from designing and implementing solutions to business and digital transformation. She holds a bachelor's degree in informatics from the University of Piraeus, a master's degree in business administration from the University of Derby, and multiple Microsoft certifications. Georgia's honors include several awards from international technology and business competitions and her journey to excellence stems from a growth mindset and a passion for technology.

I would like to express my sincere gratitude to everyone who has played a role in making this project a reality, especially George and my parents. Your support, encouragement, and contributions have been invaluable, and I couldn't have done it without you. Thank you!

About the reviewer

Amreth Chandrasehar is an engineering leader in cloud, AI/ML engineering, observability, and SRE. Over the last few years, Amreth has played a key role in cloud migration, generative AI, AIOps, observability, and ML adoption at various organizations. Amreth is also the co-creator of the Conducktor platform, serving T-Mobile's 100+ million customers, and a tech/customer advisory board member at various companies on observability. Amreth has also co-created and open sourced Kardio.io, a service health dashboard tool. Amreth has been invited to speak at several key conferences and has won several awards.

I would like to thank my wife, Ashwinya Mani, and my son, Athvik A, for their patience and support provided during my review of this book.

Table of Contents

3

Planning for Regulatory Compliance   55

Part 2: Securing Your Data

4

5

Part 3: Securing and Monitoring Your AI Environment

6

Managing and Securing Access   137

7

Managing and Securing Your Azure Machine Learning Workspace   165

8

Managing and Securing the MLOps Life Cycle   195

9

Logging, Monitoring, and Threat Detection   219

Part 4: Best Practices for Enterprise Security in Azure Machine Learning

10

Setting a Security Baseline for Your Azure Machine Learning Workloads   253

Preface

Machine learning (ML) and **artificial intelligence** (AI) have continued to evolve rapidly in the past two years, with significant advancements and applications in various fields. AI and ML systems often process vast amounts of sensitive data, including personal information. Ensuring the security of this data is crucial to protect against breaches that could lead to identity theft, financial fraud, and other privacy violations. On top of this, governments and regulatory bodies are implementing stricter data protection and privacy laws. Compliance with these regulations is essential for legal and ethical operations. This is why securing those systems has become more vital than ever. As cyber threats evolve, AI and ML systems must be designed to adapt and respond to new and emerging security challenges, ensuring long-term resilience and reliability.

If you are working with Azure Machine Learning, this book will help you assess the vulnerability of data, models, and environments and implement the best practices to manage, secure, and monitor Azure Machine Learning workloads throughout the ML life cycle.

This book starts by providing an overview of what you need to protect. This includes learning about the Zero Trust strategy, using the MITRE ATLAS framework to understand ML attacks, and learning how to work ethically and responsibly, by using multiple services to help you stay compliant with industry standards and regulations. If you have never worked with Azure Machine Learning, you will also find a project in the beginning to get started. From there on, the book focuses on data and all the best practices to protect it. That includes everything from developing a data management framework to data encryption, backup, and recovery best practices. Following that, the book focuses on any infrastructure that surrounds Azure Machine Learning workloads, starting from identity and access and then going through networking and compute best practices. Finally, it provides all the needed information to automate these processes and monitor the system to prevent, detect, and mitigate any issues, and provides an overview of threat modeling to help you re-assess and keep your Azure Machine Learning workloads secure.

By the end of this book, you will be able to implement the best practices to assess and secure your Azure Machine Learning assets throughout the ML life cycle.

Who this book is for

If you are interested in Azure Machine Learning and security, you will learn the basic components of Azure Machine Learning, the most common ML attacks, and how to work with Azure to develop and implement a strategy to secure Azure Machine Learning and any associated services. This book is written for the following:

Machine learning developers, administrators, and data scientists: Anyone who has an active role in an Azure Machine Learning project, or is planning to, and is looking to gain expertise in securing their machine learning assets.

IT administrators and DevOps or security engineers, who are required to secure and monitor Azure Machine Learning workloads on Azure. They will benefit from learning the basics of Azure Machine Learning along with the best practices outlined in this book, as the book includes all the information needed to develop a security strategy across multiple resources.

Basic Azure knowledge and experience in processing data, building, and deploying Azure Machine Learning models is advised.

What this book covers

Chapter 1, Assessing the Vulnerability of Your Algorithms, Models, and AI Environments, provides an overview of the ML life cycle and the Azure Machine Learning components and processes that go into working with ML in Azure. It will explain the Zero Trust model to develop an implementation and assessment strategy. This chapter will cover all the knowledge needed to follow the concepts and implementations outlined in the rest of the book.

Chapter 2, Understanding the Most Common Machine Learning Attacks, provides an overview of the MITRE ATLAS framework, which is adapted from the MITRE ATT&CK framework for ML and this chapter will explain the different stages of an attack and possible attacks on an AI/ML system.

Chapter 3, Planning for Regulatory Compliance, provides insight into how to develop ML models ethically and responsibly by using the six Responsible AI principles according to Microsoft and how to translate them into a responsible development strategy using Responsible AI tools. Finally, it wraps up with an overview of industry-recognized regulatory compliance standards for Azure Machine Learning and how to enforce them by using Azure services.

Chapter 4, Data Protection and Governance, provides an overview of all aspects of governing, storing, and securing data. That includes everything from developing a data management framework to data encryption, backup, and recovery practices.

Chapter 5, Data Privacy and Responsible AI Best Practices, provides best practices to recognize and protect sensitive information and privacy before and after model training. It explains how to interpret models, recognize bias, and mitigate it. Finally, it provides an introduction to federated learning and secure multi-party computation.

Chapter 6, Managing and Securing Access, provides an overview of the security aspects of Microsoft Entra ID, which is the identity management system for Azure Machine Learning. This includes an introduction to the principle of least privilege, the role-based access control, and other security features such as conditional access and privileged identity management.

Chapter 7, Managing and Securing Your Azure Machine Learning Workspace, provides the best practices for securing the Azure Machine Learning workspace and its associated services. It focuses on network isolation, compute, container registries, and container security.

Chapter 8, Managing and Securing the MLOps Life Cycle, provides an overview of MLOps best practices and the tools to implement them in Azure. It will explore **Infrastructure as Code (IaC)**, CI/CD pipelines, and event-driven workflows in Azure.

Chapter 9, Logging, Monitoring, and Threat Detection, provides implementation steps to enable logging and configuring alerts in Azure. It introduces Microsoft Defender for Cloud and Azure Sentinel to prevent, detect, and mitigate any security issues that arise.

Chapter 10, Setting a Security Baseline for your Azure Machine Learning Workloads, summarizes the best practices outlined in the book and provides more services to explore, which, although not directly related to Azure Machine Learning, can be leveraged for securing Azure resources. It wraps up by providing an overview of threat modeling and how to develop a strategy to always stay secure. Finally, it outlines our responsibilities to secure our resources compared to those of the cloud provider.

To get the most out of this book

To follow along with the examples in this book you will need an *active* Azure subscription. Knowledge about the following concepts will also be helpful in understanding the implementations presented in this book.

Basic Microsoft Azure knowledge:

- An understanding of core cloud concepts, such as what cloud computing is, the differences between **Infrastructure as a Service (IaaS)**, **Platform as a Service (PaaS)**, and **Software as a Service (SaaS)**, and the benefits of using Azure cloud services.

- Familiarity with the Azure Portal, which is the primary user interface for interacting with Azure services. This includes navigating the dashboard, creating and managing resources, and understanding the layout and tools available in the portal.

- Familiarity with basic commands in Azure **Command Line Interface (CLI)** and PowerShell for managing Azure resources.

Machine learning:

> An understanding of fundamental ML concepts, including supervised and unsupervised learning, along with basic algorithms such as linear regression, logistic regression, decision trees, and k-means clustering.

Programming Skills:

> Basic proficiency in a programming language commonly used in data science, such as Python or R, including familiarity with libraries such as Pandas, NumPy, Scikit-learn (for Python).

Basic understanding of cybersecurity:

> A basic understanding of cybersecurity involves grasping key concepts, practices, and strategies used to protect computer systems, networks, and data from cyber-attacks or unauthorized access.

If you are using the digital version of this book, we advise you to type the code yourself or access the code from the book's GitHub repository (a link is available in the next section). Doing so will help you avoid any potential errors related to the copying and pasting of code.

Download the example code files

You can download the example code files for this book from GitHub at `https://github.com/PacktPublishing/Machine-Learning-Security-With-Azure`. If there's an update to the code, it will be updated in the GitHub repository.

We also have other code bundles from our rich catalog of books and videos available at `https://github.com/PacktPublishing/`. Check them out!

Conventions used

There are a number of text conventions used throughout this book.

`Code in text`: Indicates code words in text, database table names, folder names, filenames, file extensions, pathnames, dummy URLs, user input, and Twitter handles. Here is an example: "Especially with the `azureml` SDK v2, FL features are built in."

A block of code is set as follows:

```
import pandas as pd
data_path = 'mockdata.csv'
mockdata = pd.read_csv(data_path)
actualdata = mockdata[['age','diabetic']].groupby(['diabetic']).
mean().to_markdown()
print(actualdata)
```

Any command-line input or output is written as follows:

```
az ad sp show --id <clientId from previous result>
```

Bold: Indicates a new term, an important word, or words that you see onscreen. For instance, words in menus or dialog boxes appear in **bold**. Here is an example: "By clicking on a component, we can easily change the compute target from the **Pipeline interface** button by going to the **Run settings** option and choosing **Use other compute target**."

> **Tips or important notes**
> Appear like this.

Get in touch

Feedback from our readers is always welcome.

General feedback: If you have questions about any aspect of this book, email us at customercare@packtpub.com and mention the book title in the subject of your message.

Errata: Although we have taken every care to ensure the accuracy of our content, mistakes do happen. If you have found a mistake in this book, we would be grateful if you would report this to us. Please visit www.packtpub.com/support/errata and fill in the form.

Piracy: If you come across any illegal copies of our works in any form on the internet, we would be grateful if you would provide us with the location address or website name. Please contact us at copyright@packt.com with a link to the material.

If you are interested in becoming an author: If there is a topic that you have expertise in and you are interested in either writing or contributing to a book, please visit authors.packtpub.com.

Share Your Thoughts

Once you've read *Machine Learning Security with Azure*, we'd love to hear your thoughts! Scan the QR code below to go straight to the Amazon review page for this book and share your feedback.

https://packt.link/r/1-805-12048-4

Your review is important to us and the tech community and will help us make sure we're delivering excellent quality content.

Download a free PDF copy of this book

Thanks for purchasing this book!

Do you like to read on the go but are unable to carry your print books everywhere?

Is your eBook purchase not compatible with the device of your choice?

Don't worry, now with every Packt book you get a DRM-free PDF version of that book at no cost.

Read anywhere, any place, on any device. Search, copy, and paste code from your favorite technical books directly into your application.

The perks don't stop there, you can get exclusive access to discounts, newsletters, and great free content in your inbox daily

Follow these simple steps to get the benefits:

1. Scan the QR code or visit the link below

https://packt.link/free-ebook/9781805120483

2. Submit your proof of purchase
3. That's it! We'll send your free PDF and other benefits to your email directly

Part 1: Planning for Azure Machine Learning Security

This part is all about creating a plan to secure your resources. Security is organization-specific so you will get an overview of the Zero Trust security approach designed to secure any implementation of IT systems. You will learn to leverage the MITRE ATLAS knowledge base to understand ML attacks. Finally, you will also learn how to develop AI systems ethically and responsibly and how to use Azure services to ensure regulatory compliance.

This part has the following chapters:

- *Chapter 1, Assessing the Vulnerability of Your Algorithms, Models, and AI Environments*
- *Chapter 2, Understanding the Most Common Machine Learning Attacks*
- *Chapter 3, Planning for Regulatory Compliance*

Assessing the Vulnerability of Your Algorithms, Models, and AI Environments

Welcome to your machine learning security journey with Azure! Together, we will explore all the methods and techniques to secure our AI projects and set a security baseline for our services. Let us start with a quick introduction to the **machine learning** (**ML**) life cycle and the **Azure Machine Learning** components and processes that go into working with ML in Azure. We will cover the essential knowledge you need to follow the concepts and implementations outlined in the rest of the book.

The next step will be to go through an example scenario, which we will reference throughout this book as the basis for applying the concepts of securing your data, models, workspace, and applications that use the deployed models from Azure Machine Learning. You can follow the instructions to re-create this scenario in your Azure Machine Learning environment to familiarize yourself with the Azure Machine Learning components.

We will use the **Zero Trust** model to develop an implementation and assessment strategy. This model is a security strategy based on the principle of *Never trust, always verify*. This model applies to all levels of implementation, from identities, infrastructure, and networks, to apps, endpoints, and data. This strategy is the best approach when working with multiple services and environments because we can easily adapt it to the complexity of modern cloud and hybrid environments. Since developing a strategy heavily depends on the individual scenario and use case for each organization, in this book, we will explore multiple options and demonstrate implementations of several Zero Trust aspects. Specifically, we will learn about attacks in *Chapter 2*, data governance and protection in *Part 2* of the book, how to manage and secure access to the workspace and associated resources in *Part 3*, and in *Chapter 10*, we will gather all those best practices in an ML security baseline.

In this chapter, we are going to cover the following main topics:

- Reviewing the Azure Machine Learning life cycle
- Introducing an ML project
- Exploring the Zero Trust model
- Assessing the vulnerability of ML assets and apps

By the end of this chapter, you will be familiar with the basic principles and defense areas of the Zero Trust strategy. You can use this strategy to create a high-level vulnerability assessment of **artificial intelligence (AI)**/ML project components, applications, and related services hosted in Azure.

Technical requirements

Throughout this book, we will need a few things to apply the learnings and implementations. Each chapter will outline more details if needed, but the minimal resources we need are an **Azure subscription** and an Azure Machine Learning resource with its related services.

Azure subscription and resources

Throughout this book, we will reference the scenario presented in this section and other services and implementations in Azure. You will need an active Azure subscription and an Azure Machine Learning workspace to follow along or replicate the results.

If you don't have an Azure subscription, you can activate a free trial by following this link: `https://azure.microsoft.com/en-us/pricing/offers/ms-azr-0044p/`.

If you run the project suggested in this chapter from end to end, it should not cost more than $150–$200 as long as you delete all associated resources afterward and use the lowest pricing tier of all services. However, this estimation can vary by the region that you choose, which features you choose to implement, the size of the dataset, and for how long you plan to keep the resources deployed. The trial will provide you with a sufficient balance to try it out; however, I strongly recommend using the Azure pricing calculator and working with the cost management in your subscriptions to ensure keeping the costs at a minimum and deleting or stopping resources when you no longer use or need them.

> **Note**
>
> The Azure free trial provides you with credits to spend on Azure services. After they are used up, you can keep the account and use free Azure services. You need to add your credit card, but the service won't charge your card unless you explicitly change your subscription type. Azure uses a pay-as-you-go pricing model. To make sure you don't run out of credits faster than intended, visit the Azure pricing calculator at `https://azure.microsoft.com/en-us/pricing/calculator/`.

Azure Machine Learning

To use Azure Machine Learning, you need to create an Azure Machine Learning resource. The following screenshot shows the basic options for creating one:

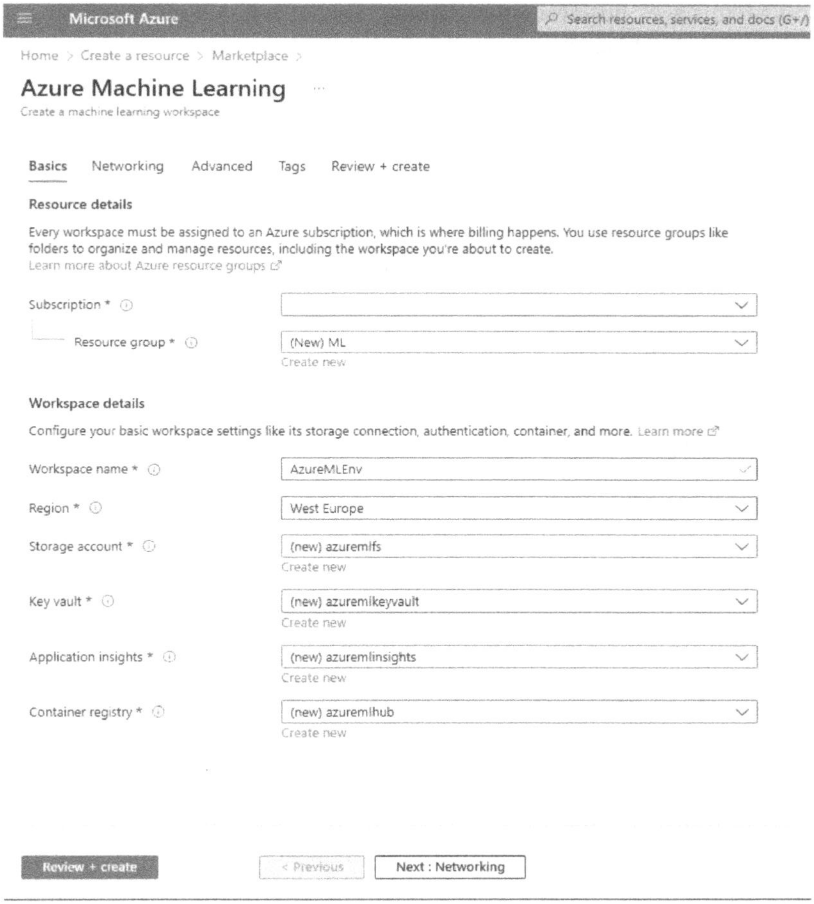

Figure 1.1 – Azure Machine Learning resource creation form

Reviewing the Azure Machine Learning life cycle

No matter what technology or framework we choose to work with to develop our ML project, there are four phases we go through. Each stage has one or more steps, depending on the individual scenario. The ML life cycle is significant because it clearly outlines every project step. Then, it is easy to break the project into tasks and assign them to the person responsible because, usually, more than one role is involved in an ML project.

Let us review all the stages before we connect them to the components of Azure Machine Learning.

ML life cycle

In ML, we identify four stages: business understanding, data operations, model training, and model deployment. As shown in the following figure, these stages are part of an iterative process:

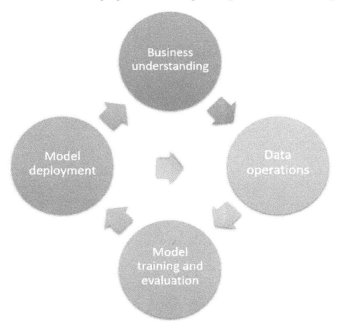

Figure 1.2 – ML life cycle

Let us go through each step of this iterative process and what it entails, starting with the business understanding stage and the gathering of the initial requirements.

Business understanding

Every project starts with a problem that needs to be solved. Business understanding (or problem understanding) is the first step in creating a plan that outlines what needs to be done. Ideally, we would like to have the requirements clearly detailed for us, but this is rarely the case. The first thing is to understand the project's goal and where it can bring real value to the business. Then, evaluate which processes can be automated using ML by narrowing down the problem to actionable tasks.

For example, let us examine the following scenario. Our client is a hospital administration looking to minimize costs by increasing doctor productivity and automating as much of their workload as possible. In an analysis of doctors' daily tasks, they found that they spend a lot of time looking through patient histories and analyzing their blood tests. By decreasing that time by 5%, the doctor could see more patients without working overtime. We can solve this problem by using supervised learning techniques, where an ML model could be trained to suggest illnesses by combining the patient's symptoms and blood test results. The doctor would still have to verify the results. However, shortening the analysis time would increase the doctor's productivity.

After narrowing down the requirements and clarifying the problem, the next step is to examine the data.

Data operations

ML is based on data. During this stage, we work with everything that has to do with data operations, from data collection to data processing. **Data gathering** or **data collection** is the part where the goal is to collect relevant data to the problem at hand. This data could come from various sources such as files, databases, APIs, or sensors. It is one of the most critical steps in the project because we identify the different data sources and collect and integrate the data. The quality and quantity of the data we gather will determine the efficiency and accuracy of the model's output.

Collected data can be messy and often not ready to be used by ML algorithms. Issues with the data include irrelevant data, noise, outliers, and missing data. This is where **data preparation** or **data wrangling** comes in. Any data irrelevant to our model should be filtered properly. When outliers are recognized, we usually eliminate them from the dataset. With missing data, the process is a little bit more complex. Once identified, the outliers should be evaluated and either removed or filled with default or calculated values. Finally, data might need to be encoded differently to be used by ML algorithms.

Model training and evaluation

An appropriate ML algorithm is selected and trained on the prepared data at this stage. The model is developed by completing multiple training iterations and the result is evaluated at the end of each iteration until a satisfactory performance level is achieved. During this stage, there might be a need to go back and work with the data again to ensure that data are relevant and that no unintended correlation might affect the results.

Model deployment

Once the results are satisfactory, the final step is deploying the model so that software engineers can integrate it into their applications and make predictions. Although it might seem like the end, this is far from it. Deployed models need to be monitored to ensure proper performance. Models can degrade over time, which would impact the accuracy of their predictions. In this case, we can retrain the model with an updated dataset to ensure this does not happen and the cycle starts over again. Changing the requirements or introducing a new business need might also cause us to retrain our model.

Now that we have a good understanding of the ML process, we can move on to the Azure Machine Learning service components that are part of each stage of the ML life cycle. Everything we need to develop Azure Machine Learning projects is part of or in some way related to the **Azure Machine Learning Studio** or workspace.

Azure Machine Learning

Azure Machine Learning is a cloud service for accelerating the ML project life cycle. It leverages the Azure infrastructure to connect to data and train, deploy, and monitor models. The service includes everything from connecting data from multiple data sources to working on developing the code and training, evaluating, and publishing models ready to be used by web applications.

The service is a complete environment for developing end-to-end ML projects. It allows collaboration for multiple roles, from data scientists to developers, security engineers, or IT (information technology) administrators. In this section, we will review how each component maps to each part of the ML project life cycle and the service capabilities.

Azure Machine Learning Studio

The Azure Machine Learning service creates several related Azure services required to use the service properly. First, you need an active Azure subscription. When you create the Azure Machine Learning resource, the following services are created alongside it: an **Azure Storage** account, an **Application Insights** resource, and **Azure Container Registry**.

An Azure Storage account serves as the filesystem. All imported files, notebooks, and so on are saved here. The Applications Insights resource can be used to monitor a deployed model and provide logs and insights when the deployed model does not work as expected. The Azure Container Registry is optional in creating the workspace, but you will probably need one if you plan to publish your models in the **Azure Container Instances** (**ACI**) service. The models can be published to different compute targets, including containers, and are created as **APIs** so any application can easily use the models and make predictions. Everything else is handled from the Azure Machine Learning Studio. Here, you can work with your data, create compute resources, train and deploy your models, manage user access, and much more.

The following screenshot shows the Azure Machine Learning Studio home page. On the left, you can find the Azure Machine Learning **Authoring**, **Assets**, **Compute**, and other resource management options:

Figure 1.3 – Azure Machine Learning Studio

Most of the work will happen in the workspace, whether that is data preparation and import, code development, or model training and inferencing. Let us see what features and assets we have available to work with.

Working with data

There are a few ways of working with data in Azure Machine Learning Studio. The first is working with data stored elsewhere by creating a **datastore**. A datastore is a reference to existing storage on Azure. That could be **Azure Blob Storage** or **Azure Data Lake**. If your data is not in Azure, you can still work with it in Azure Machine Learning. You can always upload your files as data assets into the workspace or add a reference to an external database. Then, you can use them in your project, share them with your colleagues, and keep the versioning to track changes and updates.

In the following screenshot, you can see some of the types of data assets you can import:

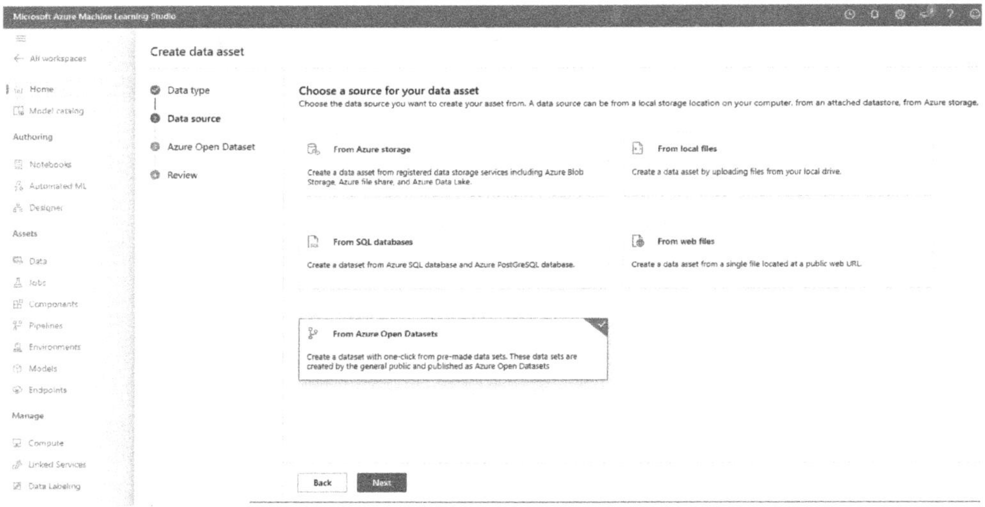

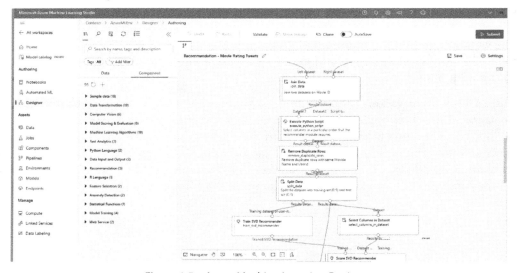

Figure 1.4 – Create data asset in Azure Machine Learning Studio

Azure Machine Learning Designer

You can use **Python** and **R** to develop your Azure Machine Learning project, but the service also provides a visual designer. You can use the designer for training and inference (production models that make predictions).

Refer to the following screenshot:

Figure 1.5 – Azure Machine Learning Designer

The designer has many out-of-the-box modules for multiple operations that you can drag and drop onto the canvas to create the training pipeline. That includes importing data, splitting datasets, SQL operations, algorithms, and model evaluation modules. If you need more, you can always use the custom script modules for Python or R and add your code as part of the pipeline. The benefit is that you can quickly go to an inference pipeline and convert it to a web service with just a few clicks.

Automated Machine Learning

The **Automated Machine Learning** (**Automated ML**) capability of Azure Machine Learning is a set of tools and techniques that automate the process of building ML models. It helps beginners or experienced data scientists by automatically selecting the best algorithm and hyperparameters for a given dataset and then training and validating the model. This process is done by applying various algorithms, such as decision trees, random forests, and deep neural networks, to the data and selecting the best-performing model. It also includes data features such as preprocessing, feature engineering, and model selection. It allows users to upload data into the Azure Machine Learning workspace and let the platform handle the rest of the ML process with minimal configuration. When the best model is selected from the list, it can be deployed to a **web service** ready to be consumed, as is the case with all models in the Azure Machine Learning workspace. Have a look at the following screenshot:

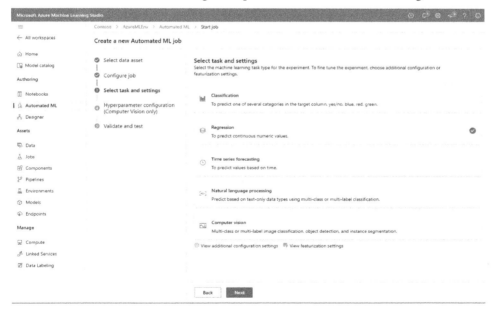

Figure 1.6 – Automated ML supported algorithms

Working with compute

When training or deploying models, computing power is required. Azure Machine Learning provides a scalable compute infrastructure for training and deployment based on Azure infrastructure. To train your experiments, you can use compute targets or compute clusters. A compute target is a dedicated virtual machine running your training jobs. If you need more power, you can create a cluster with multiple nodes to run workloads in parallel. You can also attach compute from virtual machines you are not using or from other ML services such as **Azure Databricks**. You can use ACI or **Azure Kubernetes Service (AKS)** clusters to deploy models.

Coding with Python or R

Besides the visual and automation tools, Azure Machine Learning supports **Jupyter Notebooks** for code development and collaboration. You can use the embedded notebook editor, **Visual Studio Code** with the Azure Machine Learning extension, or the Jupyter Notebook editor that you can launch from the running compute target during training. Refer to the following screenshot for this:

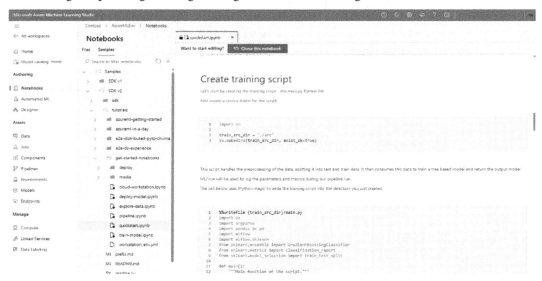

Figure 1.7 – Azure Machine Learning Studio notebook editor

Here, we can see the most fundamental components of Azure Machine Learning. The workspace is complete with multiple features and tools that can facilitate all stages of the ML life cycle and take an ML project from start to finish. In the following section, we will see how to use the features and tools outlined here to develop a sample ML project from development to production.

Introducing an ML project

If you want to follow along with the implementation examples in this book, here is an example project to get you started. If you are already an expert in Azure Machine Learning, feel free to skip this introduction. This section will help beginners with the service or those in other roles to understand the ML life cycle in action. We will create a sample project that demonstrates how to import a dataset into Azure Machine Learning, how to use the Automated ML feature to train multiple models with multiple parameters, and deploy the resulting model as an endpoint to be used for predictions. The Automated ML feature was chosen as it does not require extensive data science expertise.

Log in to the **Azure portal** (`https://portal.azure.com/`) and look for **Azure Machine Learning resource**. From **Overview**, click on **Studio web URL** or the **Launch Studio** button to access your workspace, as seen in the following figure:

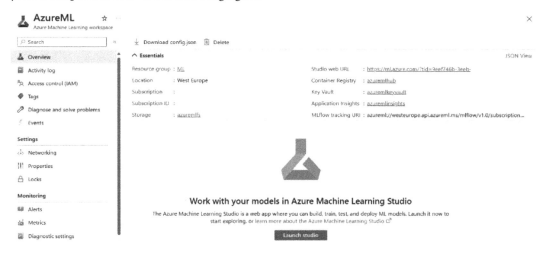

Figure 1.8 – Accessing your Azure Machine Learning workspace

Now you will find yourself on the home page of the workspace. From here on, you will find all the options in the left-hand menu outlined in the following sections.

Dataset

ML starts with data, so you will need to find a dataset to use to train a model to make predictions. There are a lot of open source datasets available for ML and you can download them for free – for example, from university repositories for learning or research purposes. Just make sure the source is reputable so that there is no malware or something similar with your download. For this example, we will use the regression task with Automated ML. If you want to follow along with the steps, you can use any dataset; just make sure you tailor the Automated ML options to match the dataset you choose. If you don't have a lot of experience and you want something close to the dataset used here, when you are looking for a dataset, pay attention to the task and data. If it can be used for regression and it contains a column with numerical data that your model will be trained to predict, any dataset will do. Automated ML does not support all types of ML tasks yet, so this is a good way to get started.

I am using a sample dataset that contains patient symptoms and a class column that notes whether the patient was diagnosed as diabetic. It will help to train a new model that predicts the probability if the patient will become diabetic or not based on symptoms.

If you have your dataset ready, all we have to do is go to the **Data** menu under **Assets** and create a new data asset. Here are the steps for it:

1.   First, we provide details for **Name**, **Description**, and set **Data type** as **Tabular**, as shown here:

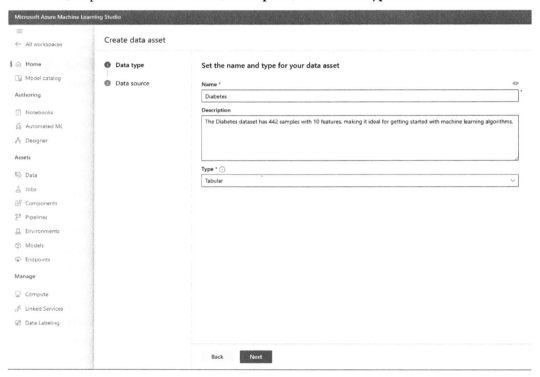

Figure 1.9 – Create data asset

2. In the next step in the wizard, choose the **From local files** option:

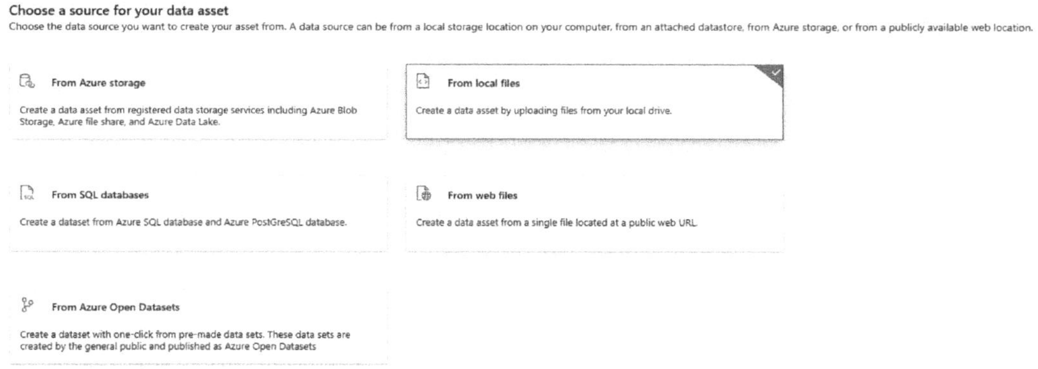

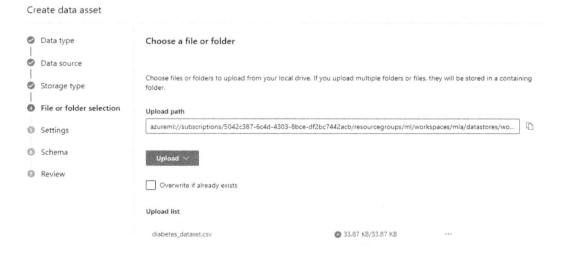

Figure 1.10 – Choosing the data source

3. Leave the default option in the **Storage type** screen and move on to upload the file in the **File or folder selection** screen:

Create data asset

Figure 1.11 – Uploading the file

4. Under **Settings**, choose the options as illustrated until **Data preview** shows the correct columns and data:

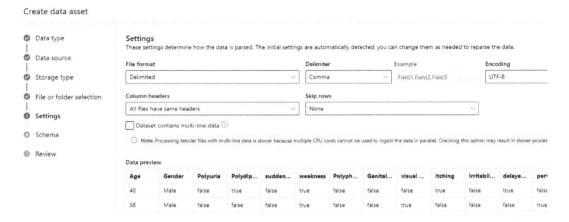

Figure 1.12 – Applying the settings

5. Under **Schema**, make sure the **Path** column is excluded from the dataset. You can also exclude any columns that you feel are not relevant to the prediction or change the **Data type** if it has been identified incorrectly:

Figure 1.13 – Choosing the columns and data type

Move on to the **Review** screen and create the dataset. Now you have a dataset available to use for your ML project! The next step is to start training a model.

Training the model

There are many ways to train our model. Here, we will use the Automated ML capability of Azure Machine Learning to run the model through multiple algorithms and parameters, let the service train, and suggest the best model based on performance. It is the fastest way to create all the components we need to demonstrate the security concepts we will talk about later in this book.

Let us begin:

1.   To get started, open the **Automated ML** menu under **Authoring**:

Figure 1.14 – Starting a new Automated ML job

2.   Select the dataset you created previously and move on to the next screen:

Figure 1.15 – Selecting the data asset

3. Give the job a name under **New experiment name** and fill in **Target column** to predict in your dataset. In this dataset, it is the **Y** column:

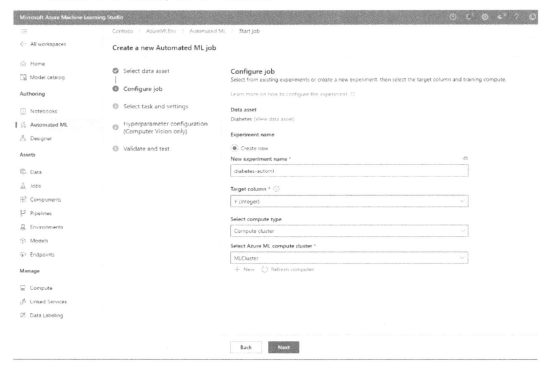

Figure 1.16 – Configure job settings

4. Select the **Compute cluster** option for the training compute and click on the **New** link to create a new cluster without leaving the wizard:

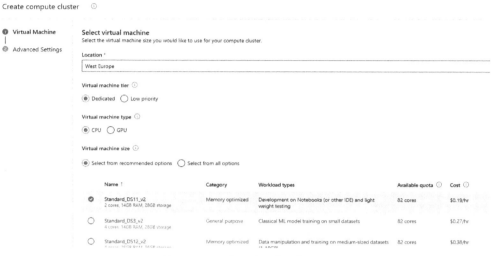

Figure 1.17 – Creating the cluster

5. Select the **Standard_DS11_v2** machine size and on the next screen, **Minimum number of nodes** as 0 and **Maximum number of nodes** as 2 should be fine:

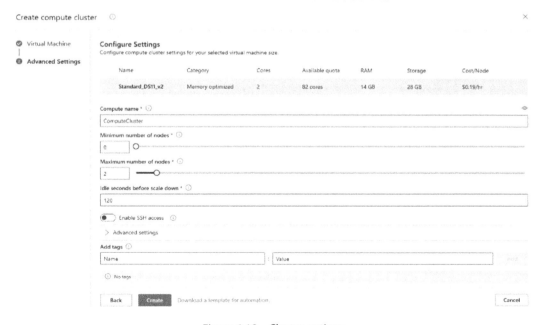

Figure 1.18 – Cluster options

6. Leave all other options to default, create the cluster, and when you get back to the Automated ML wizard, move on to the **Select task and settings** screen.

7. Since we want to predict a numeric value, we choose the **Regression** category of algorithms, as shown here. The service engine will run multiple regression algorithms that it deems to fit the data profile to generate multiple models:

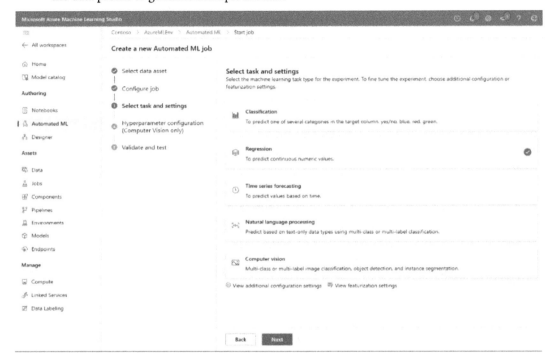

Figure 1.19 – Selecting the algorithm category and settings

8. In the **Additional configurations** settings, ensure you set **Training job time (hours)** to 1 hour under **Exit criterion**:

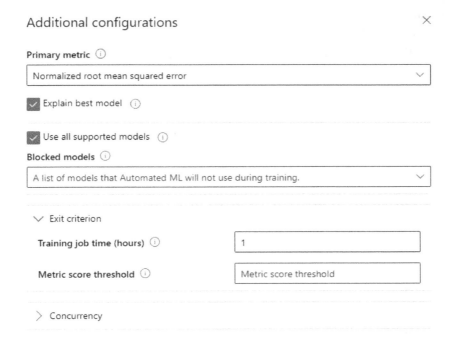

Figure 1.20 – Setting additional configuration settings

Leave all other options to default in the wizard and start the Automated ML job. Now, all you can do is wait until a performant model is found and the training stops or the maximum training time has been reached and the best model up to that point is automatically chosen. You can monitor the progress of the model's training under the new job created in the **Automated ML** menu.

Now that we have the model trained, we can deploy it.

Deploying the model

You can find the best-performing model under the **Models** menu as soon as the job is completed. Choose the one from the list that performs the most accurately based on the metrics, and it will be ready for deployment to the ACI as a web service.

Here are the steps to try this:

1. Choose the model from the list with the best score. You will recognize the best score as in the **Explained** column, it will also contain the feature explanation. You can also compare the scoring metric and it could be higher or lower, depending on the metric type:

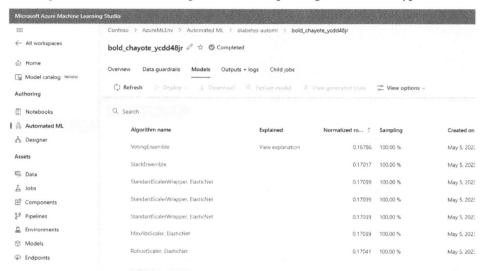

Figure 1.21 – List of trained models with different algorithms and parameters

2. Open the **Model** screen and click on the **Deploy** button. In the list, choose the **Web service** option, as shown here:

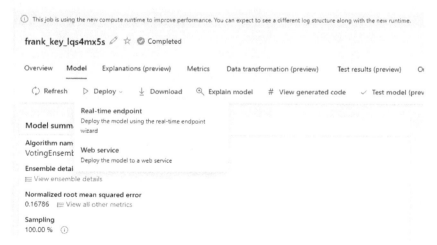

Figure 1.22 – Model deployment

3. For the deployment settings, add **Name**, choose **Azure Container Instance** as **Compute type**, and set the **Enable authentication** toggle button to true. This is depicted in the following screenshot:

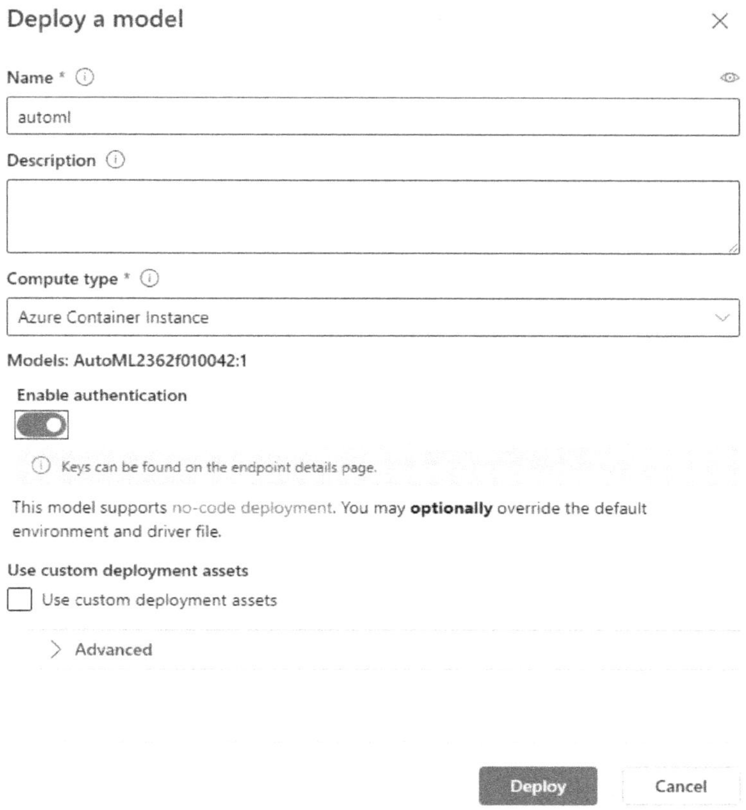

Figure 1.23 – Deployment settings

Wait for the deployment to finish and go to the **Endpoints** menu to integrate your model with an application and make predictions.

Making predictions using the deployed model

To use the deployed model for predictions, go to the **Endpoints** menu and find the endpoint deployment. Make sure **Deployment state** is **Healthy** and **Operation state** is **Succeeded**. If **Deployment state** is anything other than **Healthy** or **Failed**, it might need some more time to deploy. Refer to the following screenshot for the model:

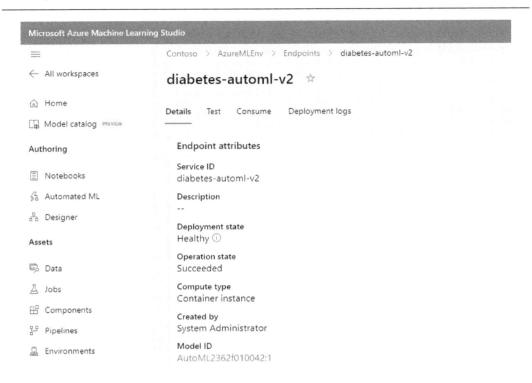

Figure 1.24 – Azure Machine Learning model endpoint for predictions

You can do a quick test of the service using the **Test** tab. Use the **Consume** tab to find the endpoint and authentication key to integrate the web service into your application for predictions.

If you have followed along with the previous steps, congratulations: you just trained and deployed a model using Azure Machine Learning. This is not over yet, though; we will use this sample project throughout this book to demonstrate the implementations to learn how to secure your own solution. But before we dive into the implementations, let us go through the strategies and techniques we are going to follow, starting with Zero Trust.

Exploring the Zero Trust model

The **Zero Trust** model is a security strategy based on the principle of *Never trust, always verify*. So, instead of assuming that our resources that are deployed behind a firewall are safe, the Zero Trust model assumes breach and every request needs to be verified as though it originates from an open network. The Zero Trust model is applied in cloud, on-premises, and hybrid environments. Implementing a Zero Trust security model can help organizations to reduce their overall attack surface, minimize the risk of data breaches, and improve their security posture by shifting from a perimeter-based security approach to a more comprehensive and adaptive security strategy.

Although Azure Machine Learning is a cloud service, the Zero Trust model still applies because a complete ML project spans across data, networks, infrastructure, and applications. We will go through an overview of the Zero Trust model. Then, we'll use this knowledge to apply it to assess the vulnerabilities in our workloads and reduce our attack surface using Azure's tools and services. We will start by familiarizing ourselves with the Zero Trust principles and defense areas.

Introducing the Zero Trust principles

The Zero Trust strategy is based on three principles – verify explicitly, use least-privilege access, and assume breach.

Let us understand each of these in the following sections.

Verify explicitly

The *Verify explicitly* principle requires that all users, devices, applications, and resources attempting to access the network must be thoroughly authenticated and authorized before being granted access.

In traditional security models, once a user or device is authenticated and granted access, they are generally trusted to some degree and allowed to move within the network without additional checks. However, in the Zero Trust model, every access request is treated as a potential threat. Access is only granted after a multi-level verification process.

This verification process includes multiple layers of authentication, such as verifying user credentials, device identity, and network location. User authentication might involve **multifactor authentication (MFA)** or other advanced authentication methods to confirm the user's identity. The verification process is not a one-time event but is ongoing and continuous. It includes checking for anomalies or changes in user behavior, device health, or other factors that may indicate a potential threat. If any changes or anomalies are detected, the system can initiate additional verification checks or even revoke access if necessary.

Use least-privilege access

The *Use-least privilege access* principle is a critical Zero Trust security model component. It states that users, devices, and applications should only be granted access to the minimum level of resources necessary to perform their job functions.

Users are often given broad access privileges to network resources and data, assuming they only access the resources required to perform their job duties. However, this approach increases the risk of data breaches and unauthorized access by allowing users to access resources they don't need, which attackers can exploit.

In contrast, the Zero Trust model takes a more granular approach to access control by limiting access based on the principle of least privilege. For example, a user in the marketing department may only need access to marketing-related files and not require access to the finance department's data or systems. Similarly, a contractor may need access to specific files or applications but not to the entire network.

Assume breach

The *Assume breach* principle assumes that a network has already been compromised and that attackers are present, or will be present, inside the network. This principle emphasizes the importance of early detection and response to mitigate the damage caused by a potential breach. We need to identify an attack as soon as it reaches our system by analyzing anomalies as soon as possible in every level of access.

Organizations typically focus on securing their network perimeters and preventing attackers from gaining access. However, with the increasing sophistication of cyberattacks, perimeter-based security is no longer sufficient to protect against modern threats. The Zero Trust model recognizes this and assumes that attackers will eventually penetrate the network through phishing attacks, malware, or other means.

Assuming a breach means that organizations must implement additional security controls to limit the damage caused by an attack, such as micro-segmentation, encryption, and network isolation. These controls help to prevent attackers from moving laterally across the network and accessing critical resources, even if they have gained access to one part of the network.

Explaining Zero Trust defense areas

The Zero Trust security model focuses on protecting network resources and data by implementing security controls across several defense areas or domains, such as the ones depicted in the following figure:

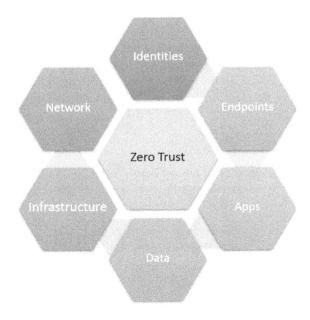

Figure 1.25 – Zero Trust defense areas

Let us understand each of these areas in the following sections.

Identities

One of the vital defense areas is **identities**, which involves securing user identities and ensuring that only authorized users can access network resources. Identity verification, least-privileged access, risk-based adaptive access, and continuous monitoring are all part of identity management and security. Identity verification involves verifying user identities before granting access to network resources. It includes multifactor authentication, passwordless authentication, and conditional access policies to ensure that only authorized users can access sensitive resources.

Let us explore some best practices:

- **Least privileged access** involves granting users the minimum access necessary to perform their job functions. It includes role-based access controls, dynamic access control, and privileged access management to limit user access to only what they need.
- **Risk-based adaptive access** involves using risk assessment tools to evaluate user behavior and determine the level of access they should have to network resources. It includes continuous authentication, real-time risk assessments, and contextual access policies to ensure that user access is appropriate and secure.
- **Continuous monitoring** involves monitoring user activity and detecting anomalies or suspicious behavior. It includes real-time alerts, behavioral analytics, and ML to identify potential security threats and take proactive measures to prevent them.

Endpoints

Another critical defense area is **endpoints**, which involves securing endpoints such as laptops, desktops, mobile devices, and servers. Microsoft's approach to securing endpoints in the Zero Trust model involves ensuring that endpoints are healthy and compliant with security policies before granting access to network resources. It includes device management tools, compliance policies, and device health checks to ensure that devices and endpoints are secure and up to date.

Apps

Another significant area is **applications**, which involves securing applications and ensuring that only authorized users and devices can access them. Applications must have a unique identity and should include authentication before granting access to network resources. This includes using certificates, tokens, and secure communication protocols to establish trust between applications and network resources.

Data

Data is a crucial component in ML and involves securing data and ensuring that only authorized users and devices can access it. Multiple methods of securing data include the following:

- **Data classification** and **labeling** involve classifying and labeling data according to its sensitivity level and implementing access controls based on the classification. Labeling can be automated or user-defined and should include monitoring the data usage to protect sensitive data.

- **Data protection** involves protecting data both in transit and at rest. This includes encryption, access controls, and monitoring data usage to prevent unauthorized access or leakage of sensitive data.

- **Governance**, **compliance**, and **regulatory requirements** mean ensuring that data is handled under appropriate governance, compliance, and regulatory requirements. This includes data retention policies, data breach notification policies, and compliance audits to ensure data is handled appropriately.

Infrastructure

Infrastructure is vital in securing compute that connects devices, host applications, and data. Infrastructure includes any physical or virtual devices.

Device security is about securing network devices such as switches, routers, and firewalls to prevent unauthorized access and ensure they are configured securely. It includes implementing device management tools, firmware, and software updates, and monitoring device activity to detect potential security threats.

Virtualization security involves securing virtualized environments such as virtual machines and containers to prevent unauthorized access and ensure they are configured securely. It includes implementing virtualization management tools, patching and updates, and monitoring virtualization activity to detect potential security threats.

The kind of cloud environment should also be considered, such as **infrastructure as a service (IaaS)**, **platform as a service (PaaS)**, and **software as a service (SaaS)**.

Network

Finally, **network** is a defense area that includes securing the network connections between devices, applications, and data. The methods to achieve this are network micro-segmentation and access control. We can implement this by dividing the network into smaller segments and restricting access between them. We can expand the safety of the network by implementing firewalls and monitoring network activity to detect potential security threats. This includes managing network traffic and log analysis to detect potential security threats and take proactive measures to prevent them.

Let us move on to see how we can apply the Zero Trust strategy to assess the security status of our ML workloads.

Assessing the vulnerability of ML assets and apps

Part of assessing the vulnerabilities of Azure Machine Learning assets involves identifying potential security risks and then implementing appropriate measures to mitigate them.

Here, we will go through Azure Machine Learning components and their possible vulnerabilities. The implementation of security measures will be explained in greater detail in the rest of the book. The assessment is based on the Zero Trust defense areas.

The first step is identifying all the assets associated with Azure Machine Learning, such as data, models, and algorithms. That does not mean the Azure Machine Learning Studio only. Several services associated with Azure Machine Learning need to be checked. Once you have identified the assets, you should assess their potential risks, including unauthorized access, data breaches, and misuse.

It is important to remember that everything in Azure operates on top of cloud infrastructure, so it is helpful to get familiar with any services that work with Azure Machine Learning and secure them. We will see in the next chapter how adversaries can leverage other systems to compromise ML projects. You might not need to use all of those systems, but if you are already using some of them it will help you assess what you need to secure.

Let us go through the Zero Trust model areas and identify each service used in each area that relates to Azure Machine Learning.

Identity management

Azure uses **Microsoft Entra ID** (previously **Azure Active Directory**) for user authentication, authorization, and **role-based access control** (**RBAC**) to manage permissions for Azure resources. The Microsoft Entra ID service is an identity management solution that provides all controls to manage and safeguard access, including capabilities such as conditional access policies, identity protection, and privileged identity management.

First, identify each user or group and what access they need to use the services. Azure Machine Learning supports multiple roles such as data scientists, developers, IT administrators, and security engineers. Note what is the least access required for each user or group. Then, we can investigate what Microsoft Entra ID features you need to enable to mitigate access risks…

Data and data sources

Data is the biggest component of any ML project. In Azure Machine Learning, you can add data from many sources. Identify all those sources and enable their security capabilities. Suppose you are importing data into the Azure Machine Learning workspace. In that case, it is stored in the Azure Storage account connected to your workspace. You must limit access to the workspace and secure the Storage account as well. If you are using a data source in Azure such as Azure SQL Server or CosmosDB, these services have multiple safeguards to limit access and protect from data breaches and data loss.

Ensure that all data is also encrypted at rest and in transit. Azure provides several encryption options, such as **Azure Key Vault** and **Azure Storage Service Encryption**. **Azure SQL Database** also supports encryption on multiple levels. Another aspect to consider is backup. Ensure you have multiple options to recover your data in case of a security incident.

Infrastructure

Azure Machine Learning works on top of Azure Infrastructure. There are four types of compute in Azure Machine Learning for training or inference, compute targets, compute clusters, AKS, and attached compute. For the deployment of models, you can use Azure Container Registry and Azure Containers. For attached compute, you can leverage virtual machines, the Azure Databricks service, and more. All those services have their own security features. Make sure you have all services or infrastructure up to date with the latest updates. Azure also provides several services for the automation of updates and monitoring.

Network and endpoints

Virtual networks are part of the Azure infrastructure services. Every service in Azure is deployed in the Microsoft network, or as it is sometimes called, the **Azure Backbone** network. Suppose your solution does not necessarily need to be available from the public internet, but only from your company office to and from Azure services, for example. In that case, multiple ways exist to keep traffic over the Azure Backbone network by encrypting and routing the network traffic between your virtual network and your on-premises infrastructure security. Identify the necessary endpoints and restrict network access to your workspace if possible. You can use anything from virtual networks, private links, and VPNs such as the Azure VPN Gateway, to even a private connection using ExpressRoute. If you already have firewalls, such as the Azure Firewall, or any networking, you can leverage those services to protect your ML projects. That could also apply to other services working with Azure Machine Learning, such as databases.

Monitoring and maintenance

Part of the assessment is also setting a plan for monitoring and maintenance in place. Now that you have identified all the services you have and the features you need to enable, you need to answer the following questions:

- Who is responsible for each security issue that arises?
- What notifications should be enabled and for which services?
- Who is responsible for responding to each notification?

Azure has multiple views and support tools for monitoring and alerting.

AI/ML applications

There are two types of applications that you can leverage to work with Azure Machine Learning. These AI applications use the Azure Machine Learning endpoints for predictions or are applications that trigger Azure Machine Learning pipelines for model training or batch predictions.

For both types of applications, using secure coding practices will ensure that the application is not vulnerable to outside attacks. Techniques include input validation, error handling, and authentication mechanisms. Use secure protocols such as HTTPS or SSL/TLS to encrypt data in transit. To assess the vulnerability of an application, you can use security testing tools and techniques, such as penetration testing and vulnerability scanning, to identify and remediate potential security weaknesses. The application should also not expose or hardcode sensitive information such as connection strings or endpoint access keys. You can mitigate this using another Azure service, the Azure Key Vault. Applications that trigger pipelines that also need access data should be continuously assessed and monitored as changes in the dataset can affect the model's accuracy.

As you might have already realized, security is not clear-cut, but rather an iterative process. We need to assess, implement, monitor, and repeat to make sure our workloads are secure in Azure. We might need to leverage multiple security features and recommendations and tailor the Zero Trust strategy to our needs.

Summary

In this chapter, we covered the basics of the ML life cycle and how it applies to Azure Machine Learning components. This knowledge is essential not only for data scientists and developers, but also for IT administrators and security engineers who are required to know the basics of ML development to ensure they can secure and monitor all associated services. For anyone wanting to get more familiar with Azure Machine Learning, you can always come back and recreate the scenario presented at the beginning as a base to follow along with the implementations and methods presented in the rest of the book's chapters.

Together, we learned what the Zero Trust strategy is and how it can be applied to Azure Machine Learning components and their associated services to assess what needs to be secured. We will need Zero Trust, as the principles and the defense areas outlined in this strategy are the same ones we will use in our security implementations in the following chapters. Now that you know how to create an initial assessment of the services you need to protect, in the next chapter, we will learn more about the methods and techniques that adversaries use to compromise our system. By learning those methods, you will be better equipped to protect your ML workloads and associated systems.

Further reading

- *Introduction to Azure Machine Learning*: https://learn.microsoft.com/en-us/training/modules/intro-to-azure-ml

- *Introduction to the Azure Machine Learning SDK*: https://learn.microsoft.com/en-us/training/modules/intro-to-azure-machine-learning-service/

- *Train an ML model with Azure Machine Learning*: https://learn.microsoft.com/en-us/training/modules/train-local-model-with-azure-mls/

- *Introduction to Zero Trust and best practice frameworks*: https://learn.microsoft.com/en-us/training/modules/introduction-zero-trust-best-practice-frameworks/

2

Understanding the Most Common Machine Learning Attacks

When getting started with securing your projects, there are many things you can use to learn security techniques quickly. The best is the **MITRE ATT&CK framework**. As a globally recognized knowledge base, it contains valuable information about a range of attack techniques that an adversary can use to attack a system and their mitigations. In this chapter, we are going to explore the **MITRE ATLAS** framework. It is adapted from the MITRE ATT&CK framework for **machine learning (ML)**.

The goal of this chapter is to familiarize ourselves with the different stages of an attack and possible attacks on our system. This is essential because, with that knowledge, we can understand how an adversary thinks and how to protect our system. As there are multiple stages of an attack, you will understand why applying the Zero Trust strategy (covered in the previous chapter) is the most effective way to protect the system. We must never forget that this is an ongoing process as new vulnerabilities and exploits are released daily.

We must always keep up to date with all new information, and the MITRE ATLAS framework will help us do exactly that. Finally, after exploring the MITRE ATLAS Matrix, we will cover the Azure services related to Azure Machine Learning and those most commonly affected by attacks.

In this chapter, we're going to cover the following topics:

- Introducing the MITRE ATLAS Matrix
- Understanding ML and AI attacks
- Exploring Azure services involved in ML attacks

By the end of this chapter, you will have a better understanding of ML attacks and their possible mitigations for ML.

Introducing the MITRE ATLAS Matrix

The MITRE ATT&CK framework is a globally recognized knowledge base and framework. Security professionals use it to understand and organize adversary behaviors in cyber threat environments. **ATT&CK®** (or ATTACK) stands for **Adversarial Tactics, Techniques, and Common Knowledge**. It is essentially a catalog of **tactics, techniques, and procedures (TTPs)** that adversaries use during different stages of a cyberattack. It covers many threat vectors, including initial access, execution, persistence, privilege escalation, defense evasion, credential access, discovery, lateral movement, collection, exfiltration, and impact.

The MITRE ATT&CK framework organizes these techniques into a matrix that classifies them based on the various stages of an attack and the platforms on which they are applicable (for example, Windows, macOS, or Linux). Each technique in the matrix is described in detail in the MITRE knowledge base, including information on how adversaries typically employ it and the potential defensive measures we can take to detect and prevent it.

> **Note**
>
> If this is the first time you are hearing about the MITRE ATT&CK® framework, you can explore the MITRE ATT&CK® knowledge base at `https://attack.mitre.org/`.
>
> (© 2023 The MITRE Corporation. This work is reproduced and distributed with the permission of The MITRE Corporation.)

The framework has become a widely adopted industry standard. It is used by security teams, security solutions vendors, and organizations to enhance their threat intelligence, develop more effective security controls, and improve incident response capabilities. It enables organizations to align their defenses with real-world adversary behaviors, helping them proactively detect, respond to, and mitigate cyber threats.

Although very comprehensive, the MITRE ATT&CK framework might not cover all possible known attack methods, but it provides a great starting point. We are going to follow the MITRE ATLAS™ framework. **ATLAS** stands for **Adversarial Threat Landscape for Artificial-Intelligence Systems**, and it is a knowledge base of adversary tactics based on the MITRE ATT&CK framework and contains techniques that apply to ML and **artificial intelligence (AI)** systems. The ATLAS Matrix shows the progression of an attack in stages and the techniques associated with each stage. The stages can be seen in the following figure:

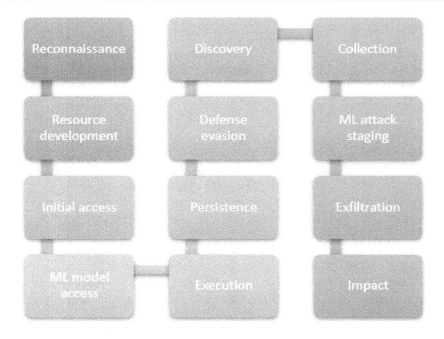

Figure 2.1 – The MITRE ATLAS stages

While the stages appear in sequence and they usually start from reconnaissance and end with impact techniques, not all stages and techniques will be used in an attack. It depends on the adversary's goal and the system architecture.

Let us understand each stage in the sections ahead.

Reconnaissance

Reconnaissance refers to the initial phase of an attack where an adversary gathers information about the target ML system. The goal of reconnaissance is to gather intelligence that can be used to identify potential vulnerabilities, plan the attack, and increase the chances of success. Information can be anything from the ML technologies used or research information that can help the adversary obtain relevant ML artifacts and tailor attacks to the victim in the next stages of the attack.

Resource development

After the initial reconnaissance, the adversary is trying to discover resources they can use to support their endgame. This stage is called **resource development** and it is usually where the adversary purchases or steals resources to target ML artifacts, infrastructure, accounts, or capabilities that can be used later in the attack.

Initial access

In the **initial access** stage, the adversary attempts to access the ML system. That can be anything from networks to devices and platforms. If the adversary succeeds in this step, they can get an initial foothold in the system.

ML model access

After the adversary gains some form of access to the system, they will try to get further by gaining access to the ML model. The techniques used in the **ML model access** stage vary as the adversary can try to take advantage of many levels of access. They can target the database or technology that houses the data, or the endpoints used to train the ML model. The endpoint used for predictions or any other product or service that utilizes ML as part of its process is also vulnerable to attack.

Execution

In the **execution** stage, the adversary manages to run or embed malicious code or commands on a targeted system to achieve their objective. This tactic focuses on the actions taken by an adversary to execute their payloads or explore the network to steal more data or gain access to more systems. Remote access tools can be run here to run scripts and discover unpatched known vulnerabilities.

Persistence

In the **persistence** stage, the adversary tries to maintain whatever access they have gained in the previous steps. Techniques include but are not limited to elevating credentials, cutting off access to other users, and leaving behind modified data or models and backdoors so they can regain their access more easily if they are discovered.

Defense evasion

Of course, no adversary wants to be discovered before accomplishing their goals. **Defense evasion** techniques are used by the adversary to avoid detection. Evading detection is something that an adversary can accomplish by turning off security features or software such as malware detectors.

Discovery

The **discovery** stage is like reconnaissance but from the inside. The adversary is trying to work out your ML environment. They are trying to gain knowledge about the system and internal network to broaden their goals or get as much information as possible before launching an attack. In this stage, the adversary will learn what they can or cannot control and what else they need to do based on their objective. Here, native operating system tools are often used to collect the information needed.

Collection

In the **collection** stage, all investigation and information-gathering processes are finished. The adversary is trying to actively collect data or ML artifacts. Suppose their goal is simply to disrupt the service. In that case, the techniques in this stage will help them collect everything they need to extract from the system before making the service unusable. Extraction is part of the exfiltration stage.

ML attack staging

For ML, data extraction or service disruption might not be the only goal of the adversary. In AI projects, attacks targeting the ML model can be deployed. **ML attack staging** techniques include training proxy models, poisoning the target model, and crafting adversarial data to feed the target model. Some of them can even be performed offline, so it would be difficult to mitigate in some cases.

Exfiltration

The **exfiltration** stage would be where data or artifacts will be extracted. The adversary is trying to steal (exfiltrate) the ML artifacts or use the information for future operations. In this case, the most targeted sources are software repositories, container registries, model repositories, and object stores. This is a challenging process, as data needs to leave the network, creating traffic that can be detected.

Impact

The **impact** stage consists of techniques that disrupt or compromise the integrity of the system and possibly manipulate business processes. The adversary can target data and corrupt or destroy it. Even worse, data might be slightly changed; not enough to trigger suspicion in the system, but just enough to disrupt the services in a way that helps the adversary with their endgame or provides cover for a confidentiality breach.

As you can see, these stages form a logical path an adversary might take to attack your system. In reality, that might not be the case as the flow heavily depends on their goal. Let us see the techniques used in each stage and examples of how they might affect our systems.

Understanding ML and AI attacks

All the stages mentioned in the previous section use multiple techniques to achieve each goal. The adversary can use these techniques alone, sequentially, or combined. Some attacks can be repeated and used in various stages for different purposes. It all depends on the adversary's goal, which is why by applying Zero Trust principles and always verifying all levels of the system, we have a better chance of protecting our services or at least detecting an incident before it has time to do any extensive damage to the system.

Here, we will describe the most common AI and ML attacks per stage. We will also talk about attacks from the MITRE ATT&CK framework that, although not ML-specific, can be used to access systems that contain ML capabilities, among other things. Although we will outline the possible mitigations for each attack, we will go through the implementations in more detail in the following chapters.

Let us explore the attack techniques per stage.

Reconnaissance techniques

There are five reconnaissance techniques that aim to gather information about the system, as seen in the following figure:

Figure 2.2 – Reconnaissance techniques

Let us understand each of these techniques in the following sections.

Search for the victim's publicly available information

Suppose the organization uses open source model architectures that they have trained on additional proprietary data in production or that are in the research stage. In that case, they might publish system details with announcements or press releases. Although not technical, these might contain details about their model's development and can help craft more realistic proxy models. To mitigate this, limit sharing information about the company's systems, software stack, or frameworks used in developing systems when announcing deals or partnerships.

Search victim-owned websites and application repositories

Company websites may have a lot of information publicly available, including names of departments/divisions, physical locations, and data about key employees such as names, roles, and contact information. These sites may also have information that shows business operation details and relationships. The same goes for papers or technical blogs published by company employees. Employees are also vulnerable to social engineering attacks where the adversary poses as another employee to get company information. Ensure that you instruct employees not to share information about the projects they are working on—even with other employees if they are not working on the project—and anonymize the information they share on personal blogs or social media.

Finally, ML-enabled applications might be available in mobile stores such as Google Play, the iOS App Store, the macOS App Store, and the Microsoft Store. The adversary might attempt to scan and analyze the app for ML-related components or endpoints. Try to obfuscate the application code where possible and ensure you secure endpoints if information gets intercepted.

Search for publicly available adversarial vulnerability analysis

As soon as the technology is identified, the adversary will research common system, model, or algorithm vulnerabilities to see whether they can use existing research to stage their attack. Identified vulnerabilities have implementations publicly available, making it easier for the adversary to gain initial access to the system and plan effectively.

Active scanning

Active scanning is not a simple reconnaissance or information gathering. The adversary is actively probing the system to identify entry points or gather more actionable information. They can also be trying to determine whether the collected information is valid.

Resource development techniques

There are six techniques in this stage that usually exploit information gathered from the reconnaissance stage:

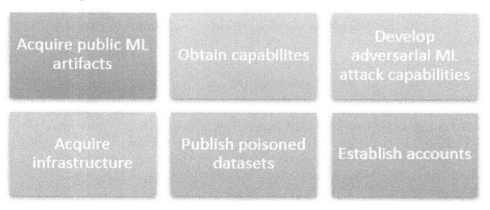

Figure 2.3 – Resource development techniques

Acquire public ML artifacts

As soon as the adversary has identified some of the details of the system, this can help them launch attacks such as creating a proxy ML model or directly crafting adversarial data, which are attack techniques that we will talk about later in this chapter. Artifacts include the software stack used to train the model, algorithms, model deployments, and training and testing datasets. The artifacts can also be in development or testing environments. Suppose they contain some logic, algorithms, or techniques that the production model uses. In that case, they can also compromise the production environment. Ensure you protect development environments as well as production environments. Access to those artifacts might require access keys or authenticated requests and you might think that this is enough, but it is not. You need to ensure that you differentiate access methods for different environments and rotate access keys so that the adversary cannot use the initial access stage techniques to acquire access to multiple environments.

Obtain capabilities

Here, the adversary may search for and get software tools to support their operations. Software tools can be either malicious or repurposed for malicious intent. Any software can be used here, and this tool or software doesn't need to be ML-enabled. For example, the adversary can use a virtual camera to add realistic effects to a feed to intercept an actual camera feed going into a system and gain access using deep fake technology.

> **Deep fake technology**
>
> Deepfake technology is a way to manipulate or generate videos, images, and audio of people using deep learning techniques. The technology uses existing audio, video, or images of a person to generate new content in the likeness of that person. The technology is so powerful that the generated content is indistinguishable from a real recorded video or audio and, as a result, can be used for various malicious purposes such as fake news, unauthorized access to systems that use biometrics, and financial fraud.

Develop adversarial ML attack capabilities

As soon as the adversary has access to the system, or at least information about it, they may choose to develop their own attacks or implement ideas described in public research. Public research papers with existing libraries as a starting point are usually well documented and explain which vulnerabilities they exploit. You can use this information to protect your system, so it's imperative not to share information publicly so that the adversary has a limited ability to tailor the attack on your system.

Acquire infrastructure

The adversary might buy or lease infrastructure they will use throughout their operation. This infrastructure can include physical or cloud servers' domains, devices, or services. Depending on the implementation, the adversary will make it difficult for you to discover their traffic in your network and they will try to blend in. They will probably use infrastructure that can be very quickly provisioned and then shut down. That means that even if you discover a suspicious endpoint and block it, that doesn't mean you are safe, as the adversary might provision new infrastructure and try again. This is why it's essential to always follow the best industry practices about security to prepare for any attack.

Publish poisoned datasets and poison training data

When it comes to ML, everything is based on data. Poisoning the training data will change the results of the algorithm and the trained model. They can introduce vulnerabilities that cannot be easily detectable. The adversary may poison training data and publish it in a public location. It can be new data or a different version of an open source dataset. Always verify the source of any open source ML artifacts you use to train or update your model to protect against poisoned datasets. Staying away from public data is not the only thing you can do since data can be introduced into your system using the ML supply chain compromise attack, which we will highlight later in this chapter. Always validate that the data has not changed in the data sources; do not encrypt data or set the data sources as read-only or immutable if possible.

Establish accounts

The adversary may create accounts with many services that they can use to target your system and gain access to the resources they need. They might also impersonate someone from your organization, such as an employee, and use this to gain access to your systems. Always verify whom you are talking to about a project and train your employees accordingly. For example, if you get a message on LinkedIn from a coworker asking you to share access or reset their password for them, always verify their identity. Even if they use a company email, if this is not the proper process for resetting credentials or requesting access, direct them to follow the appropriate process because their account might be compromised. You could unknowingly share access information about the ML endpoint or training data with a third party.

Initial access techniques

The adversary can use the following techniques to gain access to the system:

Figure 2.4 – Initial access techniques

Let us understand each of these techniques in the following sections.

ML supply chain compromise

With the ML supply chain compromise technique, the adversary is trying to gain access by compromising the unique parts of the ML supply chain. It usually includes hardware used to train the model, such as GPU hardware, data, parts of the software stack, or the model itself. When it comes to hardware, always verify that you have the latest updates and patches. When using open source libraries, always check the implementation of those algorithms. Any updates to the library should be checked for vulnerabilities or malicious code. Data can be poisoned, especially public data, and private datasets can be compromised during the labeling phase. If you are using a third-party service to label your data, make sure there are processes in place to protect against data poisoning. Also, keep versions of your datasets to compare any changes and identify issues if possible. If you're using Azure Machine Learning, some capabilities can help you with that. Finally, if you are using open source models and fine-tuning them using your own private dataset, always verify the source of the model or the libraries, especially when updates are released. Every time you incorporate new models or execute unknown code, there is the possibility it is infected with traditional malware.

Valid accounts

In this case, the adversary may obtain valid credentials from existing accounts or API access keys. Especially when using Azure Machine Learning, leaked or stolen credentials may provide access to artifacts and allow the adversary to compromise them. We should be worried about two levels of access. The first is the user credentials and user accounts with access to the trained model or pipelines, and the second is the API keys for the inference model or pipeline.

Evade ML model

Not all attacks are targeted at your ML project. An adversary can launch a craft adversarial data attack to prevent an ML model from correctly identifying data contents. This technique disrupts any task that relies on ML. Such tasks or processes can be, for example, ML-based malware detection software, network scanning software, or antivirus software that protects the system from traditional cyberattacks. Mitigations for this technique include model hardening to make ML models robust to specific inputs, behaviors, or atypical queries or using an ensemble of models for inference to increase robustness since an attack can be effective against one model type but not another.

Exploit public-facing applications

While Azure provides many security features and complies with several industry-standard protocols for its services, the responsibility for protecting anything from ML to databases, public-facing applications, and internet-accessible endpoints (such as web servers) falls on the customer. So, when protecting your ML assets, you must think of all the related services using your model. In this book, we will talk a lot about security practices that have nothing to do with ML just because they apply to related services that use the ML environment, such as networks and applications.

ML model access techniques

There are four techniques that can be leveraged to access your ML model:

Figure 2.5 – ML model access techniques

Let us review each of the ML model access techniques.

ML model inference API access

The ML model inference API access technique refers to legitimate access to the inference API. The goal of creating models is to make predictions. More often than not, those predictions are leveraged from web applications. The way to accomplish this is to publish the model as a web API for use from the service. This API can provide an adversary with information about the model type or the data.

Usually, models are retrained to learn based on input. That means if you are using the production environment to retrain and improve your model based on actual usage, ensure there is an approval process to check the data coming from public endpoints. Otherwise, an adversary can introduce false data to the system just by using the inference API.

ML-enabled product or service

Even if your API is not public, the service using it still contains some information about the model and its data. An application that has access to an inference endpoint still has to send some data to it, which may reveal details of the ML model in logs or metadata. Hijacking the application opens up the ML service, making it vulnerable to multiple attacks.

Physical environment access

Attacks are not only digital. Suppose the model or the application interacting with the model uses real-world data somehow. In that case, the adversary can influence the model by accessing the environment where the data has been collected. For example, if you have an application that streams data from sensors or cameras by accessing the camera feed and poisoning it, the adversary can influence the model. Ensure that when you are using sensors, they are properly secured in their communication with any form of system and that there's not a single point of failure in the hardware.

Full ML model access

Sometimes, although it's more secure to have the model in a centralized system and query it every time you need a prediction in real life, that's not always sustainable or performant. You might be tempted to upload or repackage a mobile version of your model and add it to your edge device, such as your sensors or mobile device. While this might increase performance and provide faster predictions, this increases the attack surface area. If possible, consider uploading your model to the cloud with a single access point to reduce the attack surface area.

Execution techniques

There are two execution techniques available, both of which rely on specific actions or scripts executed by a user or a tool:

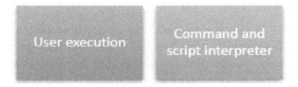

Figure 2.6 – Execution techniques

Let us explore each of these techniques in the following sections.

User execution

The adversary will usually rely on specific actions made by a legitimate user to gain execution. A system user may unknowingly execute unsafe code introduced by the ML supply chain compromise technique or social engineering. To mitigate this, train your users not to open suspicious or malicious links or documents from unknown sources. Part of the training should also be for checking the ML artifacts used throughout the ML process, as those can also be poisoned. Always check the checksum of the file or source and verify that it is secure and unchanged.

Command and scripting interpreter

Adversaries may use command and script interpreters to execute commands in the target system. Those interfaces provide many ways of interacting with the system, and it's a standard feature of different technologies. Depending on the operating system, there are tools included. For example, in Windows, the Windows Command Shell and PowerShell can be exploited. There are also interpreters for programming languages such as Python. Commands and scripts can be embedded in payloads delivered to the target system as documents or downloaded from poisoned sources. Remote services can also be used.

Persistence techniques

Two persistent techniques are available, one of which we've already discussed in the *Resource development* section. The poison training data technique can be used to embed vulnerabilities or insert a backdoor trigger. Depending on the goal, this can be either a resource development or a persistence technique:

Figure 2.7 – Persistence techniques

Backdoor ML model

The adversary can introduce a backdoor into the ML model based on other techniques, such as the poison training data technique. A model that includes a back door usually works as expected but will produce a different output when triggered by an input associated with a specific request from the adversary. This technique gives the adversary a persistent artifact on the system. The back door can be either a model response tailored to the input from the adversary or the invocation of an injected payload that bypasses the model and returns a different set of results.

Defense evasion techniques

There's only one defense evasion technique we've already discussed: the evade ML technique. It can also be used as an initial access technique, and after initial access has been granted, the adversary is not detected by any other software that might be using ML by disrupting its process.

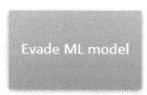

Figure 2.8 – Defense evasion techniques

Discovery techniques

There are three discovery techniques that all target getting more information about the model, its ontology, its family, or the artifacts:

Figure 2.9 – Discovery techniques

Let us explain these techniques in the following sections.

Discover ML model ontology

To discover the ontology of the ML model output, the adversary can analyze the types of objects the model can take as input. The ontology of the model can also be found in either documentation or configuration files. To mitigate against this, you can try obfuscating the model's output and restricting the number of requests the user can make to a model. Usually, the adversary would have to create a large number of requests for the model to produce multiple outputs and get useful information from a range of results.

Discover the ML model family

The adversary may use examples from the responses and outputs to discover the general family of the model. Ensure that the family of the model is not public information and cannot be easily guessed by the inputs and outputs of the model. Passive ML output obfuscation can be used here to mitigate this and restrict the number of requests a user or application can make to the model in a specific amount of time. Anything you can do to limit knowledge about the model can make it more difficult for the adversary to tailor an attack to your individual technology or model family.

Discover ML artifacts

At any point, the adversary will try to discover the private or public artifacts you are using in your model. This process usually starts in the resource development stage, but in this stage, we focus more on private ML artifacts. To mitigate this, collect and secure any artifacts, such as the software stack, testing and training data, data management systems, container registries, and software repositories. Encrypt sensitive information and systems where possible. Azure provides the management of encryption not only in data but also in whole services, such as Azure storage accounts.

Collection techniques

In the collection stage, we have three techniques that focus on data collection:

Figure 2.10 – Collection techniques

ML artifact collection

The adversary might collect any useful data or company information for exfiltration as soon as the artifacts are identified. Suppose the adversary's goal is not to disrupt the service but to gather information, such as proprietary data, by using your models and datasets. In that case, the adversary will be interested in getting as many ML artifacts as possible. Encryption of sensitive information at rest and in transit will help mitigate this to some extent because even if the adversary collects data, they won't be able to read or use it.

Data from information repositories

Data for ML is not always stored in databases or used as datasets. Machine learning projects usually require collaboration and planning. Information can also be stored in several information repositories and can be mined to get valuable information. Information repositories include document-sharing services or project management systems such as SharePoint, Confluence, and Jira. To mitigate this technique, ensure that the users are trained and informed not to share model endpoints or information on the project management software. Documentation about the service should also be secured and shared only with people required to possess that information using secure channels.

Data from the local system

Any data stored in any local systems must be secured as well. After gaining access to the network, an adversary may search filesystems' configuration files and local datasets to extract data, especially sensitive data such as SSH keys, encryption keys, and connection information.

ML attack staging techniques

After data collection, it makes sense that the adversary will move on to exfiltration to get that data out of the system. But for ML, there's a different stage. We also have to consider the ML attack staging. Depending on the adversary's purpose, they might want to leverage their knowledge to disrupt the service by using several techniques that target the ML model before they try to extract ML data. Here, we can identify four techniques, one of which is the backdoor ML model technique that can also be used as a persistent technique. We've already discussed it in the *Backdoor ML model* section, so here, we will talk about the rest:

Figure 2.11 – ML attack staging techniques

Create a proxy ML model

The adversary might create an ML model as a proxy for the target model. Proxy models can be used in a variety of ways. The adversary might train models from similar datasets, use available pre-trained models, or train a proxy model from ML artifacts they have gathered in previous stages. The proxy model then can serve to replicate the victim's inference API or to replicate access to target another model within the organization.

Verify attack

Before the launch of the attack, the adversary might need to verify that the strategy they have developed works. That means getting an offline or a replicated model and trying out the techniques they have planned. This gives them the confidence that the attack is effective. Then, they are free to deploy it in the physical environment or keep it and use it at a later time. When the adversary has gathered enough information and has the capability to verify the attack in a replicated system they have built that mirrors the victim organization system, it presents a new problem. The actual attack won't trigger any significant traffic in the victim's systems, making the use of this technique potentially undetectable.

Craft adversarial data

The craft adversarial data technique that was already mentioned in the *Evade ML model* section needs information and artifacts collected in multiple stages. Typically, the result is data poisoning. Depending on the adversary's goal, the inputs have been modified, which causes effects such as missed predictions, misclassifications, or the maximizing of the system's energy consumption. This attack depends greatly on the adversary's knowledge of the system. You can use many different algorithms to develop the adversarial data attack, such as white-box optimization, black-box optimization, black-box transfer, or manual modification.

Exfiltration techniques

The data is usually extracted in the exfiltration stage, which involves two techniques that apply to ML:

Figure 2.12 – Exfiltration techniques

Exfiltration via ML inference API

The ML inference API, if vulnerable, can lead to a leak of private information about the training, the model itself, or private intellectual property. If the model inference API needs to be public, ensure that you secure it as much as possible and limit the number of queries a user can do in production so that they cannot figure out different ways of getting that information.

Exfiltration via cyber-means

Of course, the ML project is not the only thing that is vulnerable here. Depending on the overall security of the environment and the systems, an adversary might choose traditional exfiltration techniques to steal data from your network. Exfiltration can be accomplished by just transferring data over the network, transferring data over a physical medium such as a removable or cloud drive, or via the internet to a web service, a code repository, or directly to cloud storage.

Impact techniques

There are seven impact techniques available where the adversary manipulates or interrupts the service for your ML systems or data. We have already covered the evade ML model technique. Let us look at the rest of the techniques of this stage:

Figure 2.13 – Impact techniques

Denial of ML service

Denial-of-service attacks target ML systems with multiple requests to disrupt the service. Since endpoints have finite resources, by using a denial-of-service attack, an adversary can create bottlenecks which can be expensive and disrupt the service so that it cannot serve other requests, rendering the service useless. There are a couple of things you can do to mitigate them that involve deploying third-party Azure services, but the first step would probably be to restrict the number of ML model requests.

Spam ML systems with chaff data

This technique requires the adversary to know that the system probably uses the data for predictions to retrain the service. Spamming the system with many requests and data that does not make sense will increase the number of predictions or false predictions. It will cause analysts or data scientists working on improving the system to waste much time reviewing and correcting those incorrect inferences. There are capabilities of Azure Machine Learning that we will talk about to mitigate this. However, the obvious choice here is to restrict the number of ML model queries or block traffic from suspicious endpoints that make multiple unrelated requests.

Erode ML model integrity

This technique combines spamming the system with data and using adversarial data to degrade the model's performance. This doesn't have to be a one-time event. The attack can be ongoing for quite some time, so the ML system is eroded and predictions are inaccurate. This attack might be more difficult to detect since it does not have the goal of disrupting the service; it wants to subtly make changes to the model that are not detectable over a long period of time.

Harvest cost

Systems have finite resources, and usually, when someone is launching multiple requests bombarding the system with so much data, it interrupts the service. With cloud computing, infrastructure doesn't have to be a finite resource. Cloud systems can scale to accommodate increased traffic, but at the same time, auto-scaling affects the costs of those resources. Restricting the number of queries per application or detecting those kinds of attacks can mitigate this technique, which targets the operational costs of the victim's organization.

ML intellectual property theft

Sometimes the target is the model itself. Let's say you provide ML as a service. Someone who has managed to extract that model now has unlimited use of your service without paying. That can have a significant impact, as the intellectual property is unsafe and can cause economic harm to your organization. Mitigations for this technique include controlling access to your models and data at rest, securing your models and data in transit, and encrypting services and data where possible.

System misuse for external effect

If the adversary cannot extract the model, they might still attack the system and use it for their own purpose. Hijacking the system and using their own data to get results or predictions could be an example. By gaining access to a system that monitors and protects financial data, the adversary might be able to pass invoices that otherwise would be flagged as invalid. As a result, this prohibits the system from preventing fraud.

> **Case studies and examples**
>
> For more case studies, you can check the *Further reading* section of this chapter or access the complete knowledge base at `https://atlas.mitre.org/`.

After seeing the types of generic techniques used in attacks, let us explore the actual services that can be affected in the case of an attack.

Exploring Azure services involved in ML attacks

As you can see, attacks are multi-level and primarily based on the adversary's goal. Since we do not know what that is, we can deploy multiple mitigation techniques to lessen the impact. As Azure Machine Learning is based on the Azure platform, we can deploy numerous tools to detect an incident, and by using automation, the platform will deploy mitigation steps before we are even aware that something has happened. Although we focused on ML attacks, attacks on related systems, virtual machines, and databases are still a concern. Let us look at associated services that can be used together with **Azure Machine Learning**.

Access

Microsoft Entra ID usually handles access in Azure. Microsoft Entra ID is Microsoft's cloud-based identity and access management service. It provides a range of features and capabilities to manage user identities and secure access to various resources in the Azure cloud and other Microsoft services. Besides identity and access management, it also provides **Federation**, **single sign-on** (**SSO**), a developer platform, and various features for security and governance. Different services might also offer different ways of authentication, such as via service credentials, access keys, and shared access signatures. We will focus on learning how to secure and mitigate all those services in the following chapters.

Data

ML is based on data. Azure Machine Learning supports multiple data sources, specifically **Azure Blob** and **File Storage**, **Azure Data Lake**, **Azure SQL Database**, **Azure PostgreSQL** database, and **Azure MySQL** database, each with individual security and monitoring features. We will be working with their security and monitoring features, including encryption at rest and encryption in transit, in the upcoming chapters.

Network

Although not directly related to Azure Machine Learning, many attacks happen by infiltrating the on-premises or cloud network. In the following chapters, we will discuss securing the service using network services. These include virtual networks, network security groups, **Azure Firewall**, and hybrid solutions such as **VPN gateways** and **ExpressRoute**. The **Service Endpoints** and **Private Endpoints** features can also be used for better security and isolation.

An Azure **virtual network** (**VNet**) is a fundamental component of Microsoft Azure's networking architecture. It is a logically isolated network environment that allows you to securely connect and control Azure resources, including **virtual machines** (**VMs**), **Azure App Service**, and databases.

Azure VNets usually work together with **network security groups** (**NSGs**), which provide granular network security and act as a basic firewall, allowing you to define inbound and outbound traffic rules to filter and control network traffic. NSGs do not maintain state but are the first step to securing the network traffic.

Azure Firewall is a cloud-based network security service offered by Microsoft Azure. It provides centralized, high-level network security and protection for VNets. Azure Firewall acts as a fully stateful network traffic filtering and routing solution, allowing you to control and monitor both inbound and outbound traffic to and from your Azure resources.

An Azure VPN gateway is a networking component that enables secure connectivity between on-premises networks and VNets. It provides a way to establish a **virtual private network** (**VPN**) tunnel over the public internet, ensuring secure communication and extending your on-premises network into the Azure cloud.

If the VPN gateway is not enough, you can use Azure ExpressRoute. This is a Microsoft Azure service that enables private and dedicated network connectivity between your on-premises network and Azure. It provides a reliable, high-throughput, low-latency connection, bypassing the public internet.

Service Endpoints and **Private Endpoints** are two features in Azure that provide secure and private connectivity to Azure services. Service Endpoints allows you to extend your VNet to the Azure service's backend, providing secure access to that service over the Azure backbone network. Private Endpoints allows you to access Azure services privately from your VNet using a private IP address.

Applications

Applications can be hosted in multiple services inside and outside of Azure. Most ML services are intended to be used by an application, which is another component we need to consider when we are working on implementing security. In this book, we will learn how to secure services that host applications such as Azure App Service, VMs, or **container** services, but we will also analyze some best practices for developing software applications. Of course, since the implementation of application security heavily depends on the programming language and libraries used, we will explain the high-level implementation of mitigation techniques such as SQL injection or cross-site scripting.

Compute

ML relies heavily on computational resources. You can create multiple compute targets for training or hosting inference models in the workspace. Targets can be local compute, **Azure Machine Learning compute**, **Azure Databricks**, **HDInsight**, **Synapse Spark pools**, **Azure Kubernetes Service (AKS)**, and Azure VMs. These compute targets provide the necessary resources and infrastructure to run ML workloads at scale. They must be secured and monitored properly, as they are a critical part of ML.

Local compute allows you to use your local machine or on-premises infrastructure as the compute target. This is useful for development and experimentation when you don't require large-scale resources.

Azure Machine Learning compute is a managed compute cluster provided by Azure Machine Learning. It dynamically provisions and scales compute resources based on your workload requirements. It supports both CPU and GPU instances and is optimized for running training jobs at scale.

Azure Databricks is an Apache Spark-based analytics platform that integrates with Azure Machine Learning. You can use Azure Databricks clusters as a compute target for training and deploying ML models, taking advantage of the distributed computing capabilities of Spark. If you still want to use Spark but are not using Databricks, you can use Azure Synapse Spark pools.

Azure HDInsight can also be set up as a compute target in Azure Machine Learning. Using its distributed processing capabilities allows you to execute ML tasks on HDInsight clusters.

AKS is a managed Kubernetes service in Azure. You can deploy your ML workloads as containerized applications on AKS and use them as a compute target for training and serving models. AKS provides scalability and flexibility for running distributed training and inference workloads.

Azure VM instances can also be a compute target. You can provision VMs with the required specifications and use them for training and deploying ML models.

Azure Machine Learning

All previously mentioned services relate to or can be used with the **Azure Machine Learning workspace**. The workspace is the main point of management for Azure Machine Learning; however, the workspace itself can be used for security or isolation, for example, if multiple workspaces might be needed for different scenarios. The workspace provides multiple features for monitoring and organizing assets such as model and dataset versioning and data drift. We will also explore security features in algorithms, data, and models, such as fairness, data anonymization, and more.

Now, we've learned about the services related to Azure Machine Learning that we need to protect. They might not be the only ones—it depends on your system architecture—but they are a great start to your security journey.

Summary

There are many attacks to be prepared for and vulnerabilities are discovered daily, so we must follow a framework that helps us keep up to date with current vulnerabilities and their mitigations where possible. The MITRE ATLAS framework is a great resource to get started as it is adapted to ML. We need to be aware of the 12 stages and multiple techniques per stage to protect our ML assets. However, as ML assets work with numerous other systems, the implementations we will see in the following chapters will include securing Azure Machine Learning and all its related services.

But before diving into those implementations, in the next chapter, we will learn about the security industry compliance standards we must adhere to and how to implement compliance controls together with responsible AI development practices.

Further reading

- DeepPayload: Black-box Backdoor Attack on Deep Learning Models through Neural Payload Injection: `https://arxiv.org/abs/2101.06896`

- Imitation Attacks and Defenses for Black-box Machine Translation Systems: `https://arxiv.org/abs/2004.15015`

- Explaining and Harnessing Adversarial Examples: `https://arxiv.org/abs/1412.6572`

3

Planning for Regulatory Compliance

When working with **artificial intelligence** (**AI**) systems, there are a couple of things that come to mind when we talk about compliance. The first is the process of adhering to laws, regulations, and standards that are usually set by governments, industry associations, or any other regulatory authorities, and the second is ethical considerations.

In this chapter, we will learn how to develop **machine learning** (**ML**) models ethically and responsibly by using the six Responsible AI principles according to Microsoft and how to translate them into a responsible development strategy using Responsible AI tools. Then, we will do an overview of the industry-recognized regulatory compliance standards for Azure Machine Learning and how to enforce them by using Azure Policy. These standards are not only Microsoft benchmarks but also globally accepted frameworks such as the **National Institute of Standards and Technology Risk Management Framework** (**NIST RMF**).

In this chapter, we're going to cover the following main topics:

- Exploring Responsible AI development
- Regulatory compliance in Azure Policy for Azure Machine Learning
- Compliance auditing and reporting
- Compliance automation in Azure

By the end of the chapter, you will not only become familiar with the regulatory and security compliance standards, but you will learn how to handle auditing, reporting, and automation.

Exploring Responsible AI development

As AI systems gain popularity and are used by many people around the world, it raises the question of how ethically these systems perform. This is evident, for example, by the public release of OpenAI's ChatGPT model. Everyone or almost everyone has used it so far, and it has had some interesting reactions. Many have been impressed, excited, and even loved this new product that can help them be more productive in their work and in their everyday lives. Others have been concerned or even scared of the prospects of this powerful model and how it can very easily mimic human behavior.

The focus of technology has always been to solve problems. We are amid a new technological revolution, and AI has the capability to improve people's lives very quickly; however, that does not mean that there are no dangers involved. Every individual organization that uses and creates advanced AI systems will need to create a governance system for ethical and Responsible AI development.

In the following sections, we will explore the Responsible AI principles and learn how to apply them to our organization.

Responsible AI principles

In this book, we will follow Microsoft's approach to **Responsible AI**, which is based on six ethical principles—fairness, reliability and safety, privacy and security, inclusiveness, transparency, and accountability.

We will translate these six principles into more specific governance policies, and in the following section, we will discover the tools we can use to maintain governance and compliance in our systems. Here is a depiction of these principles:

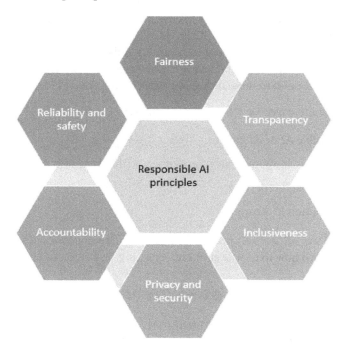

Figure 3.1 – Responsible AI principles

Let us discuss each of these in the following sections.

Fairness

AI-enabled systems and applications should treat all people fairly. Any system in development or production should avoid unfair bias and promote equal treatment and opportunities for all people who use it. This includes unbiased decision-making. We need to ensure that AI systems do not discriminate against individuals or groups based on attributes such as race, gender, age, or disability. So, when collecting data, we need to ensure we have a wide range of values for each category and that sensitive labels do not affect the predictions. When, for example, we need to include sensitive data in the dataset for the predictions, we should also be careful not to perpetuate existing inequalities or unintended correlations in the data.

Mitigations include techniques for every step of the ML process but mostly in data preprocessing. For example, if we are training an application to approve a loan, we need to exclude all sensitive features, if possible, as demographic data can perpetuate biases. There are fairness libraries available to identify and prevent biases, such as the Fairlearn library we will see in the next chapter.

Reliability and safety

AI systems should not only be reliable and safe for their users but also throughout the development process. This principle focuses on ensuring that AI systems are dependable, perform as intended, and mitigate potential risks. Safety and reliability have to do with many aspects of a system and its processes.

A system must have reliable performance and deliver reliable and accurate predictions. We should strive to minimize errors, inconsistencies, or unexpected behaviors. Service disruptions, no matter how big or small, can affect other systems as well. ML models are usually part of other processes, so a model that analyzes and makes predictions to detect cybersecurity threats should have safeguards in place so that it does not fail.

We should always address risks that could lead to negative consequences for individuals or society. The extent to which we will ensure the safety of the system heavily depends on the system's purpose. For instance, it is acceptable for an entertainment application that employs automated generation to produce subpar images without causing any harm, but the same standard does not apply to critical systems such as a self-driving vehicle or a surgery robotic arm. Finally, for a system to be reliable and safe it needs to be up to date and continuously monitored to ensure that it maintains or improves the standards it was built on. This means that there should be human interaction in the production process, or if the system learns from feedback, there should be an approval process in place.

Privacy and security

Any AI system or ML-enabled application is no different than any other application that is based on data. Privacy and security are even more important as there are attack techniques that will make the trained model reveal the data used to train it.

Before we even start, we need to consider data regulations so that we can decide where to store the data. When working with Azure, you need to be aware of the data center regions around the world to ensure your data is protected by the proper regulations and abides by any compliance requirements you have. When you are creating your Azure Machine Learning environment, you can choose your preferred region.

The second part is securing the data and the system. We will see the best practices to implement for the security and privacy of our workloads that are hosted in Azure extensively throughout this book. Always remember when securing your ML model and its data and algorithms that you must also ensure related systems are also secure, to prevent adversaries from using lateral access techniques to gain access to your resources.

The biggest issue besides security is also privacy, especially in sectors such as finance or healthcare. As ML is based on data, we need to use the absolute minimum of **personally identifiable information** (**PII**) in our models. There are several techniques we can use to anonymize our data and libraries to help minimize identification, even from aggregated results such as the SmartNoise SDK we will see in the next chapter.

Inclusiveness

An AI system should be inclusive and promote equal access, participation, and benefits for all individuals and communities. During the development stage, it is particularly important to have diverse perspectives and experiences. When you include a wide range of stakeholders and experts from diverse backgrounds and demographics, you ensure that AI systems reflect the needs and values of diverse communities.

Accessibility is also a great consideration, and I am not talking about disabilities only. Of course, we need to incorporate features that accommodate various accessibility needs, such as support for screen readers, keyboard navigation, and other assistive technologies. Additionally, we need to consider the **user experience** (**UX**) and usability. If your target audience includes salespeople who are on the move all day, adding voice capabilities is also important for inclusiveness.

By using a user-centric approach in AI development, actively seeking feedback, and collaborating with a diverse group with a focus on understanding and addressing needs, you can be confident that you are contributing positively to social, economic, and cultural inclusion.

Transparency

Every AI system should be understandable in every aspect. That does not mean sharing all information about how it was created publicly because, as we saw in the previous chapter, this is potentially dangerous, and an adversary can use that information to compromise the system. However, it should be clear to the user how the system works, its limitations, and potential implications for individuals and society.

Explainability is a major part of AI and ML. ML models, especially ones that provide predictions that involve complex decision-making, should provide insights into which features affect the predictions and to what degree. There are a lot of libraries available, and we will see some implementations in the next chapter.

The use of AI disclosure is also vital. Most of the time, models are deployed as part of another system of process. Users need to be aware of when the system uses AI automation and when the process is handled by a human to avoid any confusion. Clear communication of system capabilities and limitations helps manage user expectations and avoid potential misunderstandings.

Accountability

Accountability complements the other five principles and is a fundamental aspect of any system. It must be clear what the roles and responsibilities are of everyone that is involved in the ML process. This includes assigning accountability for the development, deployment, and continuous monitoring of ML models and related services. We need to be adaptable as AI systems continuously learn from feedback, and we need to be ready to acknowledge and address any incidents that result from our model's predictions.

Complying with applicable laws, regulations, and ethical guidelines in the development and use of AI systems is also important as the organization that developed the technology is usually accountable for any issues. Following compliance and legal requirements will help us minimize any potential future issues. This is not a one-time check; there needs to be continuous monitoring and evaluation of our AI systems to assess their performance and identify areas for improvement. Additionally, there are very few regulations for AI and data at this moment, so we need to keep up with any updates, which is a challenge as such regulations might be location- or industry-specific. We will talk about compliance a little more extensively later in this chapter and how to use Azure's tools to ensure your development process is protected and compliance is assured.

> **Note**
>
> All principles, guidelines, and related documents can be found in the official Microsoft *Responsible AI* portal here: `https://www.microsoft.com/ai/responsible-ai`.

Getting started with Responsible AI in your organization

All the preceding points are easy in theory, but how do you start building a solid strategy? Let us review the first steps you need to take, as Responsible AI can be implemented in multiple stages.

First, you will start with an assessment. Where are you in your Responsible AI journey, and what do you need to improve? The second part is responsible development, and this stage depends on what your system's goals are. There are different guidelines and tools here to ensure fairness and performance in all the stages of the ML life cycle. Our job does not end there; we need to ensure responsible deployment as well.

In this section, we will briefly outline the tools and guidelines available. We will explore the implementation and best practices of each tool in the next chapters.

The Human-AI eXperience Toolkit

The **Human-AI eXperience (HAX) Toolkit** is a set of resources and hands-on tools to support organizations in the responsible development and deployment of AI systems. It contains multiple tools and guidelines that we can use to bring together UX, AI, project management, and engineering teams and maintain responsible and ethical AI development across all stages of the ML process.

The first step in using the HAX Toolkit is to familiarize yourself with the guidelines for human-AI interaction. They outline how an AI system should behave and interact with its users.

HAX Toolkit

Find the HAX Toolkit's latest documents and guidelines here: `https://www.microsoft.com/en-us/haxtoolkit/`.

Then, you can use the HAX Workbook, which is an Excel sheet with multiple questions that will help you prioritize work items and see which guidelines you need to implement based on your individual scenario. Especially if you are working with **natural language processing (NLP)**, you can utilize the HAX Playbook. This will help you identify possible system failures and how you can prevent them or recover from them.

If all this sounds very theoretical, in the next section, we will see an example of how we can use the HAX Workbook to develop our strategy.

Exploring the HAX Design Library

The first thing we need to do is get familiar with the HAX Design Library. You can find all the complete material here: `https://www.microsoft.com/en-us/haxtoolkit/library/`. Here you can find 18 guidelines based on the responsible AI principles for human-AI interaction. These guidelines come with design patterns to apply and examples by industry.

These are the 18 guidelines at a glance:

- **G1: Make clear what the system can do.**
  Helps the user gain an understanding of what the system's benefits or limitations are.

- **G2: Make clear how well the system can do what it can do.**
  In this guideline, we ensure that the user is aware of the system's error frequency.

- **G3: Time services based on context.**
  This plans when to take action depending on the user's task.

- **G4: Show contextually relevant information.**
  Shows the user information based on their current task or scenario.

- **G5: Match relevant social norms.**
  Here, the experiences should match the user's social and cultural environment.

- **G6: Mitigate social biases.**
  Ensure the system treats all sensitive groups fairly.

- **G7: Support efficient invocation.**
  The system should be available easily when needed.

- **G8: Support efficient dismissal.**
  Ensure there is a capability to ignore the system's services.

- **G9: Support efficient correction.**
  Ensure there is a capability to recover from errors.

- **G10: Scope services when in doubt.**
  Gracefully clarify ambiguous commands.

- **G11: Make clear why the system did what it did.**
  Ensure that the system's results can be explained.

- **G12: Remember recent interactions.**
  Maintain a short history of previous actions.

- **G13: Learn from user behavior.**
  Adjust to the user actions if needed.

- **G14: Update and adapt cautiously.**
  Limit disruption during maintenance.

- **G15: Encourage granular feedback.**
  Enable the user to provide feedback.

- **G16: Convey the consequences of user actions.**
  Make clear how user actions impact the system's functionality.

- **G17: Provide global controls.**
  Ensure that the user can customize the system's behavior.

- **G18: Notify users about changes.**
  Keep the users informed about new features.

After familiarizing ourselves with the above guidelines we need to see how we can use them to develop a Responsible AI strategy.

Let us see how to prioritize and track the implementation of each guideline.

Using the HAX Workbook to develop a Responsible AI strategy

To get started, download the HAX Workbook from `https://www.microsoft.com/en-us/haxtoolkit/workbook`. We will fill in the first row together based on the scenario presented in *Chapter 1* with the diabetes prediction model.

In the workbook, the first row presents this guideline: *Make clear what the system can do.*

> **Clarification**
>
> Usually, you would fill in all rows in a step before you move on to the next step. However, just as an example, we will go through the first guideline only.

Let us proceed to fill in the first row of the workbook, as demonstrated in the following steps. You can see how the result looks in the screenshots accompanying each step:

1. **Select relevant guidelines**: In our case, the first guideline, *Make clear what the system can do*, is critical, as the predictions involve medical data and might influence the diagnosis and the treatment of the patient, so it should be clear to the doctor that the results are an estimation and they need to verify their validity before delivering a diagnosis and treatment to the patient. In the following screenshot, you can see the first step of the guideline together with an **EXAMPLES** column of how you are supposed to fill in the rest of the cells. As this guideline for us is critical, we choose **Yes** under **STEP 1**:

GUIDELINE	EXAMPLES	STEP 1: Select relevant guidelines **Fill in each row** below before going to the next step *When complete, filter for relevance.*
Description	Examples *Show or hide as needed.*	Is this guideline **relevant**? *Select Yes, No, Maybe, Already Done*
1 Make clear what the system can do. *Set the right expectations about the AI system's capabilities.*	For an AI-powered resume assistant: **Step 1:** Yes, guideline is relevant because a user might believe the system is more or less capable than it actually is (e.g., thinking the assistant can provide feedback on content when it only advises on word choices). **Step 2:** Not applying this guideline may harm a user if they over-rely on the assistant in their job search. **Step 3:** Display a summary of the system's capabilities or show some examples of the type of feedback it can provide.	Yes

Figure 3.2 – Step 1: Select relevant guidelines

2. **Imagine impact of relevant guidelines**: In this step, you will go through all guidelines that you have set as relevant and imagine the impact of implementing or not implementing this guideline on your users. In our case, it is very important as the ML model is designed to accelerate, not replace, the diagnostic process. The doctor should be aware that the prediction is an estimation, and they should verify the results. If the doctor does not verify the results, they might prescribe the wrong treatment, which can have dangerous consequences for the patient's health:

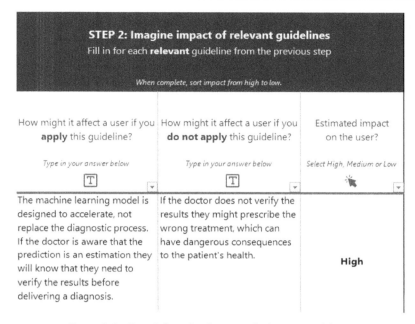

Figure 3.3 – Step 2: Imagine impact of relevant guidelines

3. **Draft implementation requirements**: In this step, we outline what we need to do to implement this guideline. In this case, we have identified three tasks that do not require a big commitment; these are visible in the next screenshot:

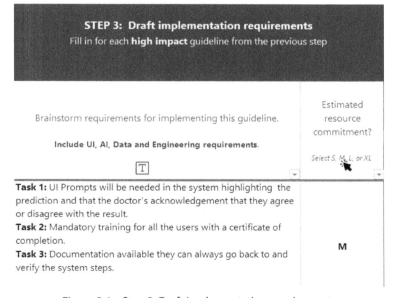

Figure 3.4 – Step 3: Draft implementation requirements

4. **Prioritize**: Prioritization is up to you. How urgent is the implementation of this guideline? Since we are working with a system in healthcare, making clear what the system can do is crucial:

Figure 3.5 – Step 4: Prioritize

5. **Track**: You can use the document or your own project management tools to assess the responsible development features you have prioritized using this document:

Figure 3.6 – Step 5: Track

This process (*steps 1* through *5*) is then to be repeated for all guidelines.

After this exercise, you will have a good idea of how to approach ethical AI development. Even if you are not sure how to fill in the document, in the **EXAMPLES** column, you will find an explanation of how each guideline can be implemented in a system, which is especially helpful.

However, applications need to be tested to ensure we have covered all our bases. When it comes to human-AI interaction there are specific things we need to look out for.

So, let us take a look at how the HAX Playbook can help us with this.

Discovering the HAX Playbook

If you are working with NLP, then you should really utilize the HAX Playbook. It is an interactive tool that is based on the scenario you present, it provides common interaction scenarios for you to test to ensure that in your application you have considered the most basic issues that arise, and plan for remediation.

The playbook can be found here: `https://microsoft.github.io/HAXPlaybook/` or if you want to tweak the survey it creates, you can build the source code from here: `https://github.com/microsoft/HAXPlaybook`.

To use the playbook, open the site and on the page and choose the AI features your application supports on the left. As soon as you click on something the playbook presents what the common usage is and the common errors and issues that can arise on the right, as seen in the next screenshot:

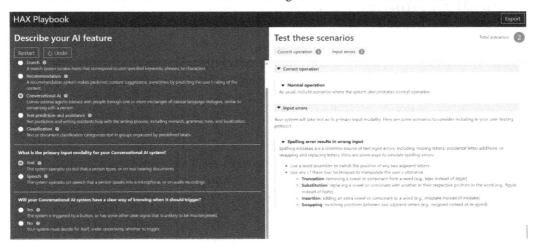

Figure 3.7 – The HAX Playbook

For example, if you choose **Conversational AI** on the left and **Text** input, the playbook will suggest that a common error is the wrong spelling in the text. The more options you choose the more scenarios will be presented. These scenarios can also be exported in various formats for later usage.

After we have completed the human-AI user experience, let us ensure that our system is inclusive using the next methodology.

The Inclusive Design methodology

One of the Responsible AI principles is inclusiveness, as we mentioned before. If you have no idea where to get started, you can use the Microsoft Inclusive Design principles, which is a methodology to ensure everyone is included and enabled in a digital environment.

> **Inclusive Design**
>
> Find Inclusive Design documents and guidelines here: `https://inclusive.microsoft.design/`.

The Inclusive Design principles are simple. First, we need to recognize exclusion and acknowledge bias. Second, we need to learn through diversity by bringing in fresh and diverse perspectives. Finally, when you provide content to accommodate people with physical or mental impairments, it creates experiences that benefit everyone. After you have a good understanding of how to approach responsible design, you can proceed to work with many tools and libraries. In this book, we will see many implementations and tools that help us integrate Responsible AI features into our systems.

After Responsible AI development, we need to learn how to ensure regulatory compliance.

Regulatory compliance in Azure Policy for Azure Machine Learning

Regulatory compliance is the process of adhering to laws, regulations, and standards that are usually set by governments, industry associations, or any other regulatory authorities. Part of regulatory compliance means that an organization operates within specific legal or regulatory frameworks that apply to the industry and or its geographical location. Regulatory compliance is essential to maintain ethical practices, protect organizations and customers, and mitigate risks. It includes laws and regulations, policies and procedures, risk assessment and management, reporting and documentation, and, finally, monitoring and auditing. Building a culture of compliance within an organization can be difficult, but it is essential. This can include employee training and ensuring that compliance is a priority. However, sometimes, the implementation of security controls might be required in order to ensure that all those processes and practices are enforced.

If your organization needs to demonstrate compliance with legal or regulatory standards, Microsoft and the Azure platform are fully compliant with multiple global, regional, and industry standards. You can find all the information in the Azure compliance documentation. However, the fact that the platform is compliant does not automatically mean that the way you implement and use the services is also compliant. You might need to implement or configure those controls properly to comply with regulations that have nothing to do with the service but, for example, with the data. Here, we will explore all the regulatory compliance controls that apply to Azure Machine Learning that we are going to see how to implement in the following chapters.

Each control is tied to one or more **Azure Policy** definitions. Azure Policy is a service in Azure that you use to create, assign, and manage policies that enforce and govern your organization's compliance and security requirements across Azure resources. These policies can be used to enforce various configurations and constraints on resources, such as resource types, regions, tagging, access controls, and more. You can use Azure Policy to bring your resources to compliance through remediation for existing resources and automatic remediation for new resources. You can group several business rules together to form a policy initiative. You can also define and implement a set of rules, called **policy definitions**, which define the desired state for your Azure resources. The policy definition or initiative can be assigned to any scope of resources that Azure supports, such as management groups, subscriptions, resource groups, or individual resources. Azure Policy evaluates resources against the defined policies and provides compliance results, allowing you to monitor and enforce the desired configurations in a central blade.

Policy assignment is quite simple. Let us see how it works:

1. Open the Azure portal at `http://portal.azure.com/` and type `policy` in the search box, as seen in the following screenshot:

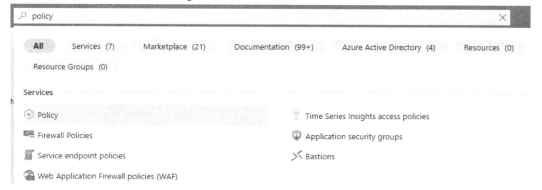

Figure 3.8 – Opening Azure Policy

2. You will find yourself in the **Overview** blade. Here, you can see a summary of your policies and the compliance of your resources:

Figure 3.9 – The Azure Policy Overview blade

3. To assign a new policy, head to the **Authoring** menu on the left and click **Assignments**. In this menu, you can assign a policy to your resources:

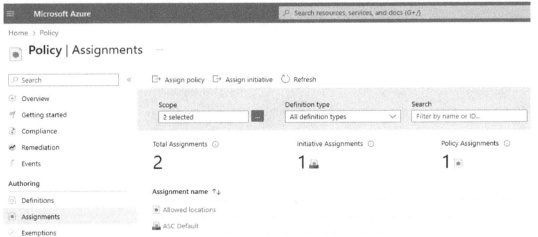

Figure 3.10 – Policy assignments

4. Click the **Assign policy** button and fill in the information as outlined in the next screenshot:

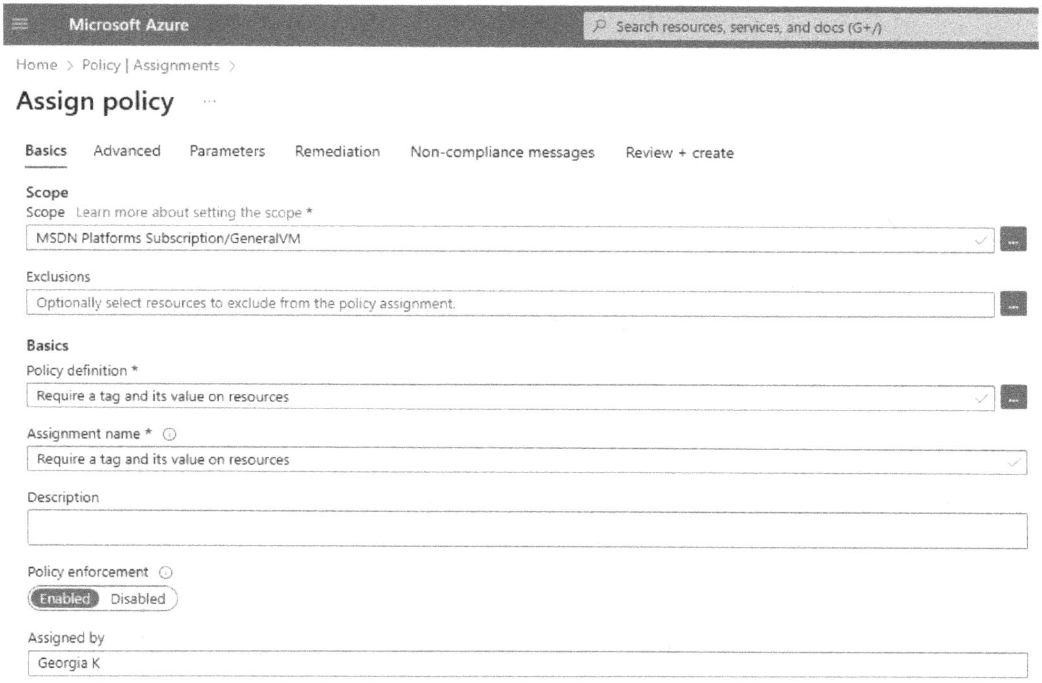

Figure 3.11 – Assign policy basics

5. **Scope** is the space where the policy is applied. You can set the scope as the management group, a subscription, or the resource group your resources exist in. I chose my subscription. If you want to exclude specific resources, you can set an exclusion here. Then, you can choose a policy definition. There are more than 1,000 in the portal; you can find more on GitHub or you can create your own. I chose a simple one that makes a tag required for all resources. If there is remediation available, you can set this up on the **Remediation** tab. The one I chose does not have a remediation for previously created resources.

If you don't want to put more than the required settings, that is it! The assignment might take up to 15 minutes to become enabled, and then it is enforced at the scope you have set for all new resources.

For Azure Machine Learning there are several policies you can implement to ensure your resources are compliant. The two I would at least recommend enabling are the *Azure Machine Learning compute instances should be recreated to get the latest software updates*, so that your compute instances are always updated and secure with the latest operating system version and that compute should have idle shutdown enabled to prevent unwanted costs using the policy *Azure Machine Learning Compute*

Instance should have an idle shutdown. The others are a little bit more scenario-specific and you can find the complete list in the following link.

> **Built-in policies for Azure Machine Learning**
> You can find the built-in policies for Azure Machine Learning in this table: `https://learn.microsoft.com/en-us/azure/governance/policy/samples/built-in-policies#machine-learning`

The fact that the preceding policies apply to Azure Machine Learning specifically does not mean that these are the only ones we can use to adhere to a compliance framework. As Azure Machine Learning uses multiple associated services to work, it is worth looking into policies for Azure Container registries, Azure Kubernetes services, databases in Azure we use, and so on. If the policy does not cover what we want to do, we can create a custom one or find more on GitHub.

The Azure Policy service integrates with **Azure Resource Manager (ARM)**, the **Azure portal**, **Azure DevOps**, and other Azure services, enabling you to enforce policies during resource creation, deployment, and ongoing management. Additionally, Azure Policy can be leveraged based on condition by using the **Azure Active Directory Conditional Access** features. In this section, we will explore industry standards and policies that apply to Azure ML specifically and use them to create a security baseline.

> **Azure compliance documentation**
> You can find details and reports for all Azure compliance offerings here: `https://learn.microsoft.com/azure/compliance/`.

Azure Security Benchmark

The **Azure Security Benchmark (ASB)** is a set of recommendations based on industry standards that guide you on how you can secure your cloud solutions on Azure. The ASB contains policies and recommendations across all Azure services. That includes security and compliance standards. If you want to see each service and how you can apply the ASB recommendations, you can find ASB mapping files in the documentation. For Azure ML, we will take into consideration the network security and data protection controls.

Federal Risk and Authorization Management Program

The **Federal Risk and Authorization Management Program (FedRAMP)** is the federal government's approach to cloud service offerings suggested by the United States government. If your organization or your customer is located in the United States, you should really take into account those regulations to be compliant with relevant laws. The fact that this is suggested by the United States government does not mean that you cannot use it to secure Azure Machine Learning workloads in other locations.

FedRAMP in Azure includes two levels of protection: FedRAMP High and FedRAMP Moderate. The high impact level is usually for systems such as law enforcement, emergency services, healthcare, or finance, where the integrity, confidentiality, and security of systems will have catastrophic effects on the operations of the organization. The moderate impact level accounts for most cloud systems, which can have serious effects, but they're not in an industry where data and operations are extremely sensitive. For Azure Machine Learning, we will use the **Access Control** and **System & Communications Protection** controls. Although those controls exist because of this approach, they are valid and can help you secure your workloads in any location or type. Throughout this book, we are going to include the best practices from multiple industry standards, including FedRAMP.

New Zealand Information Security Manual (restricted)

The **New Zealand Information Security Manual** (**NZISM**) is the New Zealand government's guidelines for information assurance and system security. Although the NZISM is intended for use by New Zealand government agencies and organizations, it contains multiple controls that are especially important for Azure Machine Learning as they apply to Azure infrastructure and cryptography.

NIST SP 800-53 Rev. 5

NIST has proposed several controls, especially about security, ranging from low-impact, moderate-impact, high-impact, and privacy controls. The *NIST SP 800-53* database contains control assessment procedures and baselines for security and privacy controls for information systems and organizations. You can find all the information under the NIST RMF. With this compliance standard, we will acquire the knowledge to implement controls in Azure ML pertaining to access control, system protection, and communication security.

Reserve Bank of India IT Framework for Banks v2016

Some controls created under the Azure policy compliance for the **Reserve Bank of India IT Framework for Banks** can also be used to secure Azure Machine Learning workloads. Although this standard is about a very specific domain, it contains controls about metrics, advanced real-time threat defense and management, patch/vulnerability and change management, and anti-phishing controls that are especially useful for Azure Machine Learning.

All the preceding compliance standards and their policies are built in with the Azure platform, so it is easy to leverage them to create our security baseline, and you will see that many of those policies can overlap as they are part of many different approaches and standards. Of course, if you want, you can always create your own policies that apply to your individual industry or organizational procedures on top of those, but in this book, we will focus on constructing a solid basis for you to build on.

Compliance auditing and reporting

Just by using the Azure Policy service, you have access to the **Compliance** and **Remediation** blades, which you can use to monitor your compliance status for free for Azure resources. All you need is an active Azure subscription. Be careful, as there might be costs associated if you enable Azure Policy to an Arc resource. In that case, you can visit the Azure pricing calculator to see associated costs.

Compliance auditing is the process of evaluating an organization's adherence to relevant laws, regulations, policies, and industry standards. It usually involves a complete inspection of an organization's practices, procedures, and controls to ensure they align with the established requirements. Compliance audits can be conducted by internal or external auditors, who must be independent of the processes being audited. Internal audits and compliance audits seem to have similar steps; however, they are very different, as compliance audits focus on whether the organization is compliant with all relevant laws, rules, and regulations and not financial or operational systems.

The auditing process involves many steps. The first is setting the scope. The audit scope defines the specific regulations, laws, standards, or policies that need to be assessed and are specific to the company location or industry. Then, there is the compliance assessment, where we assess where we are by analyzing processes, controls, and reports to determine if the organization is following the prescribed procedures. If the auditor identifies areas of non-compliance and potential risks that could impact the organization's operations or reputation, they evaluate the severity and likelihood of these risks and then prioritize recommendations based on their assessment. These recommendations may include implementing new controls, revising policies and procedures, conducting employee training, or enhancing monitoring processes. At the end of the audit, a report is created with all the results to be shared with the appropriate stakeholders. Organizations are responsible for addressing and correcting the issues, sometimes within the auditing period, and ensuring that they monitor compliance so that they remediate issues in the future.

Compliance auditing plays a crucial role in helping organizations maintain legal and regulatory compliance, mitigate risks, and demonstrate accountability to stakeholders. It assists in identifying and addressing areas of non-compliance before they lead to legal violations, financial losses, or reputational damage.

To accomplish this in Azure together with Azure Policy, we have several tools available with which we can monitor and extract reports to demonstrate compliance with our services. Let us see some of them and how to use them for reporting.

Azure portal

You can start by opening the Azure Policy service in the Azure portal. You don't need to create a new resource for this; it is already part of your subscription. All you need to do is open the portal and search in the top box for `policy`, as we saw previously in this chapter. As soon as you open the **Policy** menu, you will see something similar to the next screenshot:

Figure 3.12 – Azure Policy Overview blade in the Azure portal

Either from the **Overview** blade or the **Compliance** blade, you can see which policies you currently have assigned and which resources in your subscription are compliant or not. These are both in table form, and you can also see several graphs, as shown in the previous screenshot, to give you a quick look at the compliance percentage of your resources.

This is a great report as it gives you a summary of the information straight away. By clicking on a policy or an initiative assignment, you can see more information about the policy, view non-compliant resources, and create remediation tasks or exceptions, as seen in the following screenshot:

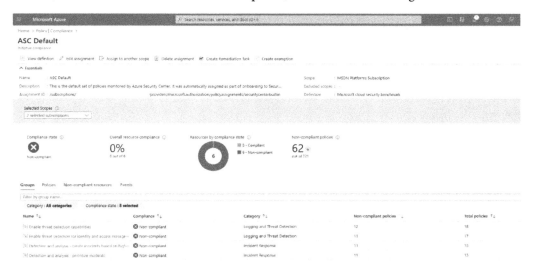

Figure 3.13 – Azure Policy assignment details using the portal

Note on the top how many options you have without leaving the reporting page.

Azure Resource Graph Explorer

Azure Resource Graph Explorer is a powerful service that gives you the ability to explore, query, and analyze your Azure resources and their properties quickly and efficiently. It's a very scalable way to retrieve information and get insights. You can create Azure Resource Graph Explorer queries with **Kusto Query Language** (**KQL**) to get information about the policies in your environment.

Let us see how we can run a simple query and extract reports:

1. To get started, open Azure Resource Graph Explorer by typing the name in the top search bar, shown as follows:

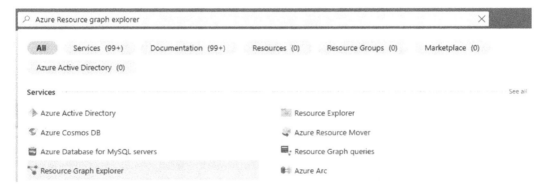

Figure 3.14 – Opening Azure Resource Graph Explorer

2. At the bottom of the page, under **Get started**, filter with the search term `policy`, as shown here:

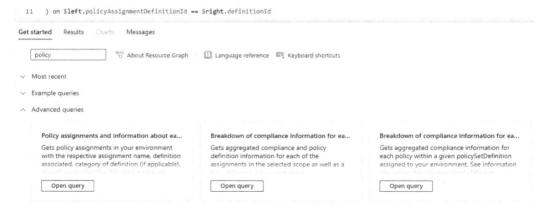

Figure 3.15 – Searching the query templates for policy-related queries

3. Run the leftmost query. You will get the active policy assignments for your subscription:

Figure 3.16 – Running a query in Azure Resource Graph Explorer

Now, you can use KQL to tailor the results and the columns to the information you want, export the data as a `.csv` file, or pin the table to an Azure dashboard.

> **KQL reference**
>
> If this is the first time you've heard about KQL, you can get started with KQL queries here as we will need it in the following chapters as well: `https://learn.microsoft.com/en-us/azure/data-explorer/kql-quick-reference`.

Additionally, there are other ways to access the compliance information generated by your policy and initiative assignments. We can use command-line scripting, the **Azure REST API**, and **Azure Monitor Logs**. Policy evaluation and enforcement reporting is real-time. As soon as each policy is enabled in your Azure subscription, any resource that is to be created is evaluated before the process is allowed to proceed.

You can integrate Azure Policy assignments with other services as well, such as Event Grid, or create alerts so that you get notified about your resources. Azure Policy works great with Azure Defender for Cloud, whereby you can actually see the compliance state of your resources based on the industry compliance standards we outlined here. However, we will talk more about those dashboards and tools later in this book when we tackle all the logging and monitoring techniques in Azure.

Understandably, handling everything manually can create some administrative overhead. In the next section, we will explore how to automate some of those processes.

Compliance automation in Azure

As we saw in the previous section, following the built-in compliance standards and enforcing policies in our resources is relatively easy. However, it is rare that we have only one resource or one subscription to apply those policies to. Usually, we will go through creating development environments and then deploying them again as production environments, and sometimes, we even maintain both with similar policies and enforcement rules.

Recreating a development environment in Azure is easy as there are several ways to replicate resources between resource groups or subscriptions by using, for example, ARM templates and command-line scripts. However, ARM templates are only used to describe one or multiple related resources. Role assignments from **role-based access control (RBAC)** and policies must be recreated and reassigned to each subscription, resource group, or resource. In this case, we have another service that helps us recreate environments in Azure: **Azure Blueprints** and **Infrastructure as Code (IaC)**.

Let us discuss both in the following sections.

Azure Blueprints

While **ARM templates** in Azure Policy need to be deployed or assigned every time you need something implemented, the Azure Blueprints service leverages role assignments, policy assignments, ARM templates, and resource groups to replicate or recreate a complete environment, preserving resources and governance. Pretty much everything you accomplish with Azure blueprints you can also accomplish with Azure ARM templates. The difference is that ARM templates deploy one or more resources. Azure blueprints preserve the relationship between what should be deployed, the template and the blueprint assignment, policies, and so on.

How that works is by creating a blueprint definition. A blueprint definition is composed of artifacts—specifically, resource groups, ARM templates, policy assignments, and role assignments that target a subscription or management group. Artifacts can also be parametric. To create a blueprint, you only need to follow two steps:

1. First, you need to assign **Blueprint name** and **Definition location** values, which would be the subscription you want this blueprint applied to. This is shown in the following screenshot:

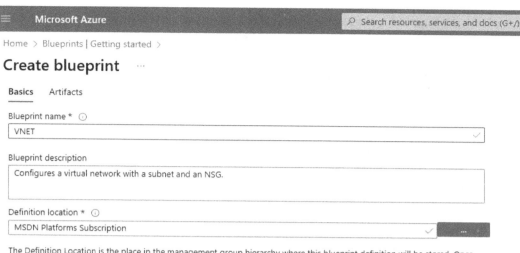

Figure 3.17 – Creating blueprint basic details

2. You need to declare artifacts and their parameters. Artifacts are resource groups, resource templates, RBAC assignments, and policies. Refer to the following screenshot:

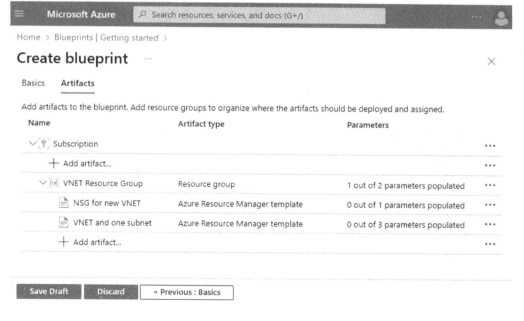

Figure 3.18 – Adding artifacts

While you are working with a blueprint, its mode is set to **Draft**. When you are ready to apply it, you need to publish the blueprint, and it is set as **Published**. Each blueprint you publish has a version number. We use the version to differentiate it from future changes to the same blueprint. If you want to make a change to a blueprint, the only thing you need to do is create a new version with any changes you would like and then apply it to the same subscription or management group.

IaC

The portal and the command-line tools are not the only way to deploy services in Azure. We can also leverage IaC as well as **DevOps** practices to ensure alignment of your environments, roles, and policies across subscriptions.

Governance through IaC on Azure refers to the practice of managing and governing Azure resources and configurations using code-based declarative templates. Azure provides tools and services that enable you to implement IaC for efficient and consistent management of its cloud infrastructure.

You can integrate IaC with version control and collaboration features, and you can also leverage continuous deployment and automation by integrating IaC with CI/CD pipelines. By integrating DevOps, you can automate the deployment, testing, and validation of any infrastructure changes.

Azure provides monitoring and auditing capabilities that can be leveraged with IaC. You can leverage and analyze logs and telemetry data so that you can monitor, and audit changes made to your infrastructure. This ensures compliance and governance in Azure. We will see how to leverage IaC and DevOps in ML (or, as we call it, **MLOps**) later in this book.

Summary

In this chapter, we learned how to develop AI systems responsibly and how to develop an ethical approach using Responsible AI tools. We became familiar with the industry security standards and learned how to enforce them using the Azure Policy service. Reporting and automation for regulatory compliance were never easier as there are a lot of tools we can use to help us view and maintain the compliance status of our services. For reporting and auditing, we have the **Compliance** and **Remediation** blades in Azure Policy, Azure Resource Graph Explorer, and command-line tools. To automate environment creation, we can leverage the Azure Blueprints service and IaC.

Now that we have a strategy and some knowledge of multiple security standards available out of the box, let us see how we can implement all those controls and guardrails in our Azure environment. As always when it comes to ML, we will start with the data.

In the next chapter, we will explain data governance and how to securely store, transmit, back up, and restore data used in our ML projects.

Part 2: Securing Your Data

Machine learning is based on data, so it is our priority to secure them. In this part, you will learn how to develop a data governance program and then how to secure data during storage and transfer. You will also learn how to work with backup and recovery services and how to identify and protect sensitive information and interpret ML models. Finally, you will explore best practices that use federated learning and secure multi-party computation.

This part has the following chapters:

- *Chapter 4, Data Protection and Governance*
- *Chapter 5, Data Privacy and Responsible AI Best Practices*

4

Data Protection and Governance

Data is a fundamental part of machine learning, so in this chapter, we will focus on all aspects of governing, storing, and securing data. We will start by explaining what data governance is and how vital it is to know what data we have. We need to know how to develop a management framework so that we can improve everything, from organizational workflows to business decisions. Data governance will also help us identify sensitive data and how we can better secure it, as part of our data governance program or our machine learning solutions.

We will begin by learning the best practices to store and retrieve data in Azure machine learning. We will see many data services that we can use to save our datasets – for example, the Azure Blob Storage and the Azure SQL database and their basic encryption and security features. Azure Machine Learning already provides us with a lot of features, such as versioning and logging, but since data is usually connected to the workspace and not saved in the workspace, it is important to familiarize ourselves with different security features from different services. Finally, we will explore backup options and recovery options because even though we will do our best to protect our assets, that does not mean we should not be prepared for the worst-case scenario, which is the need to recover our data from any data loss following human error or security incidents.

In this chapter, we're going to cover the following main topics:

- Working with data governance in Azure
- Storing and retrieving data in Azure Machine Learning
- Encrypting and securing data
- Exploring backup and recovery

By the end of this chapter, you will have a better idea of how to set up a data protection and governance framework for your organization, using the proper tools and best practices to secure your data in Azure Machine Learning.

Working with data governance in Azure

Data governance refers to the overall management and control of an organization's data assets. It involves establishing processes, policies, and guidelines to ensure availability, integrity, security, privacy, and the effective and efficient use of information. This is always important, but it is especially crucial when we're talking about ML, as ML models are based on data. Whether we're talking about data used to train our models or data generated by our models, it does not change the fact that we need to be aware of every piece of information we process and what its life cycle is.

To implement data governance effectively, organizations typically need to establish a data governance framework or strategy, which outlines the structure, processes, and responsibilities for data management. This framework should include the formation of a data governance committee or council, data governance policies and procedures, data stewardship roles, and the use of technology solutions to support data governance activities.

Data governance involves not only technical aspects but also business aspects. There are different types of information exchanged throughout different departments of an organization that all need to be a part of the company's data governance policy, which can be daunting at first. Remember that data governance is a collaborative effort involving people, processes, and technology. It requires ongoing commitment, communication, and engagement from all stakeholders to drive successful implementation, ensuring the long-term effectiveness of the data governance strategy. However, with multiple global and regional data regulations about security and privacy, not having a data governance strategy in your organization might result in financial loss and damage your reputation.

The complexity of creating those policies and processes presents us with many challenges; however, developing an efficient strategy also yields many benefits. Let us start with the challenges.

Identifying challenges

Challenges can be identified in each step as either technical, operational, or even human-oriented. Not all of them would apply to all organizations, but having an idea of the possible issues will help us prepare better for them. We will explore them together here:

- As we develop a new strategy, regardless of what it is, the most difficult part is often **company-wide acceptance**. The implementation of data governance usually requires a shift within an organization. Employees will need to change their behaviors, adopt new processes, and embrace a different mindset – a data-driven one, and that will disrupt their everyday routine. From the outset, if there is a lack of awareness and understanding, accepting a new strategy will be a struggle. Unfortunately, as data governance requires collaboration and coordination across different departments and business units, any lack of participation, misalignment of goals, and inconsistencies might hinder development and lead to fragmented data management practices that open up the organization to a lot of risks.

- Another challenge is **engaging and aligning the right stakeholders**. We need to involve relevant stakeholders from different departments and levels of the organization to ensure consistency and collaboration. This includes executives, IT professionals, data owners, data users, and legal and compliance teams. Understanding their perspectives, needs, and challenges is directly related to data management and governance and will lead to an effective data governance framework.

- Then, there is consistency or **standardization**. We really need to find the right balance between governance standards and flexibility. Creating overly complicated processes that increase data security and privacy, but hinder everyday business, is also not a welcome result. Data governance as a strategy aims to protect an organization from potential data breaches and non-compliance. Some allowances or exceptions might need to be made in some cases to allow for smooth business operations.

- If we have managed to more or less overcome the aforementioned challenges, there is then the question of the actual data. **Alignment of responsibilities** is something we really need to focus on even more if we are involved in ML development. Deciding who should and who should not have access to particular segments of data is crucial, but also only the first step. This can also be further segmented into what data should and should not be used to train an ML model.

- Finally, enabling the right **data governance tools and technologies** is also vital. We need to identify and implement appropriate tools and technologies to support data governance activities. This may include data cataloging tools, metadata management systems, data quality tools, and data security solutions. These tools help automate and streamline data governance processes, provide visibility into data assets, and facilitate data discovery and collaboration. In this and the next chapter, we will see several practices, tools, and product features that will help us do exactly that, specifically for ML.

If any of the preceding challenges are not addressed, it will lead to poor data management. That means unsecured and siloed information and incomplete and inconsistent processes. The result makes an organization vulnerable to data breaches and can even have adverse consequences in business operations, as decision-making could be impacted by a lack of information.

If we succeed in overcoming those challenges, we can reap multiple benefits. Let us review what they are in the next section.

Exploring benefits

Data governance can not only protect an organization but also improve business operations. According to Microsoft, a robust data governance strategy helps ensure that your information is audited, assessed, verified, managed, properly secured, and reliable.

The first and most obvious benefit is **improved data quality**. Data governance ensures that data is accurate, consistent, and reliable. By establishing data standards, implementing data quality controls, and assigning responsibilities, you can enhance the overall quality of your data. High-quality data enables more benefits, such as better decision-making, enhances operational efficiency, and improves business processes.

Data governance improves **decision-making**. It provides a solid foundation, and with reliable and trustworthy data available, decision-makers can make informed choices based on accurate insights, based in turn on current data. Data governance helps ensure that decision-makers have access to the right data, at the right time, in the right format, and with the appropriate context. This can also lead to reduced costs and **improved profitability**.

Additionally, as data governance focuses on protecting sensitive data and ensuring compliance with data privacy regulations, we also need **increased data compliance, security, and privacy**. By implementing data security measures, establishing access controls, and defining data handling procedures, we can greatly mitigate the risk of data breaches and unauthorized access. In Azure Machine Learning with the proper controls, you can also create compliance reports with data laws and regulations.

By creating processes and best data practices, you end up with **improved data management**. Any need, issues, or problems that arise can be found and mitigated more effectively. Data sharing and collaboration are done more efficiently and securely across different teams and departments. Data management can promote data integration and ensure data interoperability across systems and applications. By defining data standards, data formats, and data integration guidelines, organizations can achieve better data consistency and enhance data interoperability.

Finally, data management builds trust. Trust by your stakeholders and trust by your customers leads to a **stellar organizational reputation**. When it comes to trusting someone with data, an organization's reputation can be the deciding factor in their choice, as machine learning is trained and learns from old and new data.

Now that we understand how important data governance is, let us get started with learning best practices and exploring some tools and resources that can be applied with Azure Machine Learning and its related services.

Getting started using cloud data best practices

Azure Machine Learning is a cloud data service, and as you will see in the following chapters, most of the services that work with Azure Machine Learning are also cloud services or are hosted in Azure. As a result, we will focus on best practices that relate to cloud data management, and what better way to get started than to follow the **Cloud Data Management Capabilities** (**CDMC**) framework developed by a global industry council – the EDM Council.

The CDMC framework outlines the following 14 key controls to manage data risk:

- **Data control compliance** means that everything that contains sensitive data must be monitored, and notifications should be implemented should any issues arise.

- **Data ownership** must be clear on any piece of saved information, with the ability to be reported.

- **Authoritative data sources and provisioning points** should be available for all sensitive data.

- **Data sovereignty and cross-border movement** outline that sensitive data must be controlled and audited based on policies.

- **Data cataloging** should be automated consistently across departments or environments and, ideally, when data is created or ingested.

- **Data classification** should be completed and automated if possible for all sensitive data.

- **Data entitlements and access for sensitive data** should be managed by the owner and tracked.

- **Data consumption purposes** should be provided for all data, including any agreements.

- **Security controls** must be implemented to enforce data compliance.

- **Data protection impact assessments** should be in place and automated when an issue arises.

- **Data retention** is the data that is to be retained considering the data life cycle and eventually this data is deleted. This should be clearly defined and possibly automated.

- **Data quality** ensures that data is fit and classified properly, depending on its purpose.

- **Cost metrics** on how data is stored and moved must be available for reporting.

- **Data lineage** ensures that data origins and any usage can be identified.

The CDMC framework is available as a free license to all industries for internal use, including both EDM Council members and non-members. It can also be used to implement data governance, as well as an assessment tool. All you need to do is to accept their terms and conditions.

Data Management Capabilities (CDMC)

If you want to explore more about the CDMC framework and the EDM council, visit the official page: `https://edmcouncil.org/frameworks/cdmc/`.

However, no matter which framework or process you choose, completing everything at once might not be possible. Instead, you need to start small to guarantee a successful implementation. It might be good to appoint someone or a team to execute and monitor all the implementation across your organization. Then, make sure you have clear goals and a clear business case. Developing a proper metric to measure progress and keeping communication open throughout this entire process is also a vital part. The key is to realize that data governance goes beyond implementing a few IT solutions.

Also, while there is not a one-fits-all strategy that will work for every organization or industry, Azure provides multiple tools to implement controls and apply governance in your data. Let us explore some of them in the next section.

Exploring Azure tools and resources

We have already seen some tools to help us enforce compliance in our resources, such as Azure Policy and Azure Blueprints in *Chapter 3*. Let us review a couple more that apply to data governance.

Microsoft Cost Management

When working with data governance, one of the goals could be to optimize your cloud usage and spend. To monitor and get recommendations, you can use Microsoft Cost Management. This is free for Azure subscriptions, but it can be used to monitor other clouds. In the latter case, you might need to check what the management costs are.

Azure cost management includes reporting on cost and usage, multiple categorization options, creating usage budgets, and the ability to set alerts on forecasted costs.

Let us see some examples of how to use the service:

- In the next figure, you can see the **Cost analysis** blade of **Cost Management**. Some features are still in preview at the time of writing, but it gives us a good idea of what the subscriptions and each resource cost.

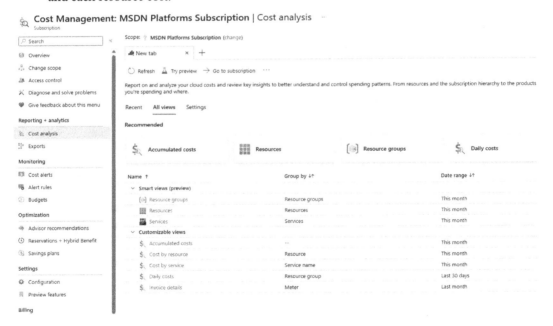

Figure 4.1 – A Cost Management overview

- Here, we can create reports by resource, service, or even time period. These reports are customizable and provide a graphic representation of the actual and forecasted cost of each billing period, as shown in the following figure:

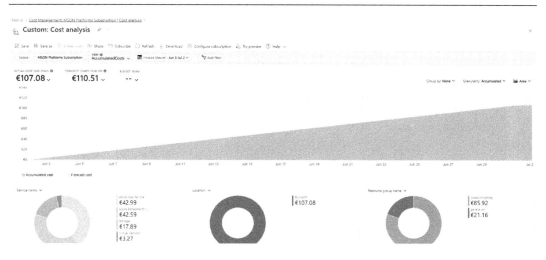

Figure 4.2 – Cost analysis

- You can create alerts to detect anomalies or based on recommendations very easily in the **Cost alerts** menu. Once you click **Add** and fill in the fields, you have your alert ready. You will receive email alerts every time something happens.

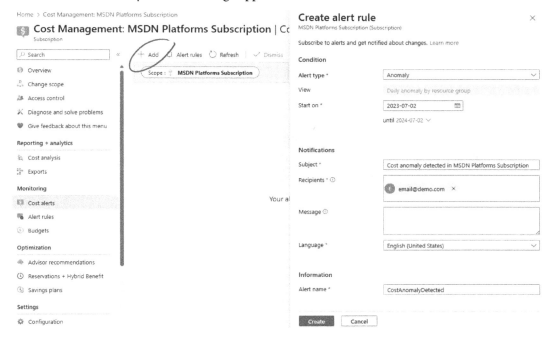

Figure 4.3 – Create alert rule

- If you want an alert based on a budget, you will need to create it through the **Budgets** menu. Once you set a budget, you can create alerts based on usage or forecasted usage so that you are always up to date, ensuring that you will never go above your budget. The process has two steps:

  I.   First, you create a **budget amount**. You get a graph with information about your past usage to help you decide what the approximate budget should be if you do not already have a predefined amount.

Figure 4.4 – Create budget

  II. The second step is to set **Alert conditions** and **Alert recipients**. The alerts are either on the actual amount or the forecasted amount, which helps you get notified before you go over a certain threshold and plan accordingly. This is shown here:

Figure 4.5 – Create budget alerts

You can also work with the Azure Advisor recommendations to find usage and cost best practices for the services you use for your subscription. Generally, any information that can optimize cloud usage should be part of your organization's governance.

Azure Advisor cost recommendations

At `https://learn.microsoft.com/en-us/azure/advisor/advisor-reference-cost-recommendations`, you can find some cost recommendations for different services. However, they will not be shown in the **Advisor recommendation** blade if you have not deployed these services.

Microsoft Purview

Microsoft Purview is a data governance, risk, and compliance solution designed to help organizations manage and govern their data assets across various sources and platforms. Its features apply both to Azure and **Microsoft 365**, and you can use it to protect sensitive data between different clouds, apps, and devices and identify and manage regulatory compliance.

Microsoft Purview offers several key features to support data governance. The basis of this support is the **Data Map**. Purview provides a data map feature that helps organizations visualize and understand the relationships and characteristics of their data assets. The data map in Purview represents a graphical representation of the data landscape within an organization, including data sources, connections, and metadata.

On top of the Data Map, you will find many apps for different purposes:

- The **Data Catalog** app finds data sources by searching your data and helping classify them
- The **Data Estate Insights** app helps you find out what kinds of data you have and where it is
- The **Data Sharing** app helps you secure your data between partners and customers
- The **Data Policy** assists with access provisioning

Microsoft Purview integrates with various Azure services, such as Azure Data Factory and Azure SQL Database, to provide end-to-end data governance capabilities. It leverages Azure's security and compliance features to ensure data protection and regulatory compliance, and any sensitive data discovered is shared with **Microsoft Defender for Cloud**. By using Purview, you can establish a comprehensive data governance framework to improve data visibility, control, and compliance. It helps to address challenges related to data sprawl, data privacy, and regulatory requirements by providing a centralized platform to manage and govern data assets effectively.

Data governance is very important, so after we have identified where sensitive data is, we will see how to work with it securely with Azure Machine Learning.

Let us start with the storage and retrieval of data.

Storing and retrieving data in Azure Machine Learning

The first task is storing and retrieving data in Azure Machine Learning. You can bring data into Machine Learning in a multitude of ways. That includes anything from your local machine, a source on the internet, or even cloud-based storage. In this section, we will explore all those concepts.

Let us see how to work with datastores.

Connecting datastores

As we mentioned in the Azure Machine Learning introduction in *Chapter 1*, **datastores** serve as a *reference* to an existing storage service, whether that is a storage account or a database. If you already have a reference or a connection to your data, this is not mandatory, as you can connect external sources as well, but connecting datastores has many benefits. Firstly, you have a common way to connect different data sources to your workspace without the need to add credential information anywhere in your scripts or your code, which is a best practice in terms of security. It is easier when you are working with a team to have the same reference available for your data sources that everyone can reuse. And, of course, this offers a common straightforward way to use APIs that can work with different storage types.

When you create a datastore, you can use different authentication methods. It can be either credential-based or identity-based. Credential-based means using a service principal or a **shared access signature (SAS)** token for authentication, while with identity-based authentication, you will use your Microsoft Entra ID identity or a managed identity. In any case, the connection and authentication information is stored in the workspace. We are not going to focus much on this now, as we will analyze all the different types of authentication options that you can use together with machine learning in the next chapters.

Every workspace has four built-in datastores, which are used by Azure Machine Learning as the system storage. There are two Azure Blob Storage datastores and two Azure Files datastores under the **Datastores** tab in the **Data** menu. You can see what the default is or set another one as the default datastore from here.

The list will look something similar to the following screenshot:

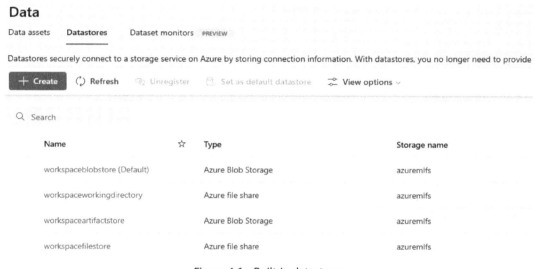

Figure 4.6 – Built-in datastores

If you want to create a new datastore, the currently available options are the ones shown in the following screenshot:

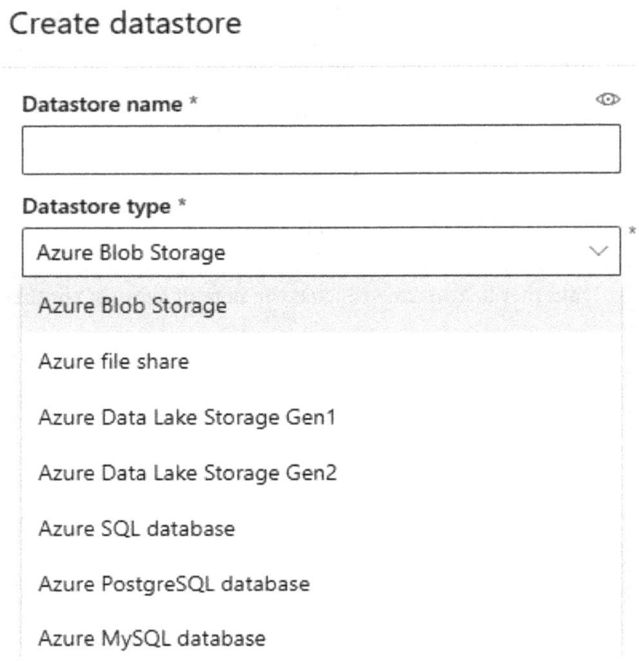

Create datastore

Datastore name *   ⊙

┌───┐
│   │
└───┘

Datastore type *

┌───┐
│ Azure Blob Storage   ∨ │
└───┘

Azure Blob Storage

Azure file share

Azure Data Lake Storage Gen1

Azure Data Lake Storage Gen2

Azure SQL database

Azure PostgreSQL database

Azure MySQL database

Figure 4.7 – The Create datastore options

You can create datastores from the Azure portal, the **command-line interface** (**CLI**), or the Python **software development kit** (**SDK**). Currently, it looks like you can only add datastores from a subscription you have access to. You can add or remove datastores at any time. Remember that they are only a connection to the service that has the data. So, creating or removing a datastore from the workspace does not actually delete or create any services and is not mandatory. Also, we still need to make sure all of the connected services are secured using their own features and best practices. What we will use in our experiments are data assets.

Let us see how we can create data assets in the workspace, either from datastores we have added to our workspace or from external services.

Adding data assets

In Azure Machine Learning, data assets refer to the several types of data that can be used and managed within the machine learning workflows. If datastores are a connection to the data source, then data assets are a reference to the actual data. You can create a data asset from datastores, local files, public URLs, or Azure Open Datasets.

Using data assets together with datastores, if possible, provides us with several security and data governance benefits. You can collaborate using the same data asset with your team and access it through your training code seamlessly, without looking for different credentials or paths. Data assets support versioning, so any updates or data processing can be saved as a new version and reused. Pipelines or jobs that use the data are recorded in the workspace, so any changes or updates can be audited.

Once you create a data asset version, it is **immutable**, which means it cannot be deleted or edited. So, if a new version of the data asset does not provide the expected results, you can always revert to a previous one to work with. You can use different asset types from older Azure Machine Learning APIs, but it is recommended to work with the latest version, which is the Azure ML v2 APIs.

In v2, there are the following three main types of data assets you can use:

- **URI file**: The URI file points to a specific file

- **URI folder**: The URI folder points to a folder

- **MLTable**: An MLTable points to a folder or file and includes a schema to read as tabular data

The choice depends on the available data you have and the type of ML project and algorithm you choose.

Regardless of the data type, you have three available sources, as shown in the following screenshot:

Figure 4.8 – Creating a datastore options

If you are choosing **From a URI** as your source, ensure the endpoint is public and not protected by any credentials. If you want to choose an existing datastore, you can choose the **From Azure Storage** option. Then, if the datastore you want is not pre-created, you can create it right through the wizard and find the file path in the list. You can also upload your own files to the datastore of your choice by choosing the **From local files** option.

> **Best practice**
>
> Use datastores in combination with data assets where supported. Datastores provide security, as credentials are stored in the workspace and not in your code. With data assets, you gain capabilities such as versioning, reproducibility, auditability, and lineage, which are all part of data governance best practices.

Now that we know how to connect data to the workspace, let us ensure that it is as secure as possible, both when it is not used and in transfer.

Encrypting and securing data

As we saw in the previous section, Azure Machine Learning relies on external services to pull in data as data assets. Depending on the service that hosts the data, there are different security and data protection features we can use, such as encryption, data classification, and data masking.

In this section, we will explore encryption and classification features that relate to our data.

Encryption at rest

Encryption at rest refers to the practice of encrypting data while it is stored or *at rest* in a storage medium, such as cloud storage. The purpose of encryption at rest is to protect data from unauthorized access if the storage medium is compromised, lost, or stolen.

When data is encrypted at rest, it is transformed into an unreadable form using an encryption algorithm and a cryptographic key. Only authorized users or processes with the proper decryption key can access and decrypt the data to its original readable form. Without the decryption key, the encrypted data remains unintelligible and useless to unauthorized individuals.

In the context of Azure services, Azure provides built-in encryption at rest for many of its storage services, such as Azure Blob Storage, Azure Data Lake Storage, and other services such as the relational databases used by Azure Machine Learning. These services automatically encrypt data at rest using industry-standard encryption algorithms. Azure manages the encryption keys and ensures the security of the encrypted data.

Implementing encryption at rest not only provides security but also forms a part of organizational compliance with data protection regulations, strengthens data security, and mitigates the risk of data breaches or unauthorized access to sensitive information.

Let us explore those features in data services that work with Azure Machine Learning.

Azure Storage

When we create an Azure Machine Learning workspace, you also create an Azure storage account. The service stores snapshots, outputs, and logs in a default storage account that is tied to the Azure Machine Learning workspace and your subscription, and it is used as the workspace filesystem. It also serves to host the training data that is used by training compute targets. It is mounted to those compute targets as a remote filesystem during the training process. Finally, if you choose to upload files, they are stored in your chosen datastore, which is usually an Azure Blob storage. So, knowing how to secure your Azure Blob storage account is necessary. The same applies to Azure Data Lake Storage, as it is essentially an upgraded Blob Storage account.

An Azure storage account is encrypted at rest using Microsoft-managed keys. In this case, Microsoft online services automatically generate and securely store the encryption keys used. If you want to control and use your own encryption key, open the **Encryption** menu in the **Storage account** blade and switch to the encryption options with **Customer-managed keys**, as shown in the following screenshot:

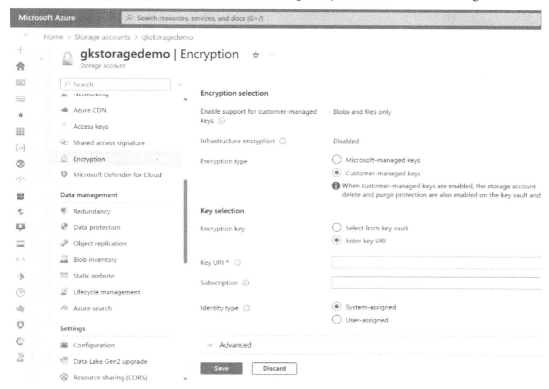

Figure 4.9 – Creating datastore options

Enter the key URI where your key is hosted and click **Save**.

> **Best practice – customer-managed keys and Azure Key Vault**
>
> Use the Azure Key Vault service to generate and store encryption keys. For more information about the service, follow this link: https://learn.microsoft.com/en-us/azure/key-vault/general/overview.

The data store connected to the Azure Blob storage uses an account access key for access. Each storage account has two access keys. Find yours on the **Access keys** menu of your **Storage account** blade:

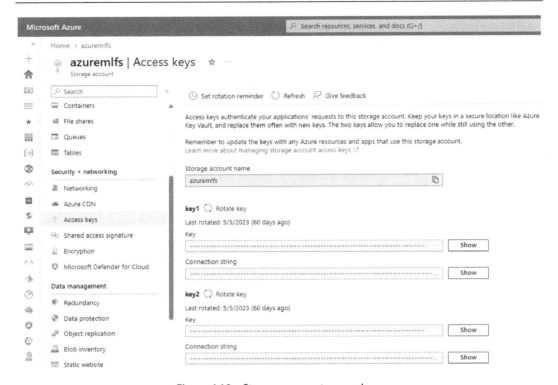

Figure 4.10 – Storage account access keys

You can use either key for authentication in Azure Machine Learning. These keys must be rotated at frequent intervals for security. This is how the process might look like when rotating access keys. This process applies to any services that authenticate using **access keys**.

Figure 4.11 – The key rotation process

You can also use an SAS token to authenticate to the storage account; however, be careful, as SAS tokens expire, and after the expiration date, you will not be able to have access to that storage account to work with Azure Machine Learning.

To create an account-level SAS token, go to the **Shared access signature** menu in the **Storage account** blade and generate a token, as shown here:

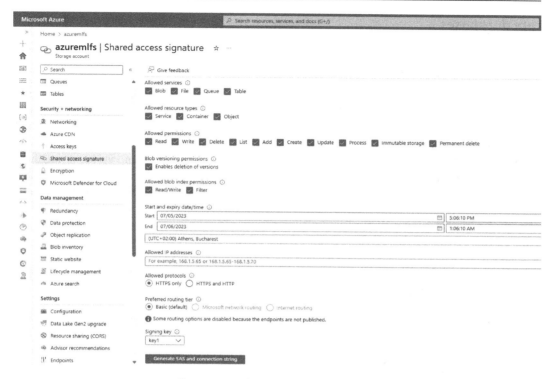

Figure 4.12 – Generating an account SAS

Be mindful to include proper permissions and service visibility. Once you are happy with your choices, you can go back to the Azure Machine Learning Studio, open the datastore, and by clicking the **Update authentication** button, you can update the datastore with the new credentials.

Figure 4.13 – Updating the authentication credentials in the workspace

However, the storage account is not our only datastore. Let us discuss more options and their features, starting with Azure databases.

Azure databases

There are a lot of database options in Azure. Most of those services offer similar security options that can be leveraged to secure data adhering to encryption and other data best practices.

Most services for relational databases use encryption similarly to an Azure storage account – for example, Azure Database for PostgreSQL and Azure Cosmos DB, the no-SQL multi-modal database. These services have encryption enabled by default, using Microsoft-managed keys, and you can always choose to use your own key by enabling the **Customer-managed keys** option and adding the key to the Azure Blob Storage account. Azure Database for MySQL also offers encryption, using the FIPS 140-2 validated cryptographic module for storage encryption of data at rest. Depending on the service, you might find more security features, such as the ones we have in the Azure SQL Database.

Let us take a closer look at the Azure SQL database security features.

Azure SQL Database

Azure SQL Database offers several encryption features to protect data at rest and during transit. When it comes to encryption, Azure SQL Database offers multiple options.

- **Transparent data encryption** (TDE): Transparent data encryption is a built-in feature in Azure SQL Database that automatically encrypts data at rest. TDE encrypts database files (e.g., data, backups, and log files) using a symmetric **database encryption key** (DEK). TDE helps protect data from unauthorized access.

> **Best practice – TDE in Azure SQL Database**
> With the TDE and **Bring Your Own Key** (BYOK) option, you can take control of the TDE by using the Azure Key Vault service and the customer-managed keys for encryption.

- **Always Encrypted**: Always Encrypted is a feature that allows you to encrypt sensitive data such as credit card information within Azure SQL Database, both at rest and during transit. With Always Encrypted, the data remains encrypted within the database, and only authorized applications and users with the necessary encryption keys can access and decrypt the data. The encryption and decryption of data occur on the client side, ensuring that the sensitive data is never exposed in plain text to the database engine or administrators.

Azure SQL Database also provides data governance and protection features for data masking and classification to help protect sensitive data and manage data privacy. Let us review these features in Azure SQL Database:

- **Data Classification**: Data Classification is a feature in Azure SQL Database that helps you identify and label sensitive data within your database. It enables you to classify columns containing sensitive information, based on predefined or custom-defined classification labels. Azure SQL Database provides built-in classification labels for common types of sensitive data, such as credit card numbers, social security numbers, or email addresses. You can then use the Data Masking feature to protect this information from unauthorized access.

- **Data Masking**: Data Masking is a feature that allows you to obfuscate sensitive data within Azure SQL Database. It helps protect sensitive information from unauthorized access by replacing the original values with masked values in query results. The masking rules include partial masking (for example, showing only the last four digits of a credit card number) or full masking (for example, replacing the original value with a constant value or random characters or stars). Data Masking operates at the database level and can be configured for specific columns containing sensitive data. This allows you to control the level of obfuscation applied to different types of sensitive data.

> **Best practice: Azure SQL Database data classification and Azure Purview**
>
> You can use the Data Classification feature in Azure SQL Database together with Azure Purview to discover, classify, and manage data across various data sources in your organization.

Data integration Services

Azure Machine Learning works with many data integration services, such as Azure Data Factory, Azure Databricks, and Azure Synapse Analytics. Azure Data Factory allows you to create data-driven workflows for data integration and data transformation at scale. It is a serverless and code-free platform for **extract-transform-load (ETL)**, **extract-load-transform (ELT)**, and data integration. Its pipelines can be used for data ingestion, so you can use them with Azure Machine Learning. Azure Databricks is a data analytics platform that runs data science workloads based on Apache Spark. Models created in Databricks can then be deployed in Azure Machine Learning. Both of these services offer built-in encryption with Microsoft-managed or customer-managed keys.

Azure Synapse Analytics is a limitless analytics service that brings together big data and data warehousing. We can use it to ingest, prepare, manage, and serve data for business intelligence and support ways of implementing machine learning and integrating with Azure Machine Learning. Depending on the type of pool you use, there are different encryption options. For dedicated SQL pools, you can use TDE, whereas for the Azure Synapse SQL serverless pool or the Apache Spark pool, since they are based on **Azure Data Lake Gen2 (ALDS Gen2)** or Azure Blob Storage, you can leverage the storage account security options.

We saw how multiple services handle encryption at rest, but data is meant to be communicated between systems, so let us talk about encryption in transit.

Encryption in transit

Encryption in transit refers to the practice of encrypting data as it is being transmitted over a network or communication channel from one location to another. It ensures that the data remains secure and protected from unauthorized access.

When it comes to Azure Machine Learning, encryption in transit is a vital aspect of securing data and communication between different components of the platform.

Azure Machine Learning enforces the use of secure communication protocols, such as **HTTPS** (short for **Hypertext Transfer Protocol Secure**) or TLS (short for **Transport Layer Security**), for data transmission. These protocols establish an encrypted connection between the client applications, Azure Machine Learning services, and other components, ensuring that data transmitted over a network is encrypted and cannot be easily intercepted or tampered with.

By implementing encryption at rest and in transit, along with other security features in Azure Machine Learning and all its related services, we can protect sensitive data and ensure its privacy and integrity during transmission. Then, we can prevent unauthorized access or interference, enhancing the overall security posture of your machine learning projects. This is only step one, however. As with any security matter, we can hope for the best, but we should always be prepared for the worst.

Let us explore in the next section how we can deploy guardrails to ensure we can recover data after an incident.

Exploring backup and recovery

Backup and recovery are closely related concepts and are both needed so that we can safeguard our data. In this section, we will explain backup and recovery options for our workspace and the data connected to them. We will also talk about how to approach situations where backup options are not available. However, before we get started, let us remember what backup and recovery are.

Backup refers to the process of creating copies or replicas of data and storing them in a separate location or medium. The purpose of backups is to provide a means of recovering data if there is data loss, accidental deletion, system failures, disasters, or other unforeseen events. Backups serve as a safety net, allowing you to restore data to its previous state or a specific point in time. Backups can be performed at different levels, such as full backups (copying all data), incremental backups (copying only the changes since the last backup), or differential backups (copying the changes since the last full backup). Different backup strategies and schedules can be implemented based on an organization's requirements and data protection needs.

Recovery, on the other hand, refers to the process of restoring data from backups after a data loss event or any other incident that results in the unavailability or corruption of data. The recovery process involves accessing the backup copies and returning the data to its original state, or a consistent state, before the data loss occurred. Recovery can take different forms, depending on the nature of the data loss and the backup strategy in place. It may involve restoring individual files or directories, recovering an entire system or database, or even restoring data to a different location or environment.

Let us explore our backup and recovery options in the next sections.

Reviewing backup options for your datastores

Since Azure Storage serves as a filesystem for a workspace, it is the most important thing that we need to secure and backup. We need to remember that the workspace does not extend any protection to its datastores, so we need to learn the basic features of each one.

Before we dive into the features of each service, we can take another step to protect our resources from accidental deletion by using resource locks.

Azure resource locks

Azure resource locks allow users to apply restrictions on Azure resources to prevent accidental deletion or modification, providing an additional layer of protection and governance for critical resources. There are two types of locks to protect against delete and read-only instances. The process is extremely simple. You create a lock on the resource, the resource group, or the subscription, and nobody can make any changes unless they have the appropriate permissions to remove the lock temporarily in order to make changes.

To create a resource lock, find the **Locks** menu on your desired resource and click the **Add** button, as shown in the following screenshot:

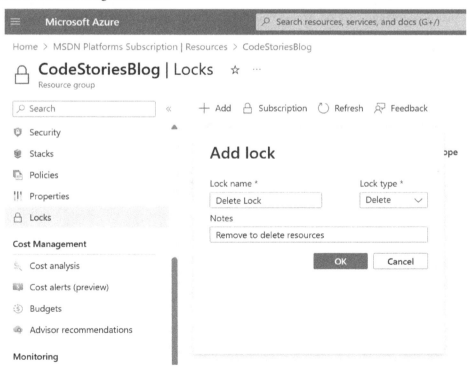

Figure 4.14 – Adding a resource lock

Add a lock name, lock type, and some notes if you want. As soon as you hit **OK**, the resources cannot be deleted or changed, depending on the Lock type. We have read-only and delete locks available.

Azure Resource locks are not exactly a backup solution, and they only protect the resources, not the data, so let us review our options.

Azure Storage

There are multiple levels to protect data in the storage account that we use for ML. There are the blob containers, the blobs themselves, and the file shares.

Some of the following features apply to one or more levels of the storage account. Let us explore each feature:

- **Immutability policies**: At the container level and the blob level, you can enable immutability policies that help you enforce a time period where your data is protected from modifications or deletions. Immutability policies are not only for data protection but also provide auditing and monitoring. They should be part of your governance process, as they can ensure compliance with legal and compliance requirements and data preservation.

  To enable immutability policies at the container level, open the chosen container blade in the storage account, and click on **Access Policy**. In the **Immutable Blob Storage** section, click + **Add policy**. Choose **Time-based retention** in the **Policy type** dropdown, add the *days* where blobs cannot be modified, and click **Save**.

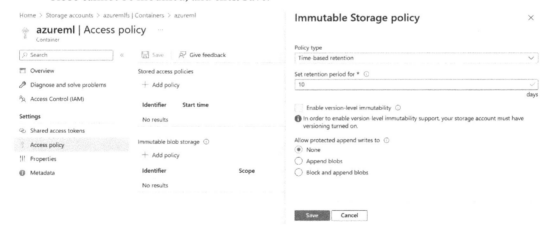

Figure 4.15 – A new immutable storage policy

- **Soft delete**: At both the container and the blob level you can also enable a soft delete. Soft delete provides an additional layer of data protection by allowing you to recover deleted blobs or containers within a specified time frame, reducing the risk of accidental data loss. It is particularly useful in scenarios where data needs to be retained and recoverable, such as compliance requirements, accidental deletions, or data recovery needs.

To enable soft delete, go to the **Data Protection** section in the **Storage account** blade, and enable soft delete for blobs and containers by checking the corresponding box, as demonstrated in the following screenshot. Fill in the retention in days for each option, and click **Save**.

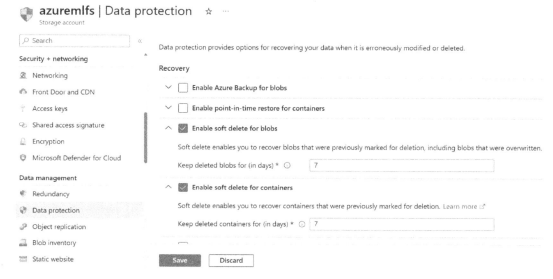

Figure 4.16 – Enabling soft delete

To restore a blob, go to the container and enable the **Show deleted** blobs button. Then, choose the deleted blob, and select **Undelete** from the three-dot menu on the right.

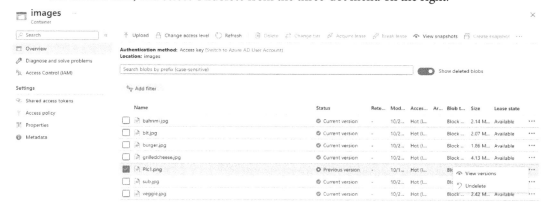

Figure 4.17 – Restoring a blob

- **Point-in-time restore**: Containers and blobs also support point-in-time restore, meaning you can restore a blob or container to a previous state before it was deleted. It is useful in scenarios where an application or a system makes multiple deletes or unintended changes, and it is difficult to find each individual file or container to restore. Backup is continuous in this case.

To enable point-in-time restore, go to the **Data protection** section in the **Storage account** blade, and enable point-in-time restore for containers by checking the corresponding box, as demonstrated in the next screenshot. Fill in the maximum restore point in days, and click **Save**.

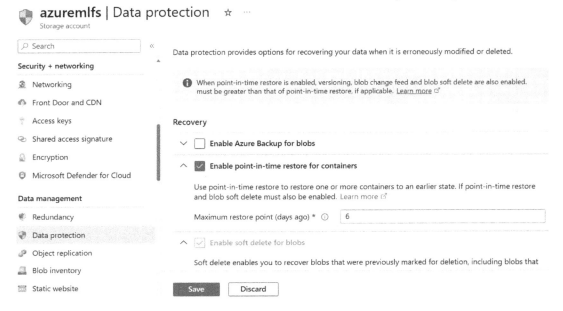

Figure 4.18 – Enabling a point-in-time restore

To restore a container to a previous point in time, select the container and click on the **Restore containers** button. Then, choose a previous point in time. This action cannot be undone, so ensure you choose wisely.

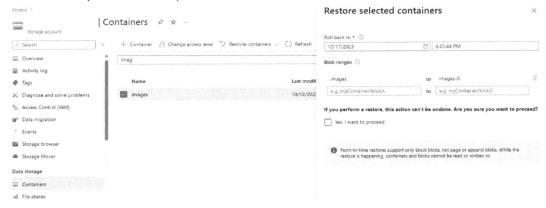

Figure 4.19 – Restoring to a previous point in time

- **Vaulted backup (operational and vaulted)**: Vaulted backup uses object replication to replicate blobs to an external backup vault. This process happens asynchronously and requires an external Azure Backup vault resource. To restore the objects, we can start a restore operation. Backups are either operational (continuous) or periodic by creating a custom policy.

To enable vaulted backups, go to the **Data protection** section in the **Storage account** blade, and click the **Enable Azure Backup for blobs** checkbox. If you already have a backup vault, you can choose it in the dropdown; otherwise, choose to create and fill in the **Vault name**, **Resource group**, and **Backup storage redundancy** options, as shown in the following screenshot.

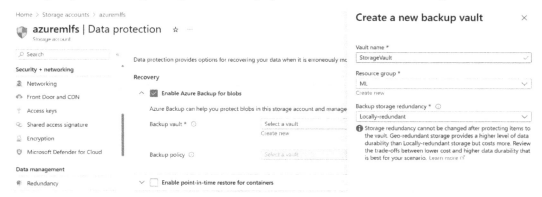

Figure 4.20 – Enabling Azure Backup

Then, choose the backup policy. If you have one, you can select it; otherwise, click **Create new**.

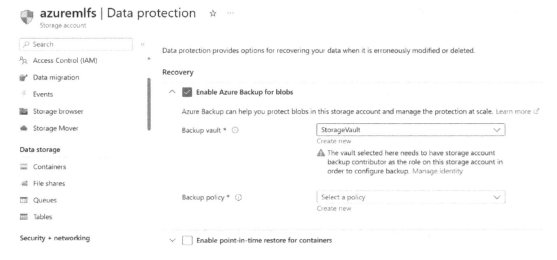

Figure 4.21 – Creating or choosing a backup vault

Provide the policy with a name, and ensure that the **Datasource type** option is **Azure Blobs**. Then, click **Next**.

Create Backup Policy ...
StorageVault

① **Basics**   ② Schedule + retention   ③ Review + create

Policy name *	WeeklyStoragePolicy ✓
Datasource type * ⓘ	Azure Blobs (Azure Storage) ⌄
Vault *	StorageVault

Selected backup vault details

Subscription
Resource group
Location   West Europe
Backup storage redundancy   Locally-redundant

Figure 4.22 – Creating a policy

Set up the schedule and retention for both the operational and vaulted backups.

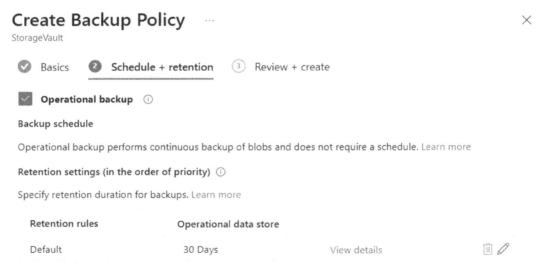

Create Backup Policy ...   ✕
StorageVault

✓ Basics   ② **Schedule + retention**   ③ Review + create

✓ **Operational backup** ⓘ

Backup schedule

Operational backup performs continuous backup of blobs and does not require a schedule. Learn more

Retention settings (in the order of priority) ⓘ

Specify retention duration for backups. Learn more

Retention rules	Operational data store		
Default	30 Days	View details	🗑 ✏

Figure 4.23 – Configuring an operational backup

For this example, we are using a weekly backup schedule, as shown in the following screenshot.

☑ **Vaulted backup (preview)** ⓘ

Backup schedule

Specify time when the backup will happen

| Backup Frequency ⓘ | ○ Daily |
| | ◉ Weekly |

Days *	Sunday ⌄
Time	1:00 AM ⌄
Timezone	(UTC) Coordinated Universal Time ⌄

Retention settings (in the order of priority) ⓘ

Specify retention duration for backups. Learn more

Retention rules	Vault-standard		
Default	7 Days	View details	🗑 ✎
Add retention rule			

Figure 4.24 – Configuring a vaulted backup

Finally, we can filter the containers included in this backup if necessary, by clicking the **Select containers** link and then clicking **Save**.

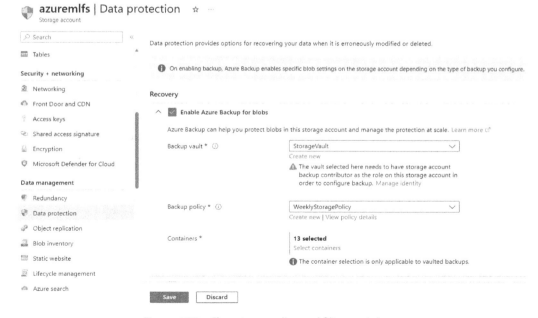

Figure 4.25 – Choosing a policy and filter containers

To restore, start a **Restore** operation from the **Overview** blade of the backup vault.

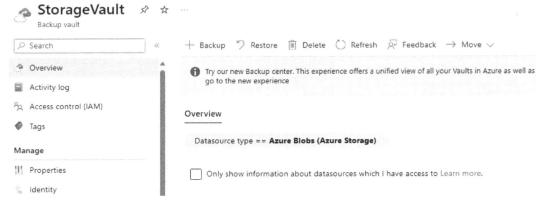

Figure 4.26 – Starting a restore operation

> **Soft delete and cost management**
>
> Soft deleted data continues to occupy storage space and is billed accordingly during the retention period. However, storage costs are usually lower compared to active data storage. After the retention period is over, the soft deleted data is automatically purged, and you will no longer have any storage costs for it.

- **Object replication**: Object replication essentially copies data from a container or the whole storage account to another storage account in the same or a different region. That way, you can keep two copies of your data if something happens. It is a great way to back up your data without downloading it into another medium and reuploading it.

  To set it up, click on the **Object replication** section of the **Storage account** blade, and then click on the **Create replication rules** button. Before you proceed, you need to have already created a second storage account to replicate the data and the necessary destination containers.

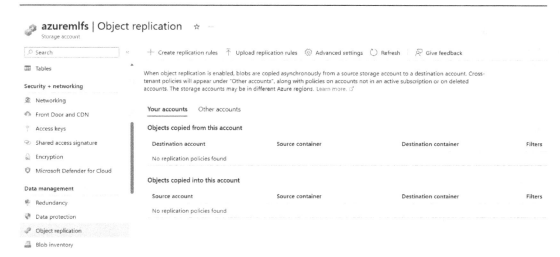

Figure 4.27 – Adding object replication

On the **Create replication** rules screen, select the destination of the storage account, create a source-to-destination container mapping so that objects are replicated to their corresponding containers, and then click **Save**, as shown in the following screenshot.

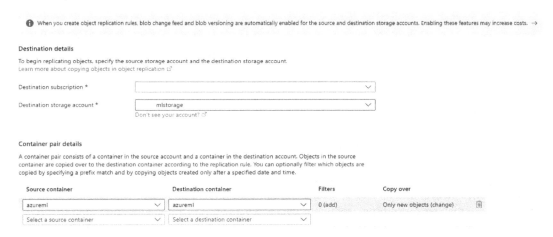

Figure 4.28 – Choose a target storage account and container mapping

> **Best practices**
>
> Out of the aforementioned options, the best combination for Azure Machine Learning would be object replication in a storage account, located in a different region or vaulted backups. These options protect us from regional disasters. Additionally, use soft delete enabled with delete resource locks to prevent resource and unintended data deletions. Immutability rules might interfere with the Azure Machine Learning workspace functions, so I would not recommend it, with the exception of legal holds.

The preceding options are fine; however, you can also use AzCopy, a cross-platform command-line tool, or data integration services such as the Azure Data Factory to accomplish the same goal. Keep in mind that, in this case, you are essentially duplicating your data in another storage account, which is accompanied by extra costs.

> **AzCopy**
>
> AzCopy is a command-line tool provided by Microsoft that allows you to transfer data to and from Azure storage services. It is commonly used for large-scale data migration scenarios, as well as to transfer data between different Azure storage accounts or Azure regions. The tool is available for Windows, Linux, and macOS, and it can be executed from the command line or integrated into scripts or automation workflows. To start using this tool, visit this link: https://learn. microsoft.com/en-us/azure/storage/common/storage-use-azcopy-v10.

If you are using relational databases or any other data services, they too have their individual backup and recovery options, so make sure you review everything. Most services do have defaults enabled, so you won't be completely unprotected, but others require more configuration than others to be secured.

Let us see how to recover the most important part of your ML project, the Azure Machine Learning workspace itself.

Recovering your workspace

External services might not be the only thing that you need to be able to recover. Perhaps the most important thing is the Azure Machine Learning studio workspace. The workspace serves as a central point where you manage everything, from your data assets to your running jobs and publishing the models to be consumed by applications.

The Azure Machine Learning workspace supports soft delete by default. This feature gives you the ability to recover your workspace data after accidental deletions. However, in this case, it does not work similarly to an Azure storage account. When you create and work in your workspace, there are a lot of components that connect to the workspace. Not everything can be soft-deleted; some of those items are permanently deleted, and there's nothing you can do to recover them. Among the recoverable items are the run history, models, data, environments, components, notebooks, pipelines, data labeling, and datastores. Any queued or running jobs, role assignments, compute, inference endpoints, and any linked Databricks workspaces are hard-deleted. This means that these items cannot be recovered even if you try to recover the soft-deleted workspace.

Soft delete has a default retention period of 14 days. After those 14 days, any remaining data is purged from the system, and the workspace can no longer be recovered. However, even between those 14 days, a full recovery isn't guaranteed. You might be able to get a lot of your data and notebooks back, but you still might need to recreate any jobs or anything else that you had running.

The process of recovering the workspace is simple. All you need to do is go to the Azure Machine Learning category, and from the top of the page, you will find the **Recently deleted** button to view workspaces that were soft-deleted and are within the retention period. From there, you can choose to either recover or permanently delete a workspace, as shown in the following screenshot:

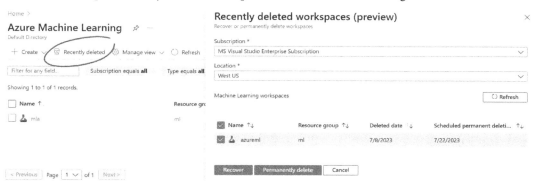

Figure 4.29 – Recovering or deleting a workspace

You can always override the default behavior of soft-deleting the workspace and choose to permanently delete it when you first attempt to delete the service, as shown in the following screenshot:

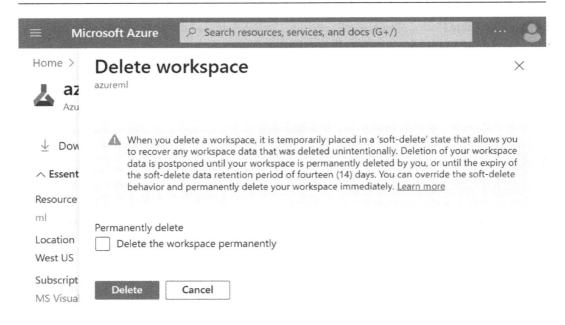

Figure 4.30 – Adding a resource lock

> **Best practice – Azure Machine Learning workspace recovery**
>
> Use resource locks to protect your resources from accidental deletions or modifications, instead of relying on soft delete for recovery. Even if the recovery is a success, you will still have lost a lot of data and configurations.

Although data backup is very important, it is only one of the preventative steps we need to take to protect our assets. We also need to know how to recover data and its associated resources as part of our security baseline, a process that must be tested at specific intervals so that we are prepared if the need arises. Testing the recovery process will also help us measure how long it takes for a full recovery and what the impact would be on everyday operations. If any downtime, for example, is not acceptable, we might need to utilize other measures.

Summary

Everything is based on data, so having a clear map of what data you have, where it is stored, how sensitive it is, and how to protect it should be your number one priority if you work with ML. So, while working with models and algorithms might be the most exciting part of ML, having a data governance and protection plan will save you from data-related issues. The CDMC framework is a very comprehensive strategy that you can use especially with cloud data, but as always, it is not the only option. Building your own data strategy policy is ultimately your decision, and the result will always be beneficial, depending on the industry and location you belong to.

As soon as you decide on a strategy, there are a lot of tools in Azure available for governance, such as Azure Policy, Azure Blueprints, Cost Management, and Microsoft Purview, each with its own benefits and limitations. As tools can come and go and data governance is not a one-off process, do not be afraid to start small and then add or improve over time as different needs arise.

Also, as exciting planning and strategizing sounds, starting a new project is the time to take action. Encrypting and securing data in Azure Machine Learning is a process affecting multiple services, and we need to leverage the benefits and features of each service to have a completely safe and performant system.

In this chapter, we only glimpsed at several connected data services and their security features. Backup and recovery options work in the same manner, and they need to be combined with the security and backup options of the Azure Machine Learning workspace. But it does not end here. We still have to cover security best practices in our network, infrastructure, DevOps, and so on. Before we can do that, let us go and see how we can extend our data protection to work with data privacy and responsible AI best practices in the next chapter.

5

Data Privacy and Responsible AI Best Practices

In the previous chapter, we talked about how to build a data governance program for our organization and how to identify types of sensitive data. Our work does not stop there. Although in some cases we can safely exclude sensitive information, other times we cannot. So, our **machine learning** (**ML**) models that solve problems might need to contain personal data. Sometimes that data can be relevant and useful, or it can create unintended correlations that make the model biased. This is the issue that we will tackle in this chapter.

We will talk about how to recognize sensitive information and how to mitigate it if it is not relevant to the model training process by using techniques such as differential privacy. We will explore how to protect individual information even from aggregated data or the model results. To help us with that, we will see how we can use the SmartNoise **software development kit** (**SDK**).

We will also discuss fairness and how you can recognize bias in your model's predictions. Here, we will apply the responsible AI principles we have learned together with the Fairlearn library and the Responsible AI dashboard. Together with bias comes model interpretability. We will analyze together how to calculate which features affect the prediction of your model for global or individual predictions by generating feature-importance values with model explainers.

Finally, we will wrap up by explaining **federated learning** (**FL**) and secure multi-party computation to protect sensitive data in cross-organizational ML scenarios.

In this chapter, we're going to cover the following main topics:

- Discovering and protecting sensitive data
- Introducing differential privacy
- Mitigating fairness
- Working with model interpretability
- Exploring FL and secure multi-party computation

By the end of this chapter, you will be able to protect your data against bias and privacy without compromising the quality of your predictions.

Technical requirements

The code for this chapter is available in this repository under the `ch5` folder:

`https://github.com/PacktPublishing/Machine-Learning-Model-Security-in-Azure/`

Working with Python

To use the libraries, you need to be familiar with Python. In this book, we will use notebooks from the Azure Machine Learning environment to run the examples, but if you prefer to use your own development environment and tools, that is fine.

> **Getting started with Python**
>
> New to Python and ML? Take a look at this learning path to learn the basics of Python: `https://learn.microsoft.com/en-us/training/paths/beginner-python/`.

Running a notebook in Azure Machine Learning

The process of running a notebook in Azure Machine Learning is very straightforward. All you need to do is import or create a workbook in the interface, attach a compute target, and then run the cells. Let us see the steps together:

1. Go to the **Notebooks** section and upload or create your file:

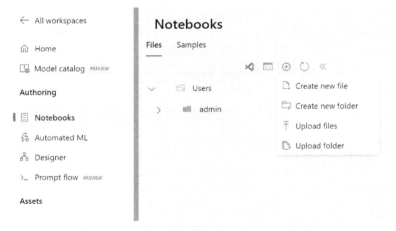

Figure 5.1 – Azure Machine Learning notebooks

2. Open the notebook file and attach a running compute target from the **Compute** dropdown:

Figure 5.2 – Attaching a compute target to a notebook

3. Run the cells in the notebook as usual.

Installing the SmartNoise SDK

The SmartNoise SDK (https://smartnoise.org/) is a differential privacy toolkit that you can use in ML or analytics. Here, we'll see how we can install the library in order to use it later in this chapter.

To install SmartNoise SQL, run the following command:

```
pip install smartnoise-sql
```

To install SmartNoise Synthesizers, run this command:

```
pip install smartnoise-synth
```

> **SmartNoise documentation**
> Find the complete documentation here: https://docs.smartnoise.org/.

Installing Fairlearn

Fairlearn can be installed with pip from PyPI using the following command:

```
pip install fairlearn
```

> **Fairlearn documentation**
> Find the complete documentation here: https://fairlearn.org/.

Discovering and protecting sensitive data

Although having good governance and working with multiple tools that work with data can help us with sensitive data discovery classification and profiling, more often than not, the data used in our ML experiments comes from outside sources, or maybe we are simply not developing for our own organization. In that case, we need to train ourselves on what sensitive data is and how to do a quick cleanup if we need to use Azure Machine Learning.

Identifying sensitive data

Sensitive data refers to any information that, if exposed, could cause harm, privacy breaches, or lead to identity theft, monetary loss, or other adverse consequences for individuals or organizations. This data requires special protection due to its nature and the potential risks associated with its disclosure.

There are many categories of sensitive data, many of which are outlined ahead, together with examples that we need to be aware of:

- **Personally identifiable information** (**PII**): Information that can be used to identify an individual, such as full name, date of birth, social security number, driver's license number, passport number, and so on

- **Financial information**: Credit card numbers, bank account details, financial transaction records, and so on

- **Health information**: Medical records, health insurance information, mental health records, and other health-related data

- **Passwords and authentication data**: Usernames, passwords, security questions, or any other credentials used to access systems or accounts

- **Biometric data**: Fingerprints, retinal scans, facial recognition data, and other biometric identifiers

- **Confidential business information**: Trade secrets, **intellectual property** (**IP**), financial reports, customer lists, proprietary algorithms, and so on

- **Government classified information**: Information classified by governments for national security reasons

- **Personal communications**: Private messages, emails, and other communications that individuals expect to be confidential

- **Social and demographic information**: Race, ethnicity, religion, sexual orientation, and other sensitive demographic data

- **Geolocation data**: Precise location data of individuals or assets

Some of that data we can exclude from our ML process. For example, if we are training a model to predict diabetes, we don't need the patient data but the symptom data. In this case, we can safely exclude that information from our dataset by using the techniques we will explore in the next section. But if we are training a model to recognize faces, we need the actual biometric data.

Let us see some techniques that help us clean up sensitive data so that it is not known to the ML model.

Exploring data anonymization

Data anonymization is a process of removing or obfuscating PII from a dataset to protect the privacy of individuals while still maintaining the data's overall usefulness for analysis and research purposes. The goal is to ensure that the data cannot be linked back to specific individuals.

Here are some common techniques used in data anonymization:

- **Removing direct identifiers**: The most straightforward method is to remove direct identifiers such as names, social security numbers, phone numbers, email addresses, and so on from the dataset. We can use a unique identification number that identifies each record to maintain uniqueness or correlation, but anything that can identify a person is removed completely.

- **Pseudonymization**: The process of replacing sensitive data with pseudonyms or randomly generated identifiers is called pseudonymization. The objective is to obscure the original identity of individuals or entities in a dataset while allowing data processing and analysis to continue using the pseudonymized data. Unlike full anonymization, pseudonymization retains the structure and format of the original data, making it useful for certain purposes while still protecting privacy. This way, the original data is still present in the dataset, but the linkage to specific individuals is broken.

> **Best practice – combining pseudonymization with other techniques**
>
> Pseudonymization is a very good privacy-enhancing technique, but it's not guaranteed. If additional information or external datasets can be combined with the pseudonymized data, identification of the individual may still be possible. Therefore, it's good to combine pseudonymization with other security measures to effectively protect sensitive data.

- **Data masking or tokenization**: This technique is very similar to pseudonymization, but instead of encrypting or replacing sensitive data, data masking or tokenization replaces the values with randomly generated tokens or symbols. For example, if there is a credit card number present, all digits except the last four will be replaced by a star symbol. Data masking or tokenization might result in data that is not useful to the ML process. Therefore, you might want to remove the data altogether.

- **Generalization or aggregation**: This involves grouping data into broader categories to reduce the level of detail while still preserving overall patterns and trends. This technique is often used in data anonymization to protect individual privacy. The goal of generalization or aggregation is to strike a balance between data utility and privacy. While it reduces the risk of directly identifying individuals, it still provides valuable insights for analysis and research. However, it's important to carefully consider the level of generalization to avoid potential re-identification risks, especially when combined with other available information. Here are some examples of generalization or aggregation:

  - **Age ranges**: Instead of using exact ages, data can be generalized into age ranges such as *18-24*, *25-34*, *35-44*, and so on. This maintains the information about age groups without revealing precise ages.

  - **Geographical aggregation**: Instead of using precise addresses, data can be aggregated at the city, state, or country level. For instance, *New York* could represent data from various neighborhoods within the city.

  - **Income brackets**: Instead of exact income values, data can be grouped into income brackets such as *Low Income*, *Middle Income*, and *High Income*.

  - **Time intervals**: Temporal data can be aggregated into time intervals, such as days, weeks, or months, rather than using exact timestamps. For example, *Q1 2023* could represent data from *January* to *March*.

  - **Education levels**: Instead of specific degrees, data can be grouped by education-level categories such as *high school diploma*, *bachelor's degree*, *master's degree*, and so on.

  - **Product categories**: Sales data can be aggregated at the product category level rather than listing individual products; for example, *electronics*, *clothing*, and *furniture*.

  - **Customer segments**: Data can be grouped into segments based on customer behavior or characteristics, such as *frequent shoppers*, *new customers*, or *high-spending customers*.

  - **Transaction amount ranges**: Instead of exact transaction amounts, financial data can be grouped into ranges such as *$0-$50*, *$50-$100*, and so on.

  - **Health conditions**: Medical data can be aggregated into broader health condition categories instead of specifying individual diagnoses; for example, *cardiovascular*, *respiratory*, and *neurological*.

  - **Web browsing patterns**: Internet browsing data can be aggregated based on website categories (for example, news, entertainment, shopping) rather than recording every visited website.

Removing, combining, or masking sensitive information is not the only option. When we need to use sensitive data to train models, there are other techniques to either protect the data or manipulate the data in a way that still protects any sensitive information without limiting our model's potential.

Let us explore how to protect the privacy of individual data without removing it from the dataset.

Introducing differential privacy

Differential privacy is a concept that has the purpose of protecting the privacy of individual data contributors while still allowing useful statistical analysis. The basic idea behind differential privacy is to add noise or random perturbations to the data in such a way that the statistical properties of the dataset stay the same, but it is much more difficult to identify individual information within the dataset.

The level of privacy protection in differential privacy is controlled by a parameter called epsilon (ε). A smaller value of epsilon indicates a higher level of privacy, but it might also lead to a decrease in data utility (usefulness of the data for analysis). Striking a balance between privacy and utility is a key challenge in implementing differential privacy:

Figure 5.3 – Epsilon (Ɛ) value relationship with privacy and accuracy

A library that we can use to add noise to the data is the SmartNoise SDK. SmartNoise is an open source SDK designed to implement differential privacy in various data analysis and ML workflows. It is developed by OpenDP and aims to make it easier for data analysts, researchers, and data scientists to apply differential privacy techniques to their data without extensive knowledge of the underlying mathematical complexities.

The SmartNoise SDK provides a set of tools and utilities that can be integrated into existing data analysis and ML pipelines to ensure privacy-preserving computations. It offers an abstraction layer for adding differential privacy to computations, allowing data analysts to easily specify privacy parameters (such as epsilon) and apply privacy-preserving mechanisms without dealing directly with the intricacies of differential privacy algorithms.

There are different components you can use, and these are the official recommendations from the documentation:

- Use **OpenDP** directly when working with Jupyter notebooks and reproducible research or if you require fine-grained control over processing and privacy

- Use **SmartNoise SQL** if you are working with large datasets or data cubes over tabular data stored in SQL databases or Spark

- Use **SmartNoise Synthesizers** if you are still in the research process and you want to see what the result will look like with other collaborators

Here, we will see an example by using SmartNoise SQL:

1. First, you need to install SmartNoise SQL by running this command:

    ```
    pip install smartnoise-sql
    ```

2. We will then load some mock data and analyze the results. Our mock dataset contains 1,000 records of random data that includes a `diabetic` column that declares if the person is diabetic or not and an `age` column:

    ```
    import pandas as pd
    data_path = 'mockdata.csv'
    mockdata = pd.read_csv(data_path)
    actualdata = mockdata[['age','diabetic']].groupby(\
        ['diabetic']).mean().to_markdown()
    print(actualdata)
    ```

    By running this cell, we get the true average age for diabetics and non-diabetics.

3. Let us see what happens when we add noise to the data. First, we need to declare the epsilon variable. We will execute this code multiple times, first with a low epsilon value for greater privacy (`0.05`) and second with a high epsilon value for accuracy (`0.90`), and compare the results:

    ```
    import snsql
    from snsql import Privacy
    import pandas as pd
    privacy = Privacy(epsilon=0.05, delta=0.01)

    csv_path = 'mockdata.csv'
    meta_path = 'mockdata.yaml'
    mockdata = pd.read_csv(csv_path)
    reader = snsql.from_df(mockdata, privacy=privacy, \
        metadata=meta_path)
    result = reader.execute('SELECT diabetic, AVG(age) \
        AS age FROM mockdata.table GROUP BY diabetic')
    print(result)
    ```

We can see in the following table a comparison of multiple executions of the preceding code side by side, and the average age for non-diabetic and diabetic patients is almost the same (around 47 years old), but when we use the SmartNoise SDK library with different epsilon values, the results start to vary from 1% to 15% depending on the epsilon value used. This percentage might seem high; however, it is up to us to determine the balance between privacy and accuracy. The only thing the library guarantees is to maintain statistical uniformity:

	Actual average age	Execution 1 Average age	Execution 2 Average age	Execution 3 Average age	Execution 4 Average age
Epsilon value	N/A	0.05	0.05	0.90	0.80
Non-diabetic	47.4101	54.2823275862069	53.209829867674856	47.72727272727273	47.38953488372093
Diabetic	47.4741	42.19132149901381	44.00204081632653	47.36438923395445	47.616977225672876

Table 5.1 – Dataset results

You can see how to run this notebook in the book repository mentioned previously in the *Technical requirements* section. This way, we can protect the privacy of the data without compromising the results of our model. What happens, though, when the data we are trying to protect actually affects the predictions, resulting in a negative impact?

Let's see how we can ensure our data is private and the model also provides fair results for different sensitive groups.

Mitigating fairness

Mitigating fairness in ML models is an essential step to ensure that the model does not exhibit bias or discrimination against certain groups of individuals. Even though we can remove PII from our datasets, predictions might favor different groups based on characteristics such as race, gender, age, or religion. If the training data is not diverse and representative of the population you aim to serve, bias can creep into the model if the data does not adequately represent all groups.

Firstly, we need to learn to identify bias in our models. This is easy by conducting an analysis of the metrics of the model. Suppose you suspect that your load approval model favors people above a certain age to get their loan application approved. You can start by looking at the metrics for the complete dataset as follows:

	Selection Rate	Accuracy	Recall	Precision
Complete dataset	0.337	0.8895	0.8385650224215246	0.8323442136498517

Table 5.2 – Dataset metrics

Now, calculate the same metrics by age group. We can do this by using a library such as Fairlearn. The result from the split looks like this:

	Selection Rate	Accuracy	Recall	Precision
Age 30 or younger	0.299282	0.890668	0.818519	0.815498
Age over 30	0.698413	0.878307	0.922481	0.901515

Table 5.3 – Metrics per age group

> **Metrics explained**
>
> Metrics are specific to the type of model. The preceding metrics are for classification models. You can find a list of metrics for different models and charts with an explanation here: `https://learn.microsoft.com/en-us/azure/machine-learning/how-to-understand-automated-ml?view=azureml-api-2`.

From these metrics, you should be able to discern that a larger proportion of older individuals are predicted to be approved for the loan. Accuracy should be more or less equal for the two groups, but a closer inspection of precision and recall indicates some disparity in how well the model predicts for each age group.

In this scenario, consider **Recall**. This metric indicates the proportion of positive cases that were correctly identified by the model. In other words, of all the individuals who should get approval for their loan application and they actually do, how many did the model find? The model seems to do a better job in the older age group.

So, what do we do now? Do we try to correct the data and model to predict equally between the two groups? The short answer is *not yet*. We need to consider the context first and evaluate why the model exhibits this behavior, and whether this is justified. Remember that metrics are just metrics, and it is up to us to interpret them. Maybe our model favors the older age group because they are more financially stable. We need to investigate more before we reach a decision because this identified bias might be reasonable. Suppose we had a face recognition application that favored light-skinned people over dark-skinned people; this would be a clear bias and would need to be corrected. The context and the model's purpose will define our next steps.

Fairlearn

Fairlearn is an open source project to help ML engineers and data scientists improve the fairness of AI systems. It can assist by providing fairness-related metrics that can be compared between groups and for the overall population. To calculate those metrics and conduct an investigation, the Fairlearn SDK is immensely helpful. It breaks down the metrics from each sensitive group, and then you can use the fairness dashboard to complete your assessment, as looking at the data visually always helps.

> **Fairlearn SDK and Azure Machine Learning**
>
> This feature is in Preview at the time of writing, so you can see limitations and applications in the Azure Machine Learning environment here: `https://learn.microsoft.com/en-us/azure/machine-learning/how-to-machine-learning-fairness-aml?view=azureml-api-1`. The Fairlearn project documentation can be found here: `https://fairlearn.org/`.

Here, you can see an example process of working with the visual dashboard. You can generate the UI in your notebooks, and it looks like this:

Figure 5.4 – Fairness dashboard main page

You can also register the model and upload the dashboard data to your workspace to conduct your assessment, as seen in the following screenshot. The process is much easier with the help of the wizard:

1. The first step is to choose sensitive features; for example, the **Age** column:

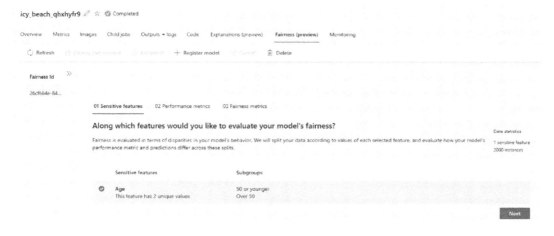

Figure 5.5 – Step 1: Choosing your sensitive features

2. The second step is to choose a metric to evaluate against in order to examine any possible bias. Depending on the model algorithm, you might get different metrics here to choose from:

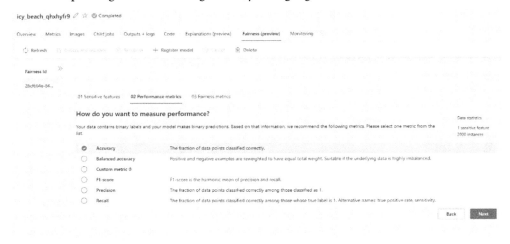

Figure 5.6 – Step 2: Choosing a primary metric to measure performance

3. In the third and final step, you set the parity constraints against which you want to measure fairness; for example, demographic parity or selection rate:

Figure 5.7 – Step 3: Choose how you want to measure fairness

The service runs an analysis based on the parameters and returns results that we can use to determine if the model favors one or more groups based on sensitive features:

Figure 5.8 – Reviewing the results

> **Note**
> The integration with the Fairlearn open source package is supported at the time of writing only on the `azureml v1` Python SDK.

Always remember that complete fairness may not always be achievable, and trade-offs may exist between different fairness goals. We need to ensure that the model performs adequately for all sensitive groups in our datasets. The key is to make informed decisions about fairness trade-offs and continuously strive to improve the model's fairness.

Another part of responsible AI is the ability to explain how a model makes predictions. Let us see some techniques in the following section.

Working with model interpretability

Model interpretability in ML refers to the ability to understand and explain how a particular model makes predictions or decisions. Interpretable models provide clear insights into the features or variables that are most influential in the model's decision-making process. This is particularly important in domains where the decision-making process needs to be transparent and understandable, such as healthcare, finance, and legal systems.

Although you can never explain 100% why a model makes a prediction, you can use explainers to understand which features affect the results. Explainers can help us provide global explanations; for example, which features affect the overall behavior of the model or local explanations that provide us with information on what influenced an individual prediction.

Let us explore some methods we can use to achieve model interpretability:

- **Feature importance** (**FI**) determines the influence of each feature in influencing the model's predictions. Techniques such as the following can be used:

  - **Permutation FI** (**PFI**): This method involves randomly shuffling the values of each feature and measuring the impact on the model's performance. Features with the highest drop in performance after shuffling are considered more important.

  - **SHapley Additive exPlanations** (**SHAP**) **values**: SHAP values provide a unified measure of FI based on cooperative game theory. They assign contributions to each feature in a prediction, considering all possible feature combinations.

  - **Local Interpretable Model-agnostic Explanations** (**LIME**): LIME creates local interpretable models around a specific prediction by perturbing the data and observing the impact on the prediction. It helps explain individual predictions for any model.

- **Partial dependence plots** (**PDP**) and **individual conditional expectation** (**ICE**) test the feature influence on the model by using different techniques:

  - PDP plots the average effect of a single feature on the model's predictions while keeping other features constant.

  - ICE plots multiple individual PDPs, one for each instance, providing a more granular view of how the feature affects different instances.

- **Rule-based models**: Decision trees and linear models are inherently interpretable as their structure can be easily visualized and understood.

- **Proxy models**: Train a simpler, interpretable model to approximate the behavior of a more complex model. This allows for better understanding without sacrificing too much accuracy.

- **Visualizations**: Visualizations such as heatmaps, saliency maps, and activation maps can help understand how the model processes and weighs different input features.

- **Layer-wise Relevance Propagation** (**LRP**): LRP is a technique used in **neural networks** (**NNs**) to understand which input features contribute most to a specific output.

The method we choose depends on our model and the flavor used to create it. Let us see the options we have for model interpretability in Azure Machine Learning.

Exploring the Responsible AI dashboard

To work with interpretability in Azure Machine Learning, you can use the Interpret-Community package for the v1 SDK, or it is recommended to use the newer version, which is part of the new Responsible AI dashboard.

Let us explore the capabilities available:

> **Model interpretability in Azure Machine Learning**
>
> Learn more about the Interpret-Community package in Azure Machine Learning and how common explainers work in the following documentation: `https://learn. microsoft.com/en-us/azure/machine-learning/how-to-machine-learning-interpretability?view=azureml-api-2#supported-model-interpretability-techniques`.

1. You can generate a dashboard in any model in the MLflow format generated with the scikit-learn by going to your registered model under the **Models** menu, choosing the **Responsible AI** tab, and clicking on the **Create dashboard** button, as shown in the following screenshot:

AutoML2362f01008:1

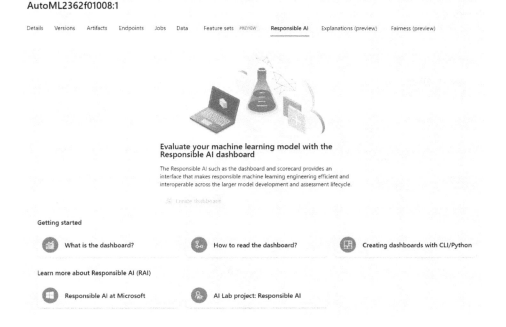

Figure 5.9 – Creating a Responsible AI dashboard

> **MLflow models**
>
> MLflow is an open source platform designed to manage the end-to-end ML life cycle by providing a consistent and easy-to-use framework, making collaboration and reproducibility more accessible for data science and ML teams. Find out more here: `https://mlflow.org/`.

2. As soon as the dashboard is generated, you can click on it on the list to view more details:

Figure 5.10 – Opening the dashboard

3. The dashboard has a lot of information to help not only with explainability but also metrics about fairness, data distribution, and individual predictions. Along with the data, there are numerous visualizations you can take advantage of to analyze your model, as seen in the following screenshot. Make sure you adhere to responsible AI development principles:

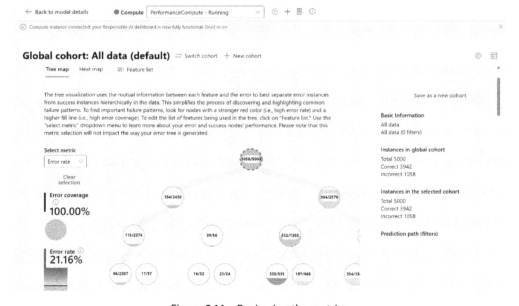

Figure 5.11 – Reviewing the metrics

4. When it comes to model interpretability, you can see FIs for the complete dataset and for individual predictions. You can tweak the class importance weights and the chart to suit your needs and understand the model better.

In the next screenshot, we can see global FIs for a sample diabetes dataset:

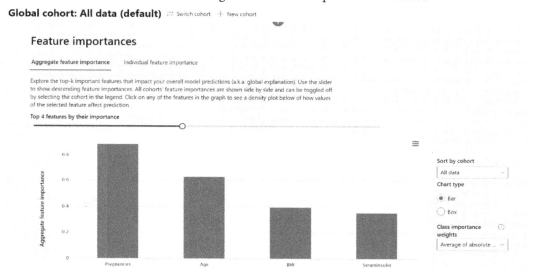

Figure 5.12 – Reviewing FIs

Model interpretability is a balance between simplicity and accuracy. Highly interpretable models might sacrifice some predictive performance, while very complex models might be difficult to explain comprehensively. The choice of interpretability method depends on the specific use case, audience, and the trade-off between model complexity and transparency.

> **Generating an AI dashboard using the SDK**
>
> For further resources to build the AI dashboard using the SDK using YAML and Python, see here: `https://learn.microsoft.com/en-us/azure/machine-learning/how-to-responsible-ai-insights-sdk-cli?view=azureml-api-2&tabs=yaml`.

All the techniques we have seen so far focus on having one dataset that is trained on one compute resource to generate the resulting model. In the next section, we will see some techniques that focus on splitting model training and datasets between different compute sources.

Exploring FL and secure multi-party computation

FL is an ML approach that enables the training of models across multiple devices or servers without centrally aggregating the raw data. In traditional ML, data is usually collected and sent to a central compute server for training, which raises privacy and security concerns, especially when dealing with sensitive or personal information.

In FL, the training process happens locally on the devices or nodes (for example smartphones, edge devices, or compute instances) that generate or store the data. These nodes collaborate by sharing only model updates (gradients) rather than the raw data itself. The central compute server aggregates these updates to create an improved global model. This process is repeated iteratively, with each node contributing to the model's improvement while keeping its data private.

The main advantages of FL are as follows:

- **Privacy**: As the raw data remains on the local nodes, there is no need to share sensitive information with a central server, reducing the risk of data leaks and breaches
- **Reduced data transmission**: FL decreases the amount of data that needs to be sent over the network, which can be beneficial when dealing with large datasets or bandwidth constraints
- **Decentralization**: The model training process can be distributed across a large number of nodes, enabling scalability and robustness in a distributed environment
- **Local adaptation**: Nodes can update the global model while taking into account their local data distribution, leading to models that are more relevant and tailored to specific local characteristics

FL is especially useful in scenarios where data privacy and security are crucial, such as healthcare and financial services, and processing can be distributed as in **Internet of Things (IoT)** applications. It gives us the opportunity to leverage the collective knowledge from distributed data sources without compromising the privacy of individual users.

Let us see a quick introduction to FL and its applications with Azure Machine Learning.

FL with Azure Machine Learning

When working in the cloud, FL can be easier than you might think. With on-demand compute and processing power come a lot of benefits. Especially with the `azureml` SDK v2, FL features are built in.

The easiest way to integrate is by using designer pipelines. The designer has a drag-and-drop interface. With the new version of the SDK come several exciting features. We can create our own component very easily, and each component that you drag and drop in the pipeline can be run on a different compute target.

In the following screenshot, we can see a pipeline created in the designer from the pre-built samples. By clicking on a component, we can easily change the compute target from the **Pipeline interface** button by going to the **Run settings** option and choosing **Use other compute target**:

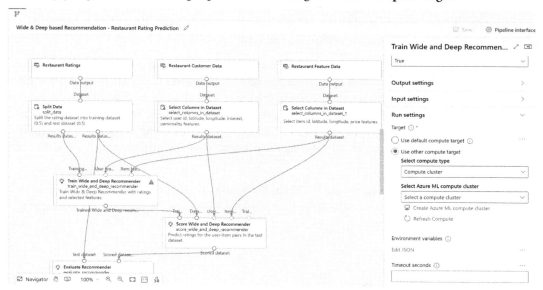

Figure 5.13 – Changing the compute target in Azure Machine Learning

If we extend the functionality and train multiple models at the same time using different datasets, we have an FL implementation and multi-party computation. For compute, we can also leverage Azure confidential computing to make the implementation even more secure, but we will talk about securing Azure compute in Azure Machine Learning later in the book. This can also be extended to using multiple workspaces connected to the same or different data stores.

The great thing about using FL with Azure Machine Learning is that you can still combine and apply all the metrics and techniques we have outlined in this chapter since we are still working within the workspace.

FL recipes and examples

Find out more on how to implement Azure Machine Learning here: `https://github.com/Azure-Samples/azure-ml-federated-learning`.

Summary

Protecting sensitive data is a multi-faceted problem. There are ways and techniques to mitigate fairness and protect privacy work ethically and responsibly with AI, but the balance between prediction accuracy and data protection is very sensitive. If you add the complexity of choosing the right combination of techniques based on your data and algorithms, it can seem daunting.

In this chapter, we learned to identify different types of sensitive data and common techniques to remove or mask them. However, it is not always possible to completely eliminate them as they are useful for the model training process. In this case, there are several libraries available to help. We can use the SmartNoise SDK to introduce noise to our data and protect privacy, work with the Fairlearn SDK to mitigate fairness, and use the Responsible AI dashboard together with explainers to interpret our models. We ended this chapter by introducing the concept of FL and how to apply it using Azure Machine Learning.

We can talk about data until the end of the book, but the truth is, there is only so much you can do in data processing. In the next chapter, we will focus on working with access to the data, the workspace, and the roles required for each part.

Further reading

- *Run a Federated Learning Demo in 5 mins*: https://github.com/Azure-Samples/azure-ml-federated-learning/blob/main/docs/quickstart.md

- *Federated Learning with Azure Machine Learning, NVIDIA FLARE and MONAI* – Build session: https://build.microsoft.com/en-US/sessions/5bd5120f-5239-450d-8a57-373efb43c0cf?source=sessions

- *Medical Imaging with Azure Machine Learning Demos*: https://github.com/Azure/medical-imaging

Part 3: Securing and Monitoring Your AI Environment

When it comes to the cloud, there is more to security than data. In this part, you will learn how to secure identity and access and all the cloud infrastructure around your Azure Machine Learning resources. Then, you will learn how to automate those processes using MLOps practices and how to set up system monitoring to detect and resolve any security issues.

This part has the following chapters:

- *Chapter 6, Managing and Securing Access*
- *Chapter 7, Managing and Securing your Azure Machine Learning Workspace*
- *Chapter 8, Managing and Securing the MLOps Life Cycle*
- *Chapter 9, Logging, Monitoring, and Threat Detection*

6

Managing and Securing Access

Up to this point, we have talked mostly about data, which is the basis of ML. But when it comes to security, there are other aspects we need to explore. Let us dive into identity and how we can manage access in Azure Machine Learning. As we embark on a journey through this chapter, we will first lay the groundwork by exploring the essence of the **principle of least privilege** (**PoLP**) and its importance. Although simple in theory, there are many things we need to consider before we start the implementation of Azure Machine Learning.

We will follow up by exploring all the identity features of Microsoft Entra. We will see authentication options available and how to work with permissions by implementing **role-based access control** (**RBAC**). We will see how to authenticate applications and services using managed identities and how to secure access using tools such as Key Vault. Finally, we will talk about how to automate the processes by using Conditional Access and **Privileged Identity Management** (**PIM**). The best practices in this chapter can be applied not only to Azure Machine Learning but to other services in Azure as well.

In this chapter, we're going to cover the following main topics:

- Working with the PoLP
- Authenticating with Microsoft Entra ID
- Implementing RBAC
- Authenticating with application identities
- Enhancing access security

By the end of this chapter, you will have learned how to apply access management effectively by implementing PoLP in Azure Machine Learning.

Working with the PoLP

As we mentioned in *Chapter 1* when we talked about the Zero Trust strategy, we learned about the PoLP, which states that users, devices, and applications should only be granted access to the minimum level of resources necessary to perform their job functions. Users are often given more access privileges to network resources and data, assuming they only access the resources required to perform their daily tasks. However, this tactic imposes a greater risk of unauthorized access. When users have access to resources they don't need, attackers can take advantage of it. While providing just enough permissions to apps or users to complete their tasks sounds easy, the implementation can present some challenges. Creating overprivileged applications is never the intention, but usually the result of unplanned actions over time.

Overprivileged applications are software applications that have been granted more access rights, permissions, or privileges than they actually require to perform their intended tasks. An application is characterized as overprivileged if it includes unused as well as reducible permissions. Let us see some examples.

Suppose we have an application that includes a user profile, where the user signs in and the application pulls all the information from the identity management system. The application's usage has nothing to do with user profile updates and is just using the user's profile information to get the manager or department information to complete other business tasks, so it does not include an **Edit profile** functionality. However, the application has the permissions needed to edit the profile information. This is an example of reducible permissions, where the application needs to read the data but not write in the system. Suppose that the same application also uses an API endpoint to get predictions from an ML model, and additionally has permissions to start or stop the Azure Machine Learning compute. This would be an example of unused permissions as the application has nothing to do with model training and the Azure Machine Learning compute.

It is tempting to include permissions to an application that will apply to future releases as we are often reluctant to modify deployed applications to avoid impacting their normal business operations. However, we must always consider the risks that accompany such decisions. Applying the PoLP is more of an iterative process than a rule.

Let us review some best practices before we dive into the implementations for Azure Machine Learning:

- **Application inventory**: The first step is to keep an updated inventory of all applications in our organization. This includes both in-house developed applications and third-party applications and their required permissions. This can be part of our governance program.

- **RBAC**: We can implement RBAC to define and assign roles that align with specific application functions. The best approach is to assign permissions based on the PoLP to ensure that applications only have the access they need and re-evaluate this access when appropriate.

- **Regular reviews**: We need to periodically review the permissions granted to applications and remove any unnecessary or unused permissions that could potentially be exploited.

- **Automated tools**: It is always preferable to use automated tools to continuously analyze application permissions and identify overprivileged applications. These tools can provide insights into which permissions are actually being used and which can be revoked. For Azure, we can use Conditional Access policies and PIM as part of Microsoft Entra ID.

- **Zero Trust architecture**: As mentioned in *Chapter 1*, applying a zero-trust architecture when possible, where applications are not automatically trusted based on their location or source, is always beneficial. We should always verify the identity and permissions of applications before granting access.

- **Continuous monitoring**: After any implementation, continuously monitor application behavior and access patterns. Detecting and investigating any unusual or unauthorized activities should be one of our priorities to identify any breaches as soon as possible.

- **Training and awareness**: We should never forget the human factor. Everyone from developers and IT staff to data scientists should be educated about the importance of preventing overprivileged applications. As part of our organization's governance, we should provide guidelines for implementing secure access controls.

Adhering to the PoLP is challenging as it requires a thorough understanding of user roles, responsibilities, and system interactions, and it is an iterative and continuous process. It can also become more complicated the more applications and systems we have. However, the security benefits it provides, by minimizing the potential impact of security breaches, make it an essential practice in any organization's information security strategy.

Let us explore how to implement the PoLP in Azure Machine Learning.

Authenticating with Microsoft Entra ID

Azure Machine Learning uses **Microsoft Entra ID** (previously **Azure Active Directory (Azure AD)**) for authentication. Microsoft Entra ID is Microsoft's cloud-based **identity and access management (IAM)** service. It's designed to help organizations manage user identities and access to resources in the cloud and on-premises.

When you are logged in to the Azure portal, the same account is used to directly authenticate you to your Azure Machine Learning Studio session. So, anyone working on your ML project needs to be part of the Microsoft Entra ID workspace. That does not mean that only employees have access to the workspace. Microsoft Entra ID supports two types of users: members and guests. Members are users that are created within the Microsoft Entra ID tenant, while guests can be users that belong to other Microsoft Entra tenants or are personal accounts such as Outlook, Gmail, Hotmail, and so on. But as soon as you create or invite a user in your Microsoft Entra ID tenant, then you can assign them roles and treat them as part of your organization.

Ways to authenticate using Microsoft Entra ID in Azure Machine Learning include interactive authentication directly with your account, the Azure CLI, service principals, and managed identities, which we will explore later in this chapter.

Microsoft Entra ID is widely used across various industries and is an integral part of Microsoft's cloud offerings, including Azure, Microsoft 365, and Dynamics 365. It's a critical component for securing and managing access to cloud resources and ensuring that users have the appropriate level of access to applications and data while maintaining a high level of security.

Here is how we can use its security features to secure our Azure Machine Learning workloads.

Implementing RBAC

RBAC is a built-in feature of Microsoft Entra ID that allows you to manage access to Azure resources using roles. This way, we can control who can perform specific actions on resources in Azure. This helps in maintaining a secure environment and ensures that users have only the permissions they need to perform their tasks.

Each role in RBAC is essentially a set of distinct permissions that operate in different scopes. We can assign a role to a management group, subscription, resource group, and resource. A role assignment at a higher scope is inherited by resources at a lower scope. For example, if we assign a role to a user at the subscription level, they will have those permissions across all resources within that subscription. Each role assignment in Azure has three distinct parts—the role, the scope, and the service principal, as we can see in the following diagram:

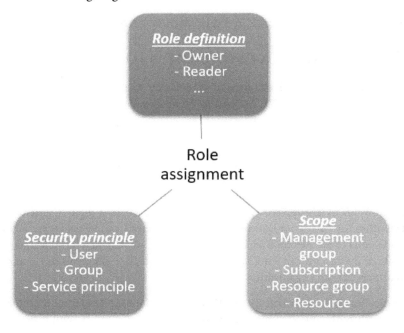

Figure 6.1 – Role assignment

The principle can be a user, a group of users, or a service principal such as an application or an Azure resource. We will explore service principals a little bit more later in the chapter when we talk about application identities and managed identities.

There are two types of roles: built-in and custom. Built-in roles are created by Azure, and we can assign them at any time. If they do not cover your needs, you can combine different roles to get the result you desire or create your own custom role to use with the service.

Let us see how we can assign or create RBAC roles specifically for Azure Machine Learning.

Working with built-in roles

Azure offers over 400 built-in roles, such as **Virtual Machine Contributor**, **Storage Account Contributor**, and more. Each built-in role corresponds to specific scopes, actions, and services in Azure.

There are three roles that are a must-know and apply to all Azure services—the **Owner**, **Contributor**, and **Reader** roles. Here are their descriptions in the following screenshot:

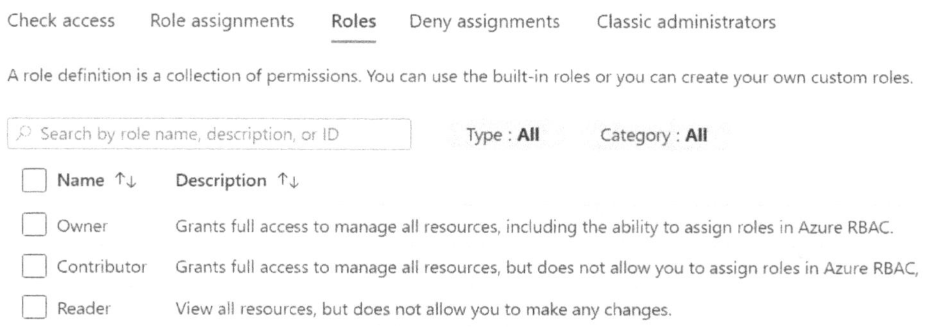

| Check access | Role assignments | **Roles** | Deny assignments | Classic administrators |

A role definition is a collection of permissions. You can use the built-in roles or you can create your own custom roles.

| Search by role name, description, or ID | | Type : **All** | Category : **All** |

Name ↑↓	Description ↑↓
Owner	Grants full access to manage all resources, including the ability to assign roles in Azure RBAC.
Contributor	Grants full access to manage all resources, but does not allow you to assign roles in Azure RBAC,
Reader	View all resources, but does not allow you to make any changes.

Figure 6.2 – Core RBAC roles for Azure resources

Then, we have Azure Machine Learning-specific roles that we need to be aware of. Here are descriptions of the most important roles we need to know when we are working with Azure Machine Learning:

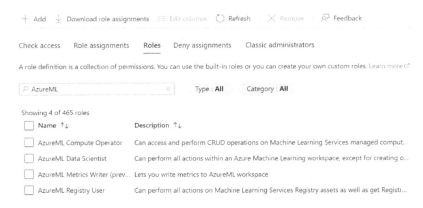

Figure 6.3 – RBAC roles for Azure Machine Learning

As you can see, the roles have been built around specific employee roles and encompass certain tasks around data scientists or compute operators for ML. Of course, if you have a different structure in your organization, you can assign two roles to the same person and have them complete all the relevant tasks in Azure.

Let us review how to work with role assignments.

Adding a role assignment

As owners of the workspace, we can assign or remove roles to/from users and the workspace at any time using the Azure portal, the command-line tools, and even **Azure Resource Manager** (**ARM**) templates if we have complex assignments that we want to repeat. The process is simple. In every resource blade on the top left, we can see that there is an **Access control (IAM)** menu:

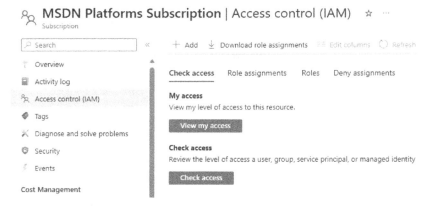

Figure 6.4 – Azure Access control (IAM) menu

From this blade, you can see existing role assignments and roles, and you can add or remove access to the resource. In this case, we have opened the **Subscription** blade, which means that any role assignments we change are going to be inherited by any resource groups and resources under this subscription.

To add a role assignment, click the **Add** button on the top. Follow the three-step wizard to add your role assignment:

1. The first step is to choose a role. For this example, I will choose **Reader**:

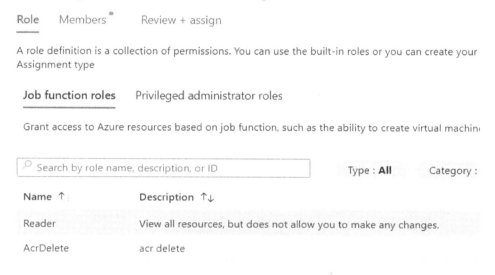

Figure 6.5 – Step 1: Choosing a role

2. The second step is to choose members for the selected role. You can add multiple members by clicking the **Select members** button:

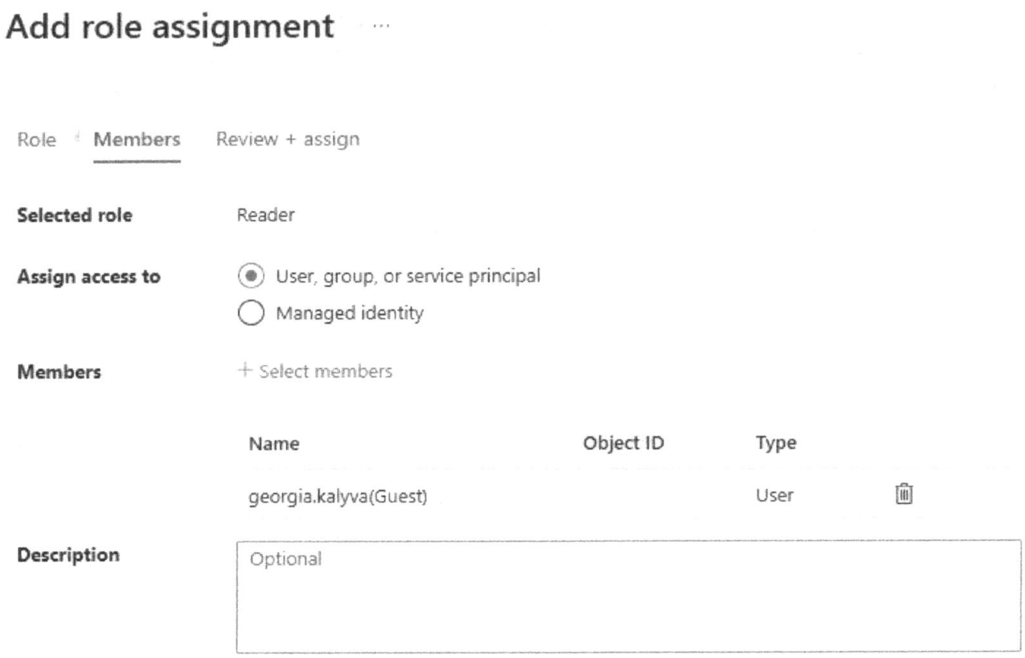

Add role assignment ···

Role | **Members** | Review + assign

Selected role   Reader

Assign access to   ⦿ User, group, or service principal
                        ◯ Managed identity

Members   + Select members

Name	Object ID	Type	
georgia.kalyva(Guest)		User	🗑

Description   Optional

Figure 6.6 – Step 2: Adding members

3.   That is it! The final step is to review and complete the assignment.

    If you want to use the command-line tools, here is an example in the CLI:

```
az role assignment create --role "Reader" --assignee
"georg***@*****.com" --subscription "00000000-0000-0000-0000-
000000000000"
```

Role assignment documentation

To view more options to assign roles using the Azure tools, follow the corresponding link to the tool of your choice:

CLI: https://learn.microsoft.com/en-us/azure/role-based-access-control/role-assignments-cli

PowerShell: https://learn.microsoft.com/en-us/azure/role-based-access-control/role-assignments-powershell

REST API: https://learn.microsoft.com/en-us/azure/role-based-access-control/role-assignments-rest

ARM templates: https://learn.microsoft.com/en-us/azure/role-based-access-control/role-assignments-template

Adding role assignments is just one part of the story. Let us see how to review our existing assignments and remove them when necessary.

Viewing and removing role assignments

The process to view and remove role assignments is just as simple. The first step is to visit the resource you want to check the role assignments for and open the **Access control (IAM)** menu. There, on the **Role assignments** tab, you can see existing role assignments, as shown in the following screenshot:

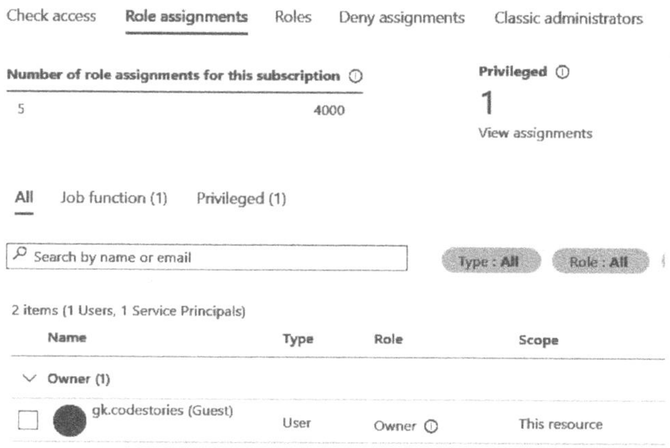

Figure 6.7 – Removing a role assignment

By clicking on the box on the left of the role assignment in the user list, the **Remove** button on the top is enabled. You can click **Remove** and **Confirm** to remove the assignment.

As with adding an assignment, you can use the command-line tools. Here is an example of removing an assignment using the CLI:

```
az role assignment delete --assignee "georg***@*****.com" \
--role "Reader" \
--subscription "00000000-0000-0000-0000-000000000000"
```

> **Role assignment documentation**
>
> To view more options to remove role assignments using the Azure tools, follow this link: https://learn.microsoft.com/en-us/azure/role-based-access-control/role-assignments-remove

Built-in roles are not the only way to assign permissions. Let us review custom roles.

Creating a custom role for Azure Machine Learning

The built-in roles are great, but sometimes they do not provide exactly what we need to properly restrict permissions of our users. In that case, we have the option of creating our own custom roles that have the exact permissions we need to complete the tasks necessary. A role is essentially a set of permissions. This set of permissions is described as a JSON file. You can find an example of the Contributor role in JSON format here: `https://learn.microsoft.com/en-us/azure/role-based-access-control/role-definitions-list`.

> **Custom role overview**
>
> If you want to learn more about Azure custom role properties, see the information provided in this link: `https://learn.microsoft.com/en-us/azure/role-based-access-control/custom-roles`

In this section, we will not go into much detail on RBAC, but we will focus on how to create custom roles for the Azure Machine Learning service. If looking at that JSON file seems daunting, you do not have to worry. We can create our own custom role using the Azure portal. As done previously, we go onto the resource blade we want to assign a new role to and find the **Add** button. Click the Add button and then follow the **Add custom role** menu:

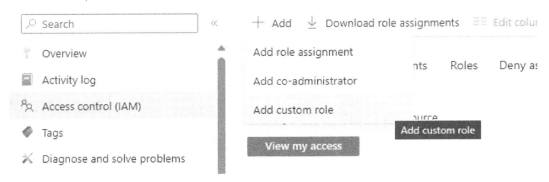

Figure 6.8 – Adding a custom role

The custom role wizard will pop up. The first step is to create a name for our role. In this case, I chose the name **AzureML Data Scientist Extended**, because my goal is to clone the existing role and simply add more permissions. You can, of course, start from scratch or from a saved JSON file. We then add a good description and we are ready to proceed, as shown in the following screenshot:

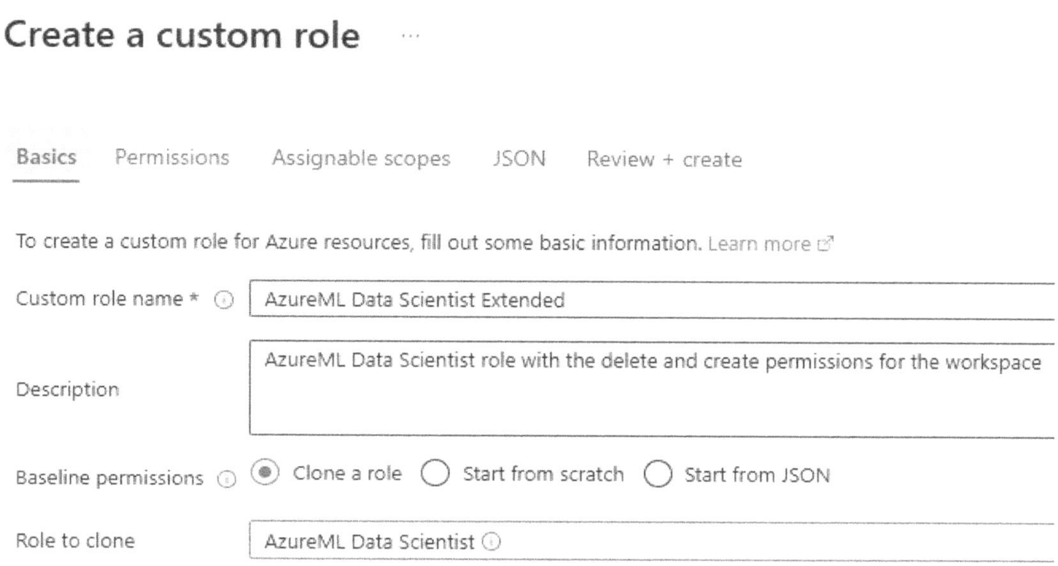

Create a custom role   ...

Basics   Permissions   Assignable scopes   JSON   Review + create

To create a custom role for Azure resources, fill out some basic information. Learn more ✷

Custom role name * ⓘ | AzureML Data Scientist Extended |

Description | AzureML Data Scientist role with the delete and create permissions for the workspace |

Baseline permissions ⓘ   ⦿ Clone a role   ◯ Start from scratch   ◯ Start from JSON

Role to clone | AzureML Data Scientist ⓘ |

Figure 6.9 – Filling in the basics

Under the **Permissions** tab, I see that this role has permissions in the workspace, but in the **Permission type** column is assigned with **NotAction** since we can see that *delete* and *write* actions in the workspace are prohibited. The **Action** section of the role describes what the role can do, and then **NotAction** describes what it cannot do. So, if I remove those permissions from **NotAction**, the role will be able to create and delete workspaces, which is what I want my data scientists to be able to do:

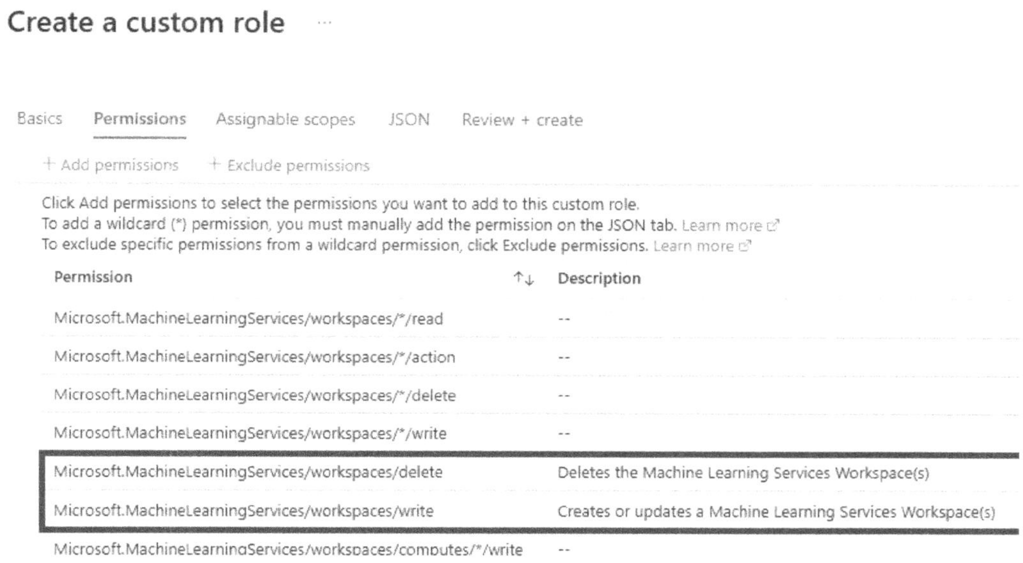

Create a custom role   ...

Basics   Permissions   Assignable scopes   JSON   Review + create

+ Add permissions   + Exclude permissions

Click Add permissions to select the permissions you want to add to this custom role.
To add a wildcard (*) permission, you must manually add the permission on the JSON tab. Learn more ✷
To exclude specific permissions from a wildcard permission, click Exclude permissions. Learn more ✷

Permission	↑↓	Description
Microsoft.MachineLearningServices/workspaces/*/read		--
Microsoft.MachineLearningServices/workspaces/*/action		--
Microsoft.MachineLearningServices/workspaces/*/delete		--
Microsoft.MachineLearningServices/workspaces/*/write		--
Microsoft.MachineLearningServices/workspaces/delete		Deletes the Machine Learning Services Workspace(s)
Microsoft.MachineLearningServices/workspaces/write		Creates or updates a Machine Learning Services Workspace(s)
Microsoft.MachineLearningServices/workspaces/computes/*/write		--

Figure 6.10 – Working with permissions

The following screenshot shows the result with the complete permissions list:

Figure 6.11 – Final permissions

Before we move on, though, you might ask: What if I want to add permissions? Where do I find them? In the preceding screenshot, we can see the + **Add permissions** button. From here, the process of adding permissions is very intuitive. When you want to add permissions, you do not need to scroll through an endless list or have the documentation at hand every time. You can simply filter to the service you want and see the relevant permissions. For Azure Machine Learning, we are interested in the **Machine Learning Services Resource Provider** or **Microsoft Machine Learning Web Services Management** permissions, as shown in the following screenshot:

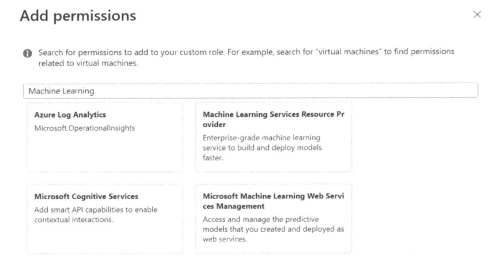

Figure 6.12 – Adding permissions

By clicking on the relevant category, we can see a list of permissions together with their description, as we can see in the next screenshot:

Microsoft.MachineLearningServices permissions

< All resource providers

ⓘ Search for permissions to add to your custom role. For example, search for "virtual machine

Machine Learning

◉ Actions   ○ Data Actions

☐ Permission

∨ Microsoft.MachineLearningServices

☐ Other : Registers the subscription for the Machine Learning Services Resource Provider
ⓘ

∨ Microsoft.MachineLearningServices/registries

☐ Read : Gets the Machine Learning Services registry(ies) ⓘ

☐ Write : Creates or updates the Machine Learning Services registry(ies) ⓘ

☐ Delete : Deletes the Machine Learning Services registry(ies) ⓘ

☐ Other : Approve or reject a connection to a Private Endpoint resource of
Microsoft.Network provider ⓘ

Figure 6.13 – Viewing Azure Machine Learning permissions

This makes it very quick to create a custom role. You just need to ensure that you have included all the permissions needed and then you can come back to the **Permissions** page and review the list.

The next step is to set the assignable scope. You can change the **Assignable scopes** option to set the scope of this custom role at the subscription level, the resource group level, or a specific workspace level:

Create a custom role ⋯

Basics   Permissions   **Assignable scopes**   JSON   Review + create

+ Add assignable scopes

Click Add assignable scopes to select the scopes (management groups, subscriptions, or resource groups) where this role will be available for assignment.
Your role must have at least one assignable scope. Learn more ↗

Assignable scope	↑↓	Type	↑↓
/subscriptions/		Subscription	🗑

Figure 6.14 – Deciding on the scope

Then, you can review and download the generated JSON or proceed to the final step to create the new custom role:

Create a custom role ...

Figure 6.15 – Reviewing and creating/downloading

After you have created the custom role, you can assign it just as with the built-in roles. You will find it on the **Roles** list in the **Access control (IAM)** menu with the **CustomRole** type:

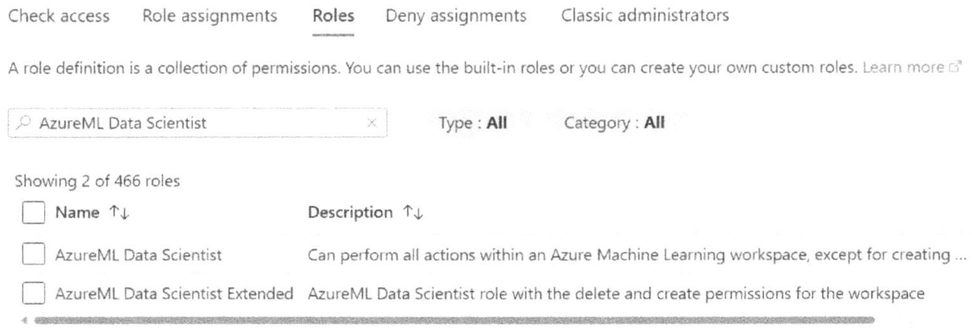

Figure 6.16 – Finding your custom role

> **Azure RBAC**
>
> Learn more about Azure RBAC here: `https://learn.microsoft.com/en-us/` `azure/role-based-access-control/overview`

Azure RBAC is a crucial component for securing Azure resources and ensuring that only authorized users and applications have access. It plays a vital role in maintaining a secure, compliant, and well-managed Azure environment. Combining it with Azure Policy, Azure management groups, and Azure Blueprints, we have all the components needed for a complete governance framework.

> **RBAC – best practices**
>
> Here are some RBAC best practices to follow when assigning roles:
>
> - Only grant the exact access users need
> - Restrict the number of subscription owners
> - Use Microsoft Entra ID PIM
> - Assign roles to groups, not individual users, so that permissions are inherited
> - Assign roles using the unique role ID instead of the role name, in case the role is renamed
> - Avoid using wildcards when working with custom roles

RBAC is not only about the users. Microsoft Entra ID is also used to authenticate users and applications. Let us see how we can work with those identities in the next section.

Authenticating with application identities

Application identities are a fundamental concept in Microsoft Entra ID IAM. They represent the security context of an application or service when interacting with Azure resources. Typically, the underlying object is the service principal. A service principal is like a user identity but is used by applications, services, or scripts to authenticate and access Azure resources securely. The process of creating a service principal depends on what it is we want to use to authenticate, and mostly, we can recognize two types—application identities and managed identities used by Azure services.

When it comes to authentication and authorization in the application or managed identity, the process is the same. If it exists in Microsoft Entra ID, it can be assigned RBAC, as with any user in the system. Service principals have life cycles, just as with user identities. They can be created, updated, and deleted. For standalone Azure AD applications, service principals can use client secrets/passwords or certificates for authentication. Client secrets should be stored securely, while certificates provide an added layer of security. Microsoft Entra ID applications can be configured as single tenant (only accessible in one Microsoft Entra ID tenant) or multi-tenant (accessible by users and applications from multiple Microsoft Entra ID tenants). Multi-tenant apps often require additional configuration to handle identity federation.

Let us review how we can create and work with service principals next.

Creating a service principal

In order to authenticate when working with applications or scripts that train and test a model, for example, you can use service principal authentication. To achieve this, we need to create a service principal in the Microsoft Entra ID workspace. If you are creating a service principal, you need to create an application registration.

Let us see both ways of achieving this.

Using the CLI

Depending on where you are running the command, you might need to authenticate your Azure subscription. Run the commands through Cloud Shell so that there is no need. The command to create a service principal is shown here:

```
az ad sp create-for-rbac --sdk-auth --name azuremldatascientist --role
Contributor --scopes /subscriptions/<subscription id>
```

The result will include several values that we must protect as they serve as credentials, but we must ensure to save them so that we can use them in our code to retrieve an authentication token. These are clientId, clientSecret, and tenantId:

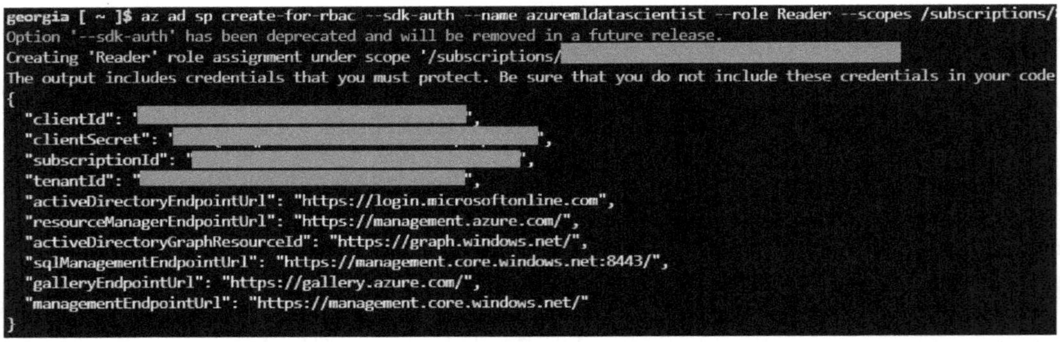

Figure 6.17 – Service principal creation result

You can retrieve more information about the service principal using the portal or the following command:

```
az ad sp show --id <clientId from previous result>
```

Now that we have created a service principal, we can use it in our code and assign more roles if necessary.

Registering an application

The CLI is not the only way to create a service principal. Another way is to use the portal. Open the Microsoft Entra ID workspace and find the **App registrations** menu. In the following screenshot, you can see a list of existing service principals, including the service principal we created in the previous section using the CLI. You can find the necessary IDs and information using the portal from here as well:

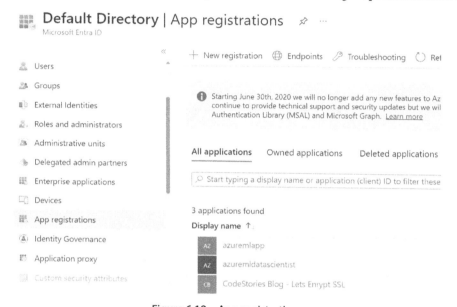

Figure 6.18 – App registrations

To proceed from here, click the **New registration** button. Fill in the details, giving the application a name and indicating what kinds of accounts can use this. For this example, we will keep the defaults and click **Register**, as we can see in the next screenshot:

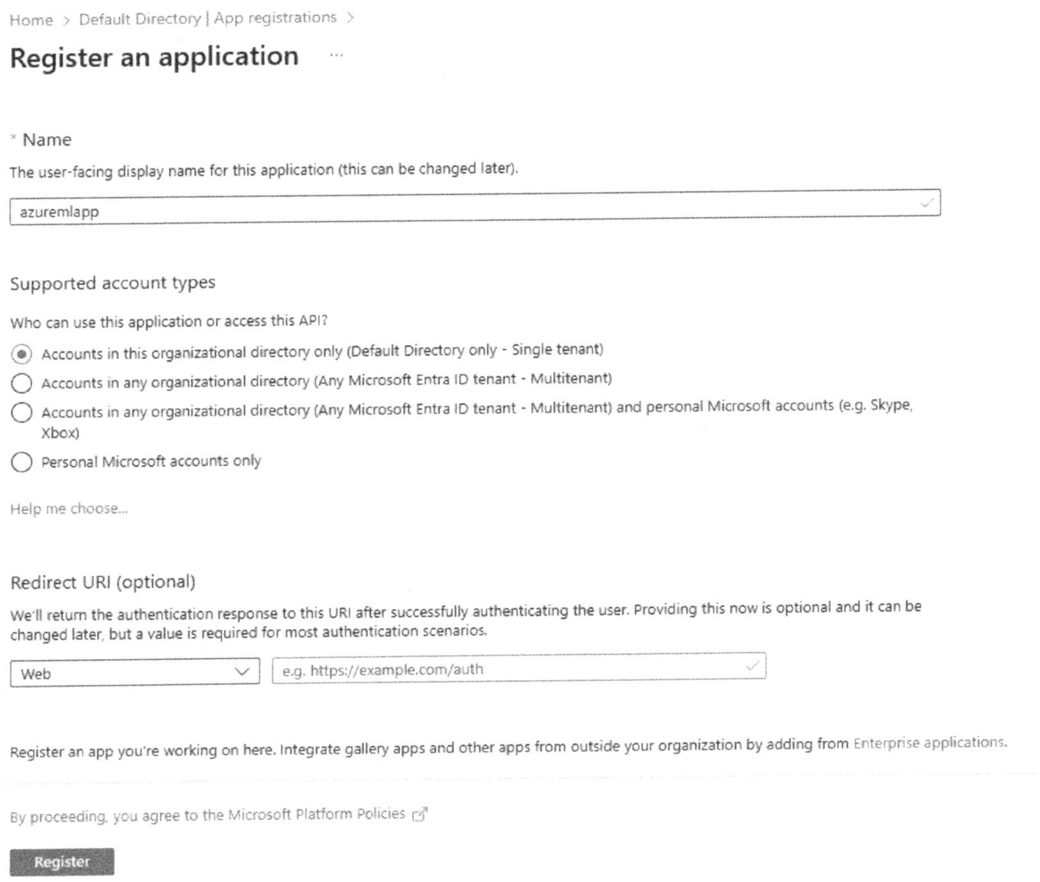

Home > Default Directory | App registrations >

Register an application   ...

* Name

The user-facing display name for this application (this can be changed later).

| azuremlapp | ✓ |

Supported account types

Who can use this application or access this API?

(●) Accounts in this organizational directory only (Default Directory only - Single tenant)

( ) Accounts in any organizational directory (Any Microsoft Entra ID tenant - Multitenant)

( ) Accounts in any organizational directory (Any Microsoft Entra ID tenant - Multitenant) and personal Microsoft accounts (e.g. Skype, Xbox)

( ) Personal Microsoft accounts only

Help me choose...

Redirect URI (optional)

We'll return the authentication response to this URI after successfully authenticating the user. Providing this now is optional and it can be changed later, but a value is required for most authentication scenarios.

| Web   ∨ | e.g. https://example.com/auth   ✓ |

Register an app you're working on here. Integrate gallery apps and other apps from outside your organization by adding from Enterprise applications.

By proceeding, you agree to the Microsoft Platform Policies ☐

[Register]

Figure 6.19 – Creating a new registration

Your registration is complete. As soon as we click **Register**, the application registration page will open, and we can configure multiple options, as seen in the following screenshot:

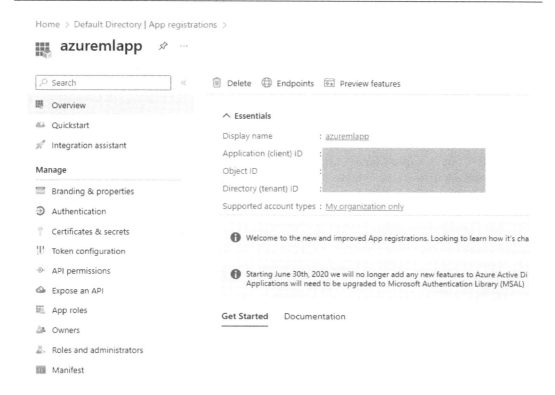

Figure 6.20 – Creating a new registration

By opening up an app registration, you can configure options such as client certificates and secrets, as well as roles and permissions.

But what about services? How does the workspace authenticate a **virtual machine** (**VM**) that wants to connect to the workspace? This is where managed identities come in. Let us see how managed identities work and how we can use everything we have seen so far to authenticate in our code.

Working with managed identities

Managed identities in Azure are a way to securely authenticate and authorize applications and services within the Azure ecosystem. They are a fundamental part of Azure's IAM capabilities and are used to authorize themselves when interacting with other Azure services and resources. This eliminates the need to store sensitive credentials or secrets in code or configuration files, making the application more secure. Managed identities can be used with a wide range of Azure services, including Azure Virtual Machines, Azure Storage accounts, Azure Key Vault, Azure Machine Learning, and more. They can be assigned specific roles and permissions in Azure RBAC. This means you can control which actions and resources the identity can access within your Azure environment. We can easily use managed identities in our applications or scripts by leveraging the Azure Machine Learning libraries and SDKs available, as we will see in the next section.

Each Azure resource that supports managed identities has a specific way of enabling and using them. There are two types of managed identities. Let us review the differences between the two.

Enabling a system-assigned managed identity

This type of identity is created and managed by Azure for a specific Azure resource, such as a VM or an Azure function. It's tightly bound to the life cycle of the resource it's associated with, meaning when the resource is deleted, the managed identity is deleted along with it and cannot be associated with multiple resources. To work with system-assigned managed identities, you simply enable them on your resources.

To enable a system-assigned managed identity, we simply need to find the **Identity** menu, as shown in the following screenshot, in the resource blade of our choice, set the **Status** toggle to **On**, and click on **Save**. For this example, I have chosen a VM, but it is supported in multiple Azure resources:

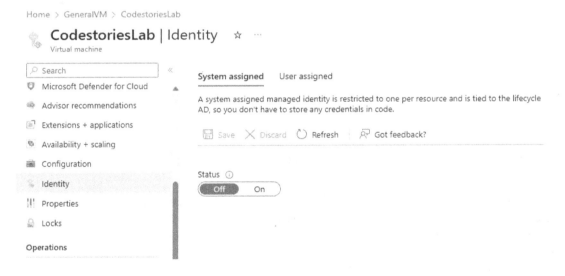

Figure 6.21 – Opening the Identity menu

As soon as we have enabled the system-assigned managed identity, we can use RBAC and assign roles or disable it by setting the **Status** toggle to **Off**. You can see the enabled system-assigned managed identity in the next screenshot:

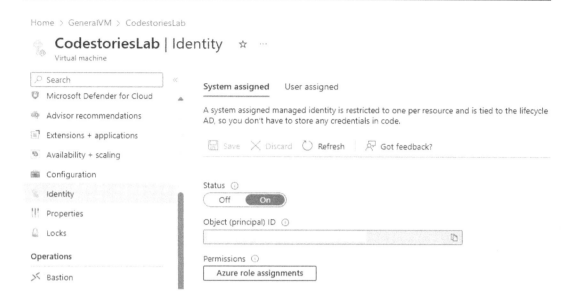

Figure 6.22 – System-assigned managed identity enabled

Creating a user-assigned managed identity

This type of identity is created and managed as a standalone Azure resource. You can then associate it with one or more Azure resources, allowing multiple resources to use the same identity. This is very useful when, for example, the life cycle of the managed identity needs to be independent of the resource life cycle or multiple resources need to share the same permissions.

Creating a managed identity is a two-step process. First, we need to create a managed identity.

To do that, open the **Managed Identities** menu from the search box on the top and click on **Create**. Fill in some basic details, as shown in the following screenshot:

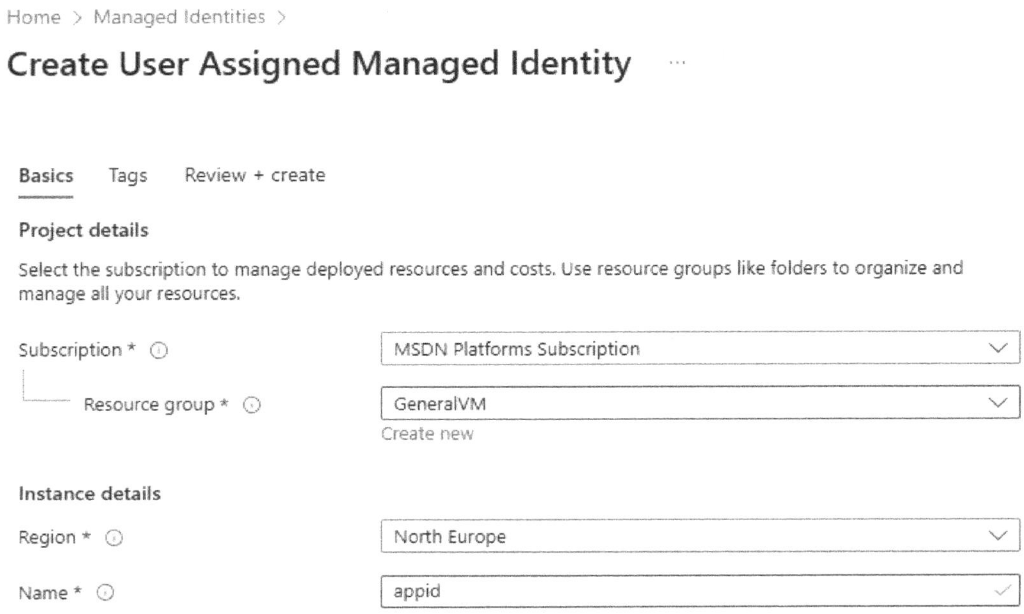

Home > Managed Identities >

Create User Assigned Managed Identity   ···

Basics   Tags   Review + create

Project details

Select the subscription to manage deployed resources and costs. Use resource groups like folders to organize and manage all your resources.

Subscription * ⓘ | MSDN Platforms Subscription   ∨ |

└── Resource group * ⓘ | GeneralVM   ∨ |
Create new

Instance details

Region * ⓘ | North Europe   ∨ |

Name * ⓘ | appid   ✓ |

Figure 6.23 – Creating a user-assigned managed identity

As soon as the identity is created, we can associate it with many resources. As previously, we will find the **Identity** menu in the resource blade, but this time we will switch to the **User assigned** tab. Then, we can click on the **Add** button and filter our identities, and as soon as we find the one we created previously, we can associate it with the resource. You can see the portal for these steps in the following screenshot:

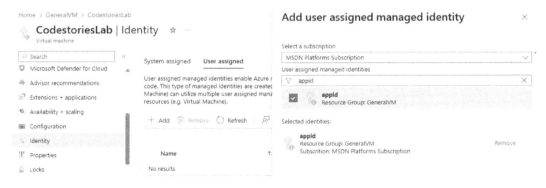

Figure 6.24 – Associating the user-assigned managed identity

Managed identities can also be created or enabled using other Azure tools such as the CLI, PowerShell, or the REST API. Then, they can be used from scripts or other Azure services we want to connect to. We can enable, disable, or disassociate them from our resources at any time.

In summary, Microsoft Entra ID managed identities are a way to improve the security and management of authentication and authorization for Azure resources by eliminating the need for storing credentials and providing seamless integration with Azure services. They help developers and administrators ensure the security and compliance of their Azure workloads.

Here is how we can set up authentication using the different identities available.

Setting up authentication

We can simplify the authentication process by using the `DefaultAzureCredential` class from the Azure Identity package for Python. This class automatically chooses the appropriate authentication method (such as Managed Identity, Service Principal, or interactive login) based on the environment it's running in. Here's how we can use it for both managed identity and service principal scenarios

When connecting with a service principal, we need to provide three environment variables and use the values when authenticating.

Here are the variables—they can all be found in the object returned when we created the service principal:

- `AZURE_CLIENT_ID` : The ID of the client

- `AZURE_TENANT_ID`: The Microsoft Entra ID tenant ID

- `AZURE_CLIENT_SECRET`: The credential secret

To set these variables, you can use the `python-dotenv` package.

> **Identity libraries**
>
> To find out more about the libraries, see here:
>
> `https://learn.microsoft.com/en-us/python/api/overview/azure/identity-readme?view=azure-python`
>
> `https://pypi.org/project/python-dotenv/`

If we are using a managed identity, the class will automatically detect the credentials, and there is no need for environment variables. Here is a code sample for both:

```
from azure.identity import DefaultAzureCredential
identity= DefaultAzureCredential() identity.get_token("https://
management.azure.com/.default")
```

After this code, you can write your desired code to work with Azure Machine Learning and train your models.

Working with application identities helps us greatly ensure that we have consistency across roles and secure our ML assets. Now that we have reviewed our authentication and role management options, let us review some other services that complement this functionality and help us secure our workloads further.

Enhancing access security

Now that we have a better idea of how to leverage Microsoft Entra ID for authentication and role management, we can see some other services that we can use to complement and further secure our users' identities.

Conditional Access

Conditional Access in Microsoft Entra ID is a powerful feature that allows organizations to set specific conditions and policies for granting or denying access to their cloud-based resources. With **Conditional Access**, you can create rules and policies that consider a range of factors before allowing or blocking access, enhancing security and compliance.

Conditional Access policies are rules that you define to control access to your protected resources. These policies are based on conditions and can be tailored to specific users, groups, applications, IP location information, user or sign risk detection, and devices. The action based on those signals is either **Block/Allow**. You can combine multiple conditions based on different scenarios that apply to your organization and users.

The following are some examples of policies that are used commonly:

- Requiring for **multi-factor authentication** (**MFA**) to be enabled for users with highly privileged roles or from unrecognized locations
- Blocking users that are flagged by the system as high risk
- Allowing or blocking access from specific IPs or countries
- Requiring a password change to allow access

This is the **Overview** blade of **Conditional Access** where you can manage policies, locations, networking, and other features:

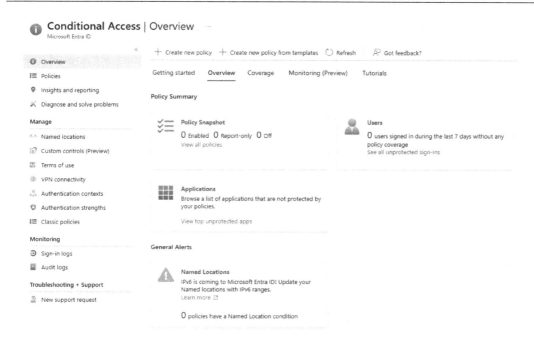

Figure 6.25 – Conditional Access Overview blade

Conditional Access in Microsoft Entra ID is a dynamic and flexible tool that helps organizations strike a balance between security and user productivity. By setting up policies that consider different factors, we can enforce access controls that adapt to the changing security landscape and the needs of your organization.

This is not the only tool we can use to enhance security. Let us see how we can use PIM together with RBAC.

PIM

Microsoft Entra ID PIM is an Azure service that helps organizations manage, control, and monitor access within their Azure AD and other Microsoft Online services. It focuses on privileged accounts, which have access to critical resources and data. PIM provides features and capabilities to help organizations protect these privileged accounts and mitigate security risks.

PIM can be used in conjunction with RBAC to enhance the security and management of privileged accounts and access to Azure resources. When used together, PIM and RBAC provide a comprehensive approach to managing access to Azure resources, especially those that require elevated privileges. We can enable **just-in-time** (**JIT**) and time-bound access for users assigned to specific RBAC roles. For example, if a user needs **Contributor** access to a resource group, Azure PIM allows them to activate this role only when necessary and for a defined duration. When a user needs to activate an RBAC role, they initiate a request through the Azure PIM interface by providing a valid justification. This request goes through an approval process, ensuring that activation is authorized by an appropriate administrator or role owner. The user specifies the duration, and access is automatically revoked when the specified time period expires, reducing the risk of prolonged elevated access.

Azure PIM logs all activations and deactivations of RBAC roles, providing audit trails for compliance and security purposes. Organizations can regularly review and certify the continued need for privileged access through access reviews. This process helps ensure that users who have been assigned RBAC roles still require them, and that access remains aligned with business needs.

By combining Azure PIM and RBAC, organizations can strengthen their IAM strategy for Azure resources. This approach minimizes risks associated with persistent, overprivileged accounts, and helps organizations maintain control, visibility, and compliance while managing access to critical Azure services and data.

Azure Key Vault

Azure Key Vault is a cloud service provided by Microsoft Azure that helps you securely manage keys, secrets, certificates, and other sensitive information used by your applications and services. It is designed to provide a centralized and secure location for storing and managing cryptographic keys and other secrets, making it easier to adhere to security best practices and compliance requirements. Here is some information about its features:

- **Key management**: Azure Key Vault allows us to generate, import, and manage cryptographic keys used for encryption, decryption, and authentication. It supports various key types, including **Rivest–Shamir–Adleman (RSA)**, **Advanced Encryption Standard (AES)**, and elliptic curve keys.

- **Secrets management**: We can use Azure Key Vault to store and manage secrets, such as connection strings, API keys, and passwords. These secrets are stored securely and can be accessed programmatically by your applications.

- **Certificate management**: Key Vault enables the management of X.509 certificates and automates tasks such as certificate renewal. It also supports integration with Azure services such as Azure Application Gateway and **Azure Kubernetes Service (AKS)** for SSL/TLS certificate management.

To retrieve keys or secrets, instead of hardcoding the secrets, we authenticate to Key Vault to retrieve them. This adds another layer of security, and we can revoke access easily at any time and have additional security options such as key versioning, logging, backup, purge protection, and more.

> **Best practice**
> Combine the Azure Key Vault service with managed identities for maximum security.

For Azure Machine Learning, we can combine the Azure Key Vault service with managed identities to retrieve secrets in our scripts. All we need is the Azure Key Vault Secrets client library for Python.

Before we get started, we need to make sure we have the following prerequisites along with our workspace:

- An Azure Key Vault resource with the secret value we want to retrieve

- A compute cluster with a managed identity enabled and assigned with the proper RBAC roles or access policies in Azure Key Vault

- The `azure-keyvault-secrets` and `azure-identity` packages installed in our Azure Machine Learning environment

If you have all the prerequisites completed, you can retrieve the secret using the following code sample. Just ensure you replace the key vault name with yours and the secret name with yours:

```
from azure.identity import DefaultAzureCredential
from azure.keyvault.secrets import SecretClient

identity= DefaultAzureCredential()

kv_client = SecretClient(vault_url="https://<key vault name>.vault.
azure.net/", credential= identity)
secret = kv_client.get_secret("secret-name")
print(secret.value)
```

Conditional Access and PIM are both Microsoft Entra ID features that, when enabled, provide additional security to our identities and keep our user credentials secure and in accordance with the PoLP. Azure Key Vault is a critical component in building secure and compliant applications in the Azure cloud environment, especially when you combine it with managed identities. These features might be optional, but they need to be considered when working to secure our ML projects.

Summary

In this chapter, we focused on all aspects of identity and adhering to the PoLP. Although simple in theory, the PoLP is an iterative and continuous process that we need to monitor in order to prevent overprivileged applications. Since Microsoft Entra ID is the identity management tool for Azure and, by extension, Azure Machine Learning, implementing its core features such as RBAC and learning to work with application identities will help us ensure that the credentials of our users and applications will not be compromised easily. Additionally, implementing features such as **Conditional Access** and PIM can provide an additional level of security to our identities. But these credentials are not the only ones that matter. In our scripts, we might be using different connection strings or secrets. We can use the Key Vault service together with managed identities where it is possible to manage them centrally and ensure that our secrets are safe.

In the next chapter, we will explore everything to do with our workspace security and the underlying infrastructure. We will learn how to secure our compute and endpoints and take advantage of any existing Azure infrastructure such as networks for added security.

7

Managing and Securing Your Azure Machine Learning Workspace

After data and access management comes infrastructure. Although Azure Machine Learning is a cloud service, it doesn't mean that we cannot leverage services together with our Azure or on-premises infrastructure to isolate our resources and secure them from public access.

In this chapter, we will learn how to implement security best practices regarding the workspace. We will focus more on practices and scenarios around virtual networking and endpoint security as well as compute. Compute in Azure Machine Learning can be used both for model training and deployment and each option available has its own security best practices. Compute includes compute instances, compute clusters, and containers. The workspace uses Azure Container Registries to deploy models that can be deployed as containers, so we will review security options for all those services.

In this chapter, we're going to cover the following main topics:

- Exploring network security
- Working with Azure Machine Learning compute
- Managing container registries and containers

By the end of this chapter, we will know how to implement best practices and isolate our Azure Machine Learning workspace and its associated resources by using virtual networking in Azure.

Technical requirements

This chapter deals heavily with networking and infrastructure in Azure. Although the tutorials can be implemented without much difficulty, properly implementing and maintaining a network architecture in Azure requires a lot of knowledge.

If you have no experience with networking in Azure, I recommend taking a look at this overview of the service before moving on with the chapter:

- **Virtual Networks overview**:

    https://learn.microsoft.com/en-us/azure/virtual-network/virtual-networks-overview

- **Networking architecture design**:

    https://learn.microsoft.com/en-us/azure/architecture/guide/networking/networking-start-here

Exploring network security

The Azure Machine Learning workspace is the main point of use. This is where you complete all your ML tasks, and by default, all endpoints and workspace have access to the public internet. However, if we are already using Azure infrastructure services for different purposes or want to restrict access to our resources, we can leverage **virtual networks** (**VNets**). Using VNets in Azure provides an extra layer of security and isolation for our Azure Machine Learning resources and better control for inbound and outbound network communications. In this section, we will explore several options we have to integrate VNets with Azure Machine Learning.

Let us start with the workspace.

Creating a VNet

The first thing we will need is a VNet. If you already have one, you can use it. If not, you can follow the next steps to create one:

1. Search for **Virtual Networks** in the Azure search bar and click to create a new one. The create form will pop up. Choose the **Subscription** and **Resource group** and provide a **Virtual network name** and **Region** as shown in the following screenshot. Choose the same region as your workspace:

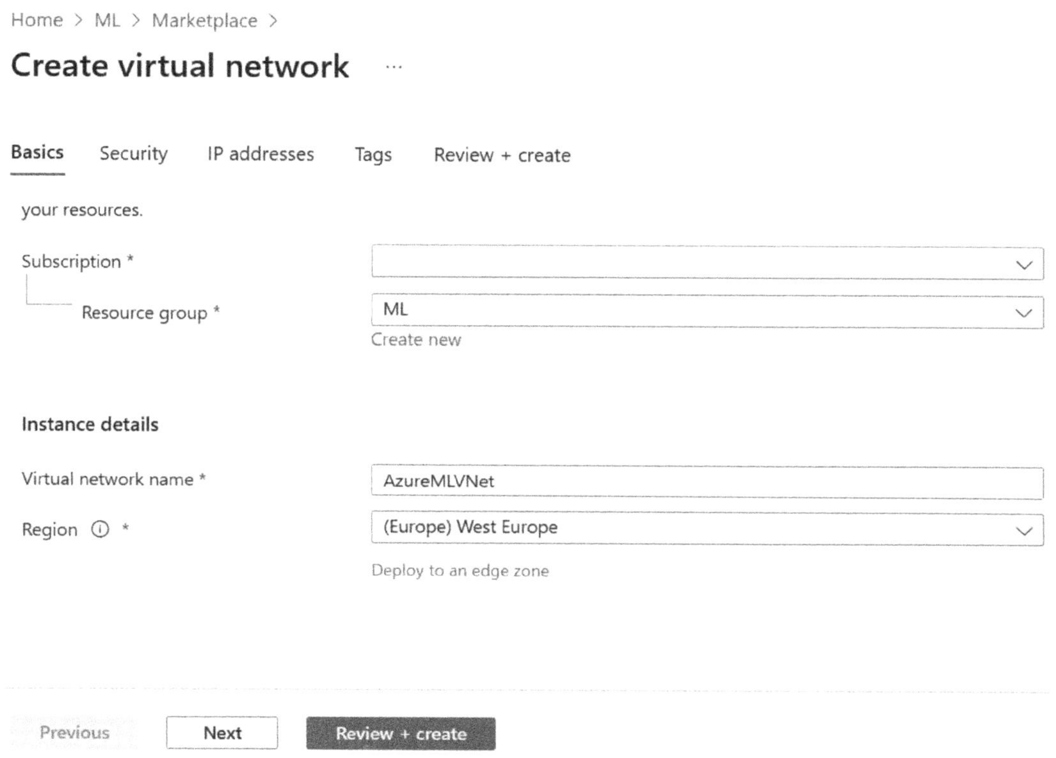

Home > ML > Marketplace >

Create virtual network ⋯

Basics   Security   IP addresses   Tags   Review + create

your resources.

Subscription *

Resource group *   ML
                                    Create new

Instance details

Virtual network name *   AzureMLVNet

Region ⓘ *   (Europe) West Europe
                                    Deploy to an edge zone

Previous   Next   Review + create

Figure 7.1 – Filling in basic details

2. Click **Next** and leave the default values until you reach the **IP addresses** tab. Make sure the address space is adequate and that there is at least one subnet available. An example is shown in the following screenshot:

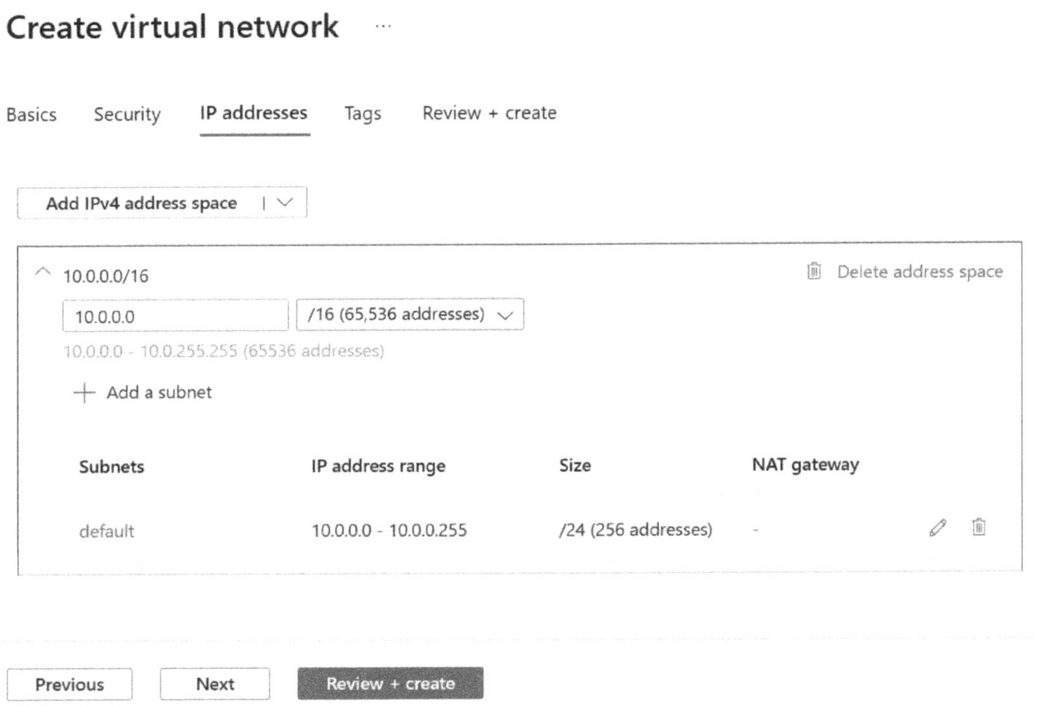

Create virtual network ···

Basics   Security   **IP addresses**   Tags   Review + create

Add IPv4 address space | ∨

∧ 10.0.0.0/16   🗑 Delete address space

    | 10.0.0.0 | | /16 (65,536 addresses) ∨ |

    10.0.0.0 - 10.0.255.255 (65536 addresses)

    + Add a subnet

Subnets	IP address range	Size	NAT gateway		
default	10.0.0.0 - 10.0.0.255	/24 (256 addresses)	-	✎	🗑

| Previous | | Next | | Review + create |

Figure 7.2 – Add the address space

> **VNet best practice**
>
> Make sure the address space and subnet do not overlap with other networks in your subscription or on-premises systems. If you need more guidance on creating a VNet architecture, see more information at https://learn.microsoft.com/en-us/azure/virtual-network/concepts-and-best-practices.

3. Click **Review + create** to create the VNet. Wait for the process to complete before you move forward with anything else.

Now we are ready to start restricting access to our workspace using VNets.

Securing the workspace

Restricting public access to the workspace is very easily configurable through the Azure portal and can restrict all inbound and/or outbound connections. When we are talking about inbound traffic, we refer to connections coming into the Azure ML workspace or associated resources from the public internet. This can be data being ingested into the Azure ML workspace from on-premises locations, from other cloud resources, or from external applications and platforms. When you submit a dataset, a job, or any other request from your local machine to Azure Machine Learning, that's considered inbound traffic. Outbound traffic is any connection leaving the workspace or associated resources to go elsewhere. This can be the results from a machine learning model, processed data, logs, and so on being sent back to your local machine, another cloud resource, or an external application or platform.

The challenge is to make sure that all associated services to the workspace are also accessible and configured properly through that virtual network and not the public internet. Something else we need to consider when designing and implementing this solution is that the workspace needs to have outbound access to specific endpoints via the public internet. If we want to restrict outbound access as well, we need to ensure that these endpoints maintain their public access.

Let us see how we can configure both options.

Restricting inbound traffic

To restrict inbound traffic from the public internet, we need to use a VNet, which we learned how to configure in the preceding section. Here is the process of disabling public access and using a VNet with our workspace.

First, open the Azure Machine Learning resource from the Azure portal and find the **Networking** section. In the first tab, called **Public access**, set the access to **Disabled** and click **Save,** as shown in the next screenshot:

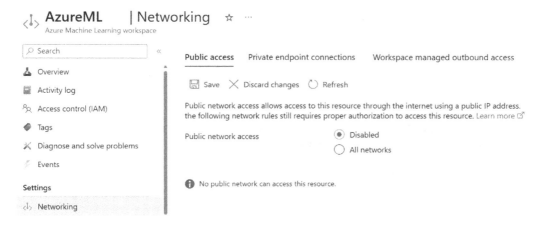

Figure 7.3 – Disable public access

Now we need to create a private endpoint connection. Azure Private Link is a service in Microsoft's Azure cloud platform that enables you to securely access Azure services over a private endpoint in your virtual network, thus avoiding data exposure to the public internet. With Azure Private Link, Azure services can be accessed over a private IP address in your virtual network. This provides several benefits. If your virtual network is connected to on-premises work environments via a **virtual private network** (**VPN**) or ExpressRoute, resources can access the Azure service over these private connections with the use of Azure Private Link. Using global VNet peering, we can connect to Azure services from any region. Azure Private Link integrates with Azure Private DNS zones, meaning that the service's private endpoint can be registered with a private DNS zone, thus making name resolution more straightforward.

Setting up a private endpoint is a straightforward process in the Azure portal. Once set up, all network traffic between the service provider and the service consumer can be routed through the private endpoint. So, now that we have disabled public access, we need to create a private link to re-establish access this time via the virtual network.

> **Virtual network peering**
>
> To learn more about Vnet peering, visit the following URL:
>
> `https://learn.microsoft.com/en-us/azure/virtual-network/virtual-network-peering-overview`

Here is the creation process for the private links/endpoints. Move on to the next tab, **Private endpoint connections**, and click on **Private endpoint** to create one:

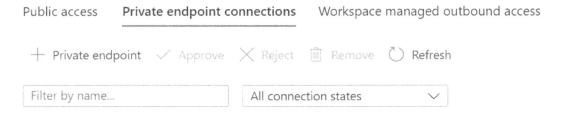

Figure 7.4 – Creating a private endpoint

On the form, fill in some basic details including **Subscription**, **Resource group**, **Network interface name**, and **Region** and click **Next** as shown here:

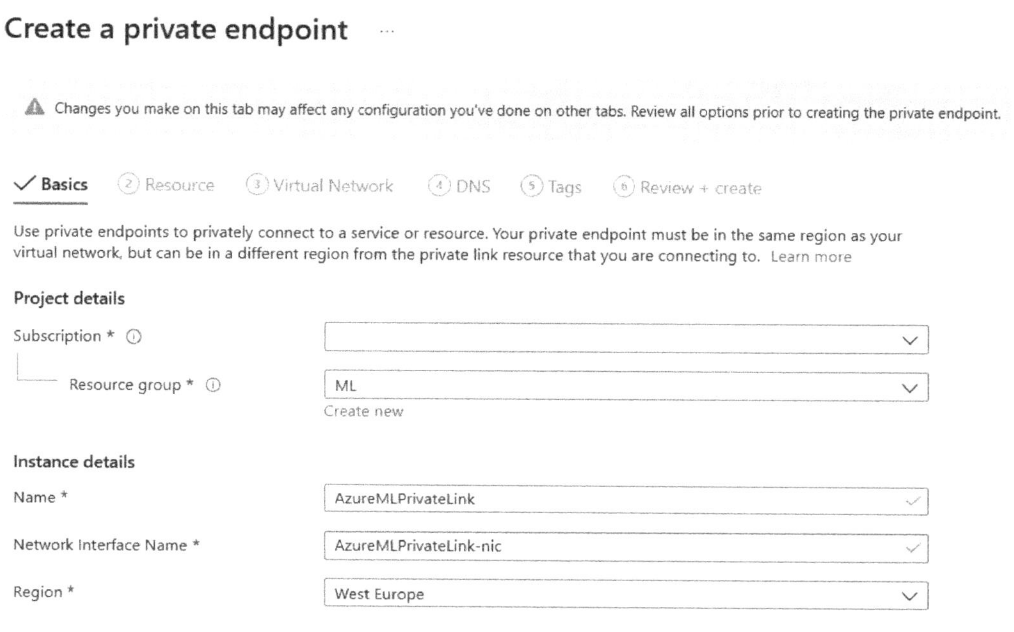

Create a private endpoint   ···

⚠ Changes you make on this tab may affect any configuration you've done on other tabs. Review all options prior to creating the private endpoint.

✓ **Basics**   ② Resource   ③ Virtual Network   ④ DNS   ⑤ Tags   ⑥ Review + create

Use private endpoints to privately connect to a service or resource. Your private endpoint must be in the same region as your virtual network, but can be in a different region from the private link resource that you are connecting to. Learn more

Project details

Subscription * ⓘ	⌄
── Resource group * ⓘ	ML ⌄
	Create new

Instance details

Name *	AzureMLPrivateLink
Network Interface Name *	AzureMLPrivateLink-nic
Region *	West Europe ⌄

Figure 7.5 – Filling in the basic details

On the **Resource** tab, choose **amlworkspace** from the dropdown and click **Next**:

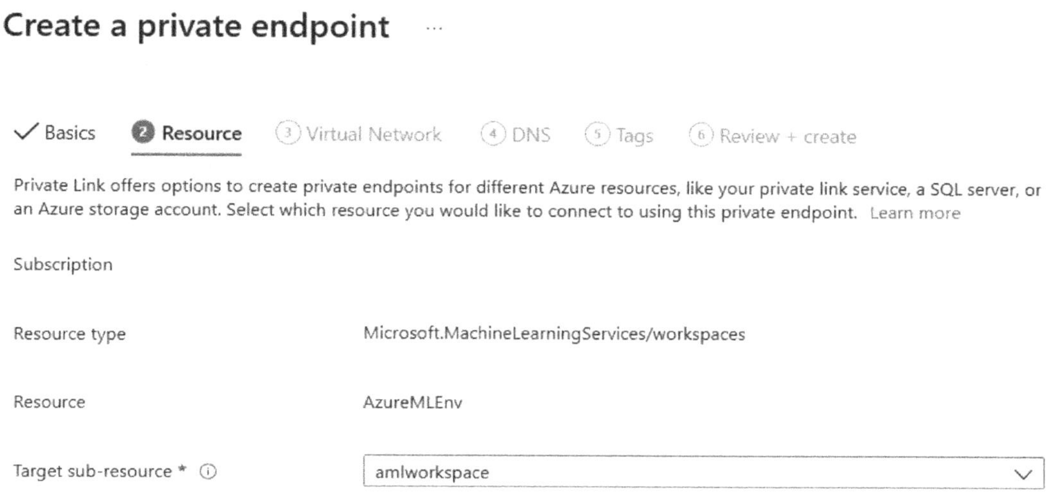

Create a private endpoint   ···

✓ Basics   ② **Resource**   ③ Virtual Network   ④ DNS   ⑤ Tags   ⑥ Review + create

Private Link offers options to create private endpoints for different Azure resources, like your private link service, a SQL server, or an Azure storage account. Select which resource you would like to connect to using this private endpoint. Learn more

Subscription	
Resource type	Microsoft.MachineLearningServices/workspaces
Resource	AzureMLEnv
Target sub-resource * ⓘ	amlworkspace ⌄

Figure 7.6 – Choosing the resource

Here, we will choose the desired VNet. You have to choose an existing one, so use the one we created previously. Make sure you select the proper subnet if your VNet has more than one. Leave the rest of the options as **default**.

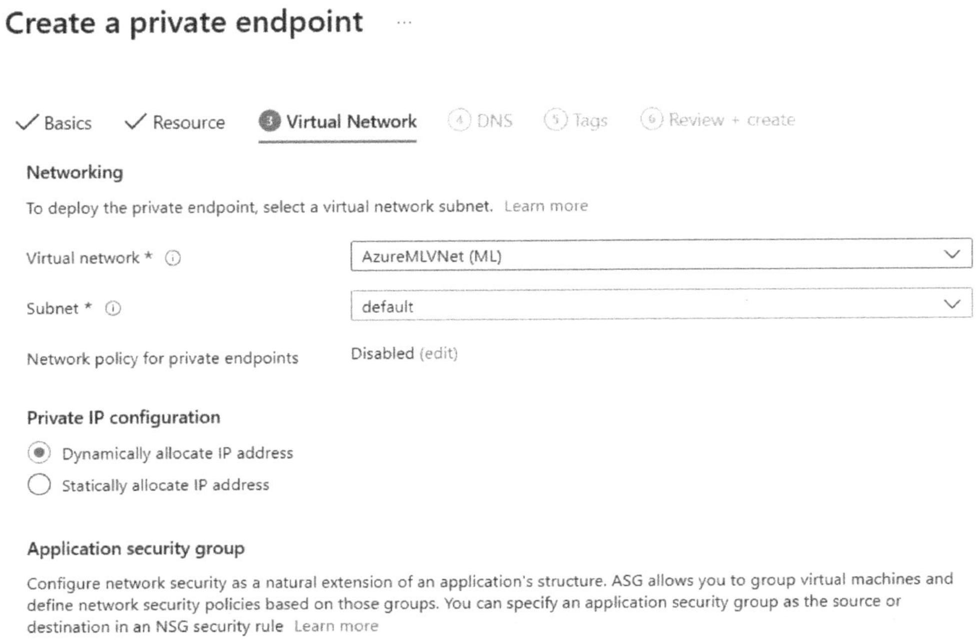

Create a private endpoint   ...

✓ Basics   ✓ Resource   ③ **Virtual Network**   ④ DNS   ⑤ Tags   ⑥ Review + create

Networking

To deploy the private endpoint, select a virtual network subnet. Learn more

Virtual network * ⓘ	AzureMLVNet (ML) ⌄
Subnet * ⓘ	default ⌄
Network policy for private endpoints	Disabled (edit)

Private IP configuration

◉ Dynamically allocate IP address

◯ Statically allocate IP address

Application security group

Configure network security as a natural extension of an application's structure. ASG allows you to group virtual machines and define network security policies based on those groups. You can specify an application security group as the source or destination in an NSG security rule Learn more

Figure 7.7 – Selecting the virtual network

Integrating with a DNS zone is optional but convenient, as it makes name resolution easier. Set the **Integrate with private DNS zone** option to **Yes** and then choose the **Subscription** and **Resource group**. The service will fill out the rest of the fields.

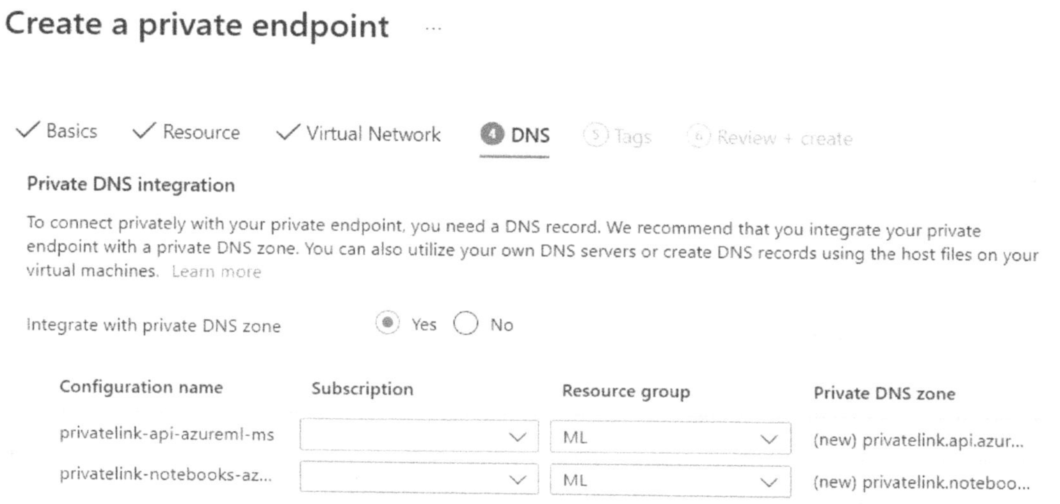

Create a private endpoint ...

Figure 7.8 – Adding DNS integration

DNS zones overview

To learn more about DNS zones check the overview here:

`https://learn.microsoft.com/en-us/azure/dns/dns-zones-records`

Now move on to **Review + create** and start the deployment of the resources. Wait for this process to be completed before moving on with any other steps.

Creating a private Link via the CLI

For creating a private link, you can learn more here:

`https://learn.microsoft.com/en-us/azure/machine-learning/how-to-configure-private-link?view=azureml-api-2&tabs=cli`

If you try to access the workspace at this point, you will get the following error because public access has been disabled.

Error loading workspace

Your administrator has disabled connectivity to your workspace from public internet. Please try to connect to your workspace with a private connection ⧉.

Figure 7.9 – Workspace public access is disabled

This was the basic configuration for the workspace's inbound access. Before we validate the access through the VNet, we should first configure outbound traffic and restrict access to associated services as well.

Let us start with outbound traffic.

Restricting outbound traffic

To restrict outbound traffic, we will go through the **Networking** blade again in Azure Machine Learning, but this time, we will click on the **Workspace managed outbound access** tab:

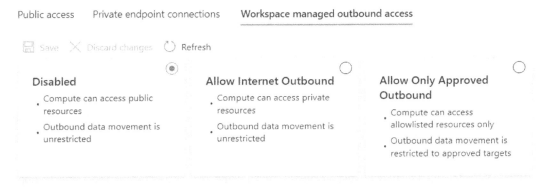

Figure 7.10 – Restricting outbound traffic

To restrict outbound traffic, we have two options: **Allow Internet Outbound** where only compute is limited and **Allow Only Approved Outbound** where both compute and all outbound data movement are limited.

Both of those options have some connection exceptions that you can see when enabling the options at the bottom of the screen. You can add some rules of your own, but the default ones cannot be disabled.

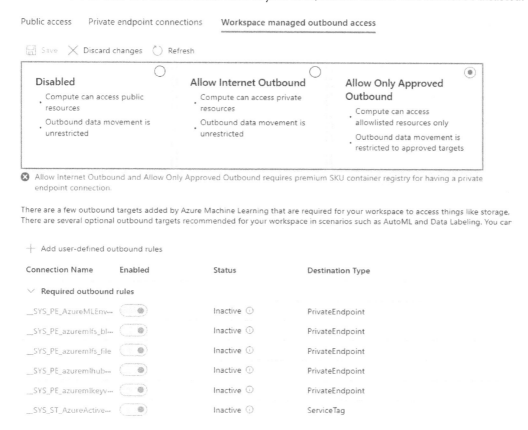

Figure 7.11 – Allowing only approved outbound option

If you are also using a firewall together with the network, make sure the connectivity is enabled through there as well, as restricting access to those resources will result in connectivity issues in the workspace and an inability to work with the services.

Securing the workspace was only the first step. Now we need to ensure that associated resources are also secured through the VNet.

Securing associated resources

As mentioned in *Chapter 1*, the workspace works closely with many resources, including storage accounts and key vaults, which are created to support the workspace. We need to configure the same networking settings if we truly want to ensure that they connect properly to the workspace through the Microsoft network but still maintain isolation from the public internet. The first thing we need to do is disable public access to those services as well.

To disable public access and restrict the account to specific networks, we can go to the **Networking** tab in the **Storage account** blade.

In the **Public network access** options, click **Enabled from selected virtual networks and ID addresses**. Then, choose the previously created VNet in the **Virtual networks** section and subnet by clicking on the **Add existing virtual network** button and click **Save**.

The final view should look like the following screenshot:

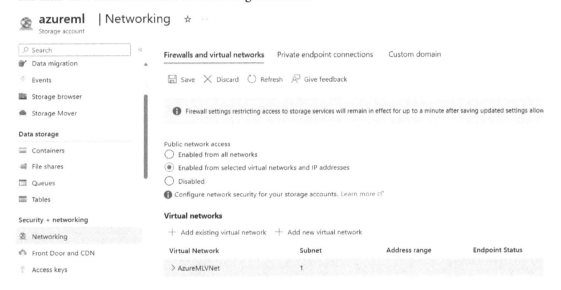

Figure 7.12 – Disabling public access in the storage account

The next step is to do something similar this time to the key vault associated with the workspace. The steps are exactly the same as previously.

To disable public access and restrict the account to specific networks, we can go to the **Networking** tab in the **Storage account** blade. For the **Public network access** option, click on **Enabled from selected virtual networks and ID addresses**. Then, choose the previously created VNet in the **Virtual networks** section and the subnet by clicking on the **Add existing virtual network** button and clicking **Save**.

The final view should look like the following:

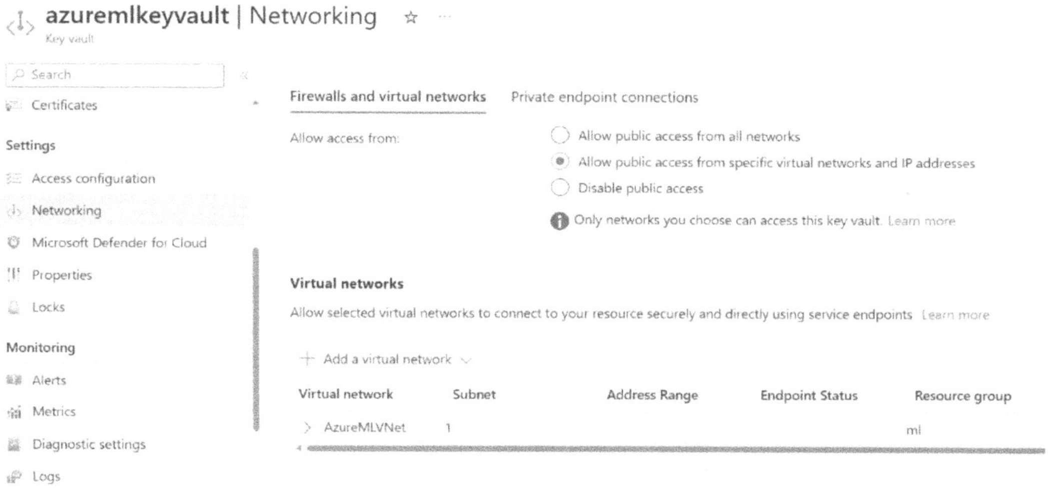

Figure 7.13 – Disabling public access in the key vault

> **Note**
>
> We can still configure service endpoints without restricting network access to the services. In this case, traffic from the workspace will go through the VNet and any other traffic will still access the services through the public internet. Doing both ensures better isolation.

Now that we have disabled public access, we have two options for configuration: enabling service endpoints or creating private endpoints for each service.

Let us explore both options starting with service endpoints.

Option 1: configuring service endpoints

This is the easiest and fastest option. Service endpoints in Azure provide enhanced security and optimized routing for VNets by extending your VNet's private address space over to Azure service resources. This allows you to secure Azure service resources to your VNet.

Open the VNet we created previously and go to the **Subnets** section. Click on the desired subnet and scroll down in the popup on the right.

Figure 7.14 – Allowing only approved outbound traffic

It is essential to note that while service endpoints are beneficial for many scenarios, there are cases where you might consider using Azure Private Link or Private Endpoints instead, especially when you want Azure services to be accessed via private IP addresses in your VNet.

So, let us see how to implement this option next.

Option 2: creating private endpoints

The process of creating private endpoints is similar to the one we use to create the public endpoint for the workspace. Let us see the steps for each service.

Azure storage account

From the **Networking** screen of the **Storage account** resource, click on **Private endpoint connections**. Click the + **Private endpoint** button and follow the tabs as we did previously for the workspace.

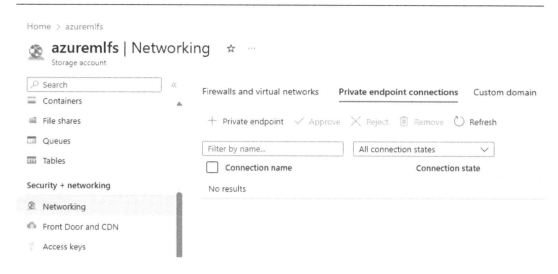

Figure 7.15 – Creating a private endpoint

Fill in some basic information for the endpoint, as seen in the following screenshot:

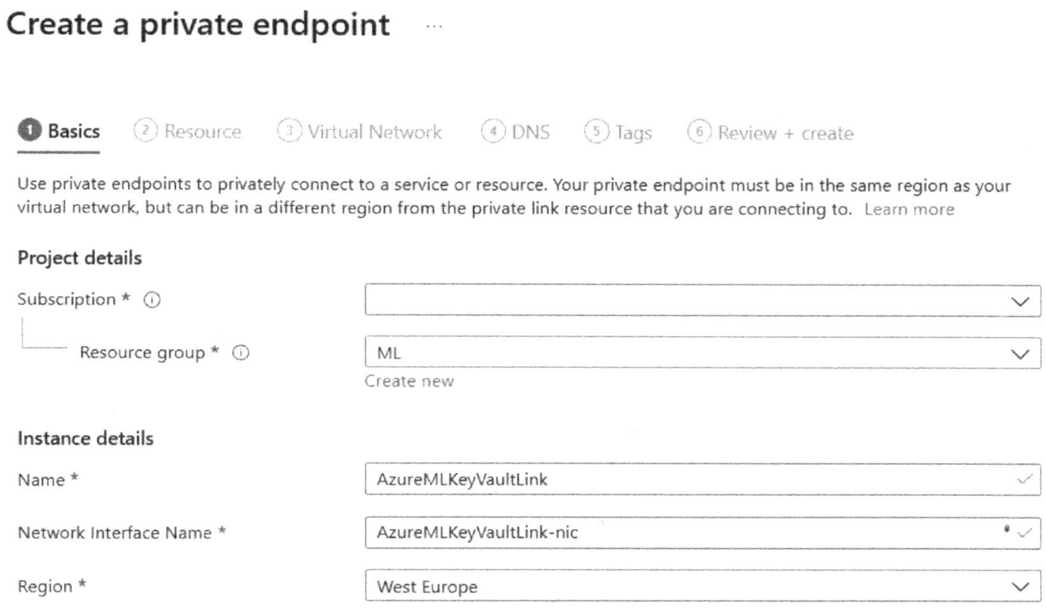

Create a private endpoint ...

① Basics   ② Resource   ③ Virtual Network   ④ DNS   ⑤ Tags   ⑥ Review + create

Use private endpoints to privately connect to a service or resource. Your private endpoint must be in the same region as your virtual network, but can be in a different region from the private link resource that you are connecting to. Learn more

Project details

Subscription * ⓘ   [⌄]

  └── Resource group * ⓘ   [ML   ⌄]
                                          Create new

Instance details

Name *   [AzureMLKeyVaultLink   ✓]

Network Interface Name *   [AzureMLKeyVaultLink-nic   • ✓]

Region *   [West Europe   ⌄]

Figure 7.16 – Filling in the basics

Then, on the **Resource** tab for the **Target sub-resource**, choose **blob** from the dropdown:

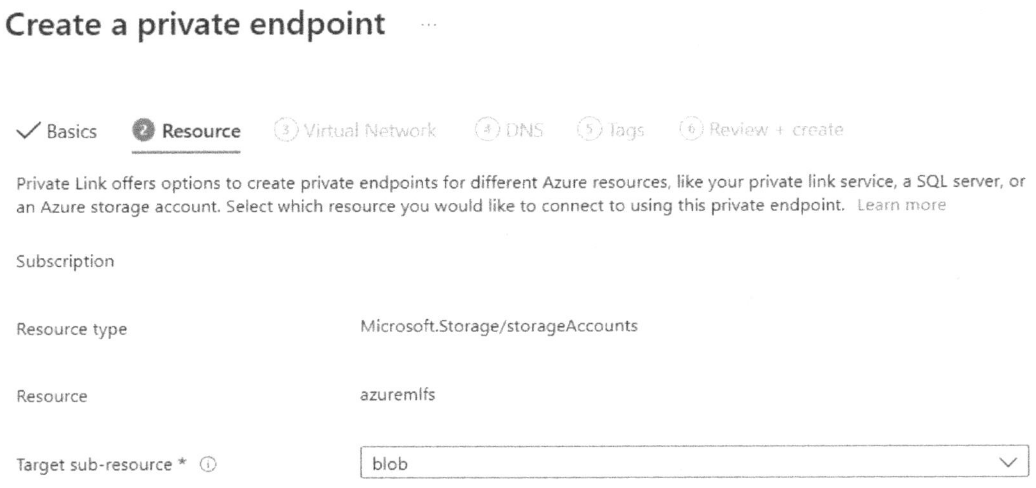

Create a private endpoint   ...

✓ Basics	❷ **Resource**	③ Virtual Network	④ DNS	⑤ Tags	⑥ Review + create

Private Link offers options to create private endpoints for different Azure resources, like your private link service, a SQL server, or an Azure storage account. Select which resource you would like to connect to using this private endpoint. Learn more

Subscription

Resource type   Microsoft.Storage/storageAccounts

Resource   azuremlfs

Target sub-resource * ⓘ | blob   ∨ |

Figure 7.17 – Choosing the blob resource

Go through the rest of the tabs exactly as for the workspace, filling in the **Virtual Network**, **DNS**, and then going to **Review + create**.

Once you have completed this process, create another private endpoint, this time choosing **file** for the **Target sub-resource**.

Once we are done with the storage account, here is how to do the same for the key vault.

Azure Key Vault

From the **Networking** screen of the key vault resource, click on **Private endpoint connections**. Click the **+ Private endpoint** button and follow the tabs as we did previously in the chapter for the storage account:

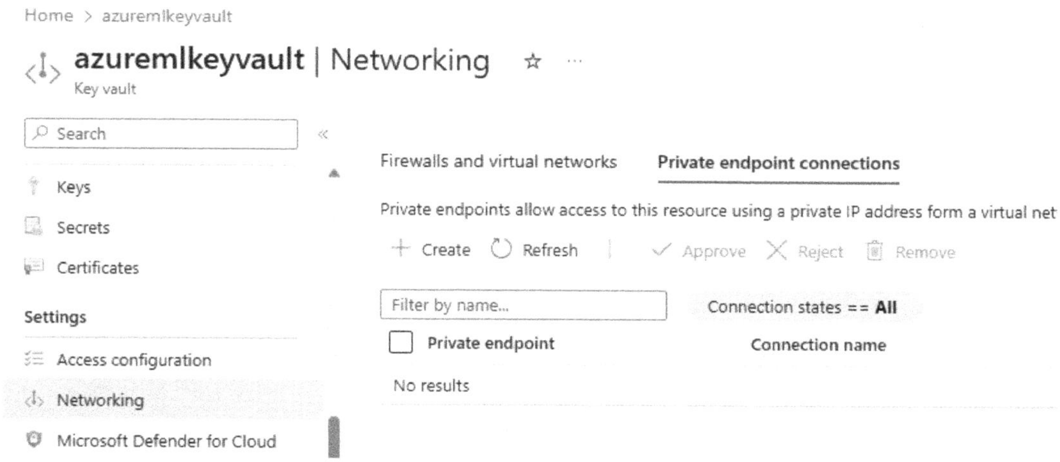

Home > azuremlkeyvault

⟨↕⟩ **azuremlkeyvault** | Networking ☆ ⋯
Key vault

| 🔍 Search | ≪ |

▲

Firewalls and virtual networks   **Private endpoint connections**

▾ Keys

Private endpoints allow access to this resource using a private IP address form a virtual net

🔲 Secrets

╋ Create   ◯ Refresh   ∣   ✓ Approve   ✕ Reject   🗑 Remove

🔲 Certificates

| Filter by name... | | Connection states == **All** |

Settings

☐ Private endpoint   **Connection name**

▤ Access configuration

No results

⟨↕⟩ Networking

🛡 Microsoft Defender for Cloud

Figure 7.18 – Creating a private endpoint

Fill in some basic information for the endpoint, as seen in the following screenshot:

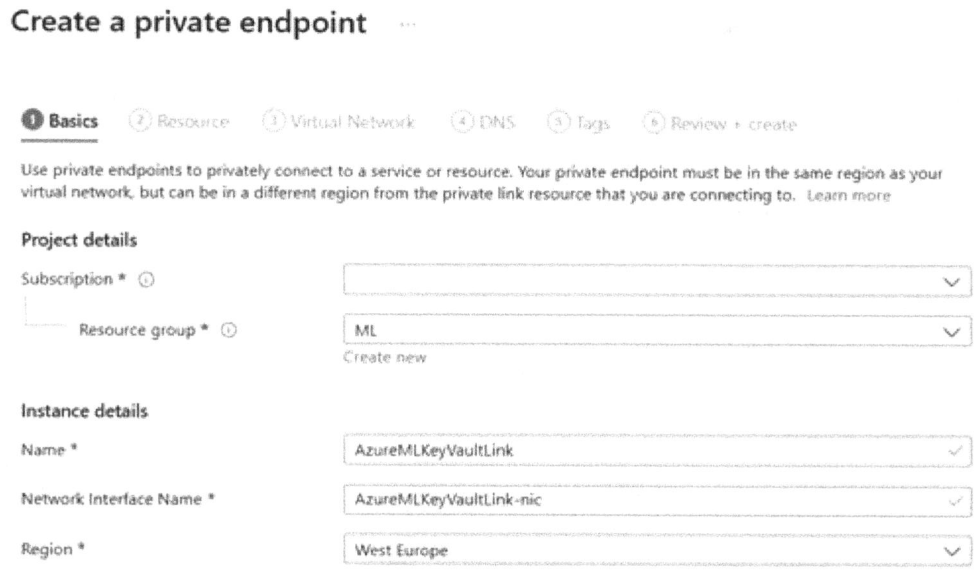

Create a private endpoint ⋯

❶ **Basics**   ② Resource   ③ Virtual Network   ④ DNS   ⑤ Tags   ⑥ Review + create

Use private endpoints to privately connect to a service or resource. Your private endpoint must be in the same region as your
virtual network, but can be in a different region from the private link resource that you are connecting to. Learn more

Project details

Subscription * ⓘ   [▾]

Resource group * ⓘ   [ML ▾]
                     Create new

Instance details

Name *   [AzureMLKeyVaultLink ✓]

Network Interface Name * [AzureMLKeyVaultLink-nic ✓]

Region *   [West Europe ▾]

Figure 7.19 – Filling in the basics

Then, on the Resource tab for the **Target sub-resource**, choose **vault**.

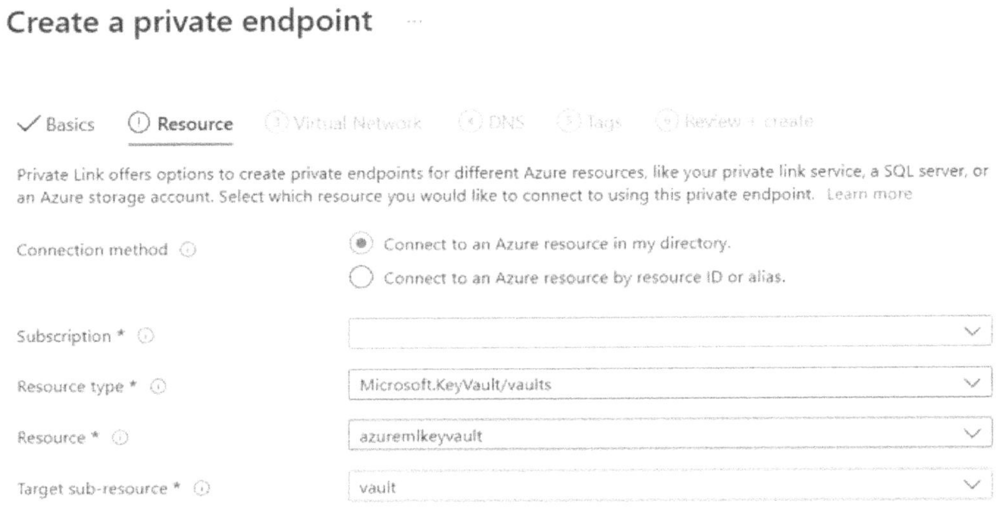

Create a private endpoint

✓ Basics   ① **Resource**   ③ Virtual Network   ④ DNS   ⑤ Tags   ⑥ Review + create

Private Link offers options to create private endpoints for different Azure resources, like your private link service, a SQL server, or an Azure storage account. Select which resource you would like to connect to using this private endpoint. Learn more

Connection method ⓘ   ⦿ Connect to an Azure resource in my directory.
                               ○ Connect to an Azure resource by resource ID or alias.

Subscription * ⓘ   [⌄]

Resource type * ⓘ   [Microsoft.KeyVault/vaults   ⌄]

Resource * ⓘ   [azuremlkeyvault   ⌄]

Target sub-resource * ⓘ   [vault   ⌄]

Figure 7.20 – Choosing the vault resource

Again, go through the rest of the tabs exactly as for the storage account, filling in the **Virtual Network** and **DNS** and then going to **Review + create**.

We have completed the minimum required configurations. Now it is time to test it! Let us review some options to test connectivity.

Validating connectivity

In order to connect to a workspace that is behind a firewall, we have many options. They depend mostly on your individual Azure infrastructure and requirements.

Let us review those options:

- **Connecting from on-premises systems**: There is one option to establish secure, encrypted communications between your on-premises networks and Azure. It is done via a VPN gateway through the public internet. Azure offers two types of gateways: **VPN Gateway** and **ExpressRoute**. It's important to choose the appropriate VPN solution, as they will have access to your internet activity, and not all VPN options offer the same level of security, privacy, and speed.

> **VPN solutions on Azure**
> Here, you can find more information about the VPN gateway and ExpressRoute services in Azure.

For VPN Gateway, see `https://learn.microsoft.com/en-us/azure/vpn-gateway/vpn-gateway-about-vpngateways`.

For ExpressRoute, see `https://learn.microsoft.com/en-us/azure/expressroute/expressroute-introduction`.

- **Connecting from cloud infrastructure**: We can always create a virtual machine—also sometimes referred to as a **jump box**—that we will connect to. From there, we can access the services restricted by the network. In addition, you can enable **Azure Bastion** in the VM and access the machine through the browser without configuring public IPs on the VM, which reduces exposure to security vulnerabilities.

  For our example, we will use a VM in Azure deployed in the same VNet that the Azure Machine Learning workspace and associated services are behind. All you need to do is create a VM deployed in the same network or a peered network and try to access the workspace.

> **Quickstart: create a VM in the portal**
>
> If you need to get started with VMs, check this quickstart guide here:
>
> `https://learn.microsoft.com/en-us/azure/virtual-machines/windows/quick-create-portal`

The result is as expected. We can access the workspace from the device inside the network, but everything outside the network is disabled. Here is a screenshot with a VM that is in the same VNet as the workspace accessing the page (left) and a browser trying to access the same workspace (right) through the public internet:

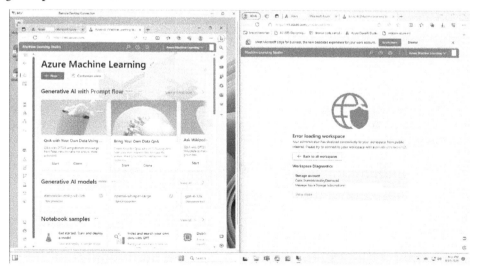

Figure 7.21 – Public access disabled

VM security best practices

To increase isolation and security, there are multiple ways to secure either the network itself or the VMs that belong to it. As an example, you can review the following services:

- **Network security groups**: https://learn.microsoft.com/en-us/azure/virtual-network/network-security-groups-overview

- **Azure Firewall**: https://learn.microsoft.com/en-us/azure/firewall/overview

- **Azure Bastion**: https://learn.microsoft.com/en-us/azure/bastion/bastion-overview

We can secure associated resources in a similar way, such as in databases and other types of data storages that can be used in Azure Machine Learning. If the services are already part of other VNets, we can always connect different networks via network peering as long as our VNets do not have overlapping addresses. We can connect networks by using VNet peering in the same or different subscriptions so ultimately your decision on how to segregate the networks in Azure is based on individual organizational requirements.

Network architecture in Azure

Find out more about network architectures by exploring network peering, the hub-spoke topology, and Azure landing zones:

- VNet peering: https://learn.microsoft.com/en-us/azure/virtual-network/virtual-network-peering-overview

- Hub-spoke: https://learn.microsoft.com/en-us/azure/architecture/reference-architectures/hybrid-networking/hub-spoke?tabs=cli

- Azure landing zones: https://learn.microsoft.com/en-us/azure/cloud-adoption-framework/ready/landing-zone/

By integrating Azure Machine Learning with Azure VNets, we are adding an essential layer of security that will help in safeguarding our data, models, and other resources from unauthorized access and threats. Let us not forget to always monitor and regularly review the security measures to adapt to the evolving threat landscape.

Let us now explore further security practices for the workspace, starting with Azure Machine Learning compute.

Working with Azure Machine Learning compute

Azure Machine Learning provides a scalable cloud environment to build, train, and deploy ML models. It offers different computational targets for running experiments, training models, and serving predictions.

There are four targets overall, with two of these being managed internally from the workspace: **compute instances** and **compute clusters**. A compute instance is a managed VM that you use for development, training, and inferencing needs. It's essentially a dedicated, personal workstation in the workspace. It can be used to run Jupyter notebooks and scripts. A compute cluster is a managed scalable set of virtual machines that are used for the large-scale training of ML models. Compute clusters automatically scale up or down (within the limits you set) based on the workload. So, for example, you can declare a minimum and maximum node and the machine will scale based on demand, which helps us optimize costs. There is also external compute, which you can use for inferencing, specifically the Azure Kubernetes service. You can also attach compute for training from external services to the workspace like Ubuntu VMs or Databricks compute.

In this section, we will focus on securing the internal resources. For external services, you must find the best practices for securing each service. Here are some links to give you more information about securing inference and attached compute:

- Azure Kubernetes Service: https://learn.microsoft.com/en-us/azure/aks/concepts-security

- Virtual Machine security: https://learn.microsoft.com/en-us/azure/virtual-machines/security-recommendations

- Azure Databricks security guide: https://learn.microsoft.com/en-us/azure/databricks/security/

- Azure Data Lake security baseline: https://learn.microsoft.com/en-us/security/benchmark/azure/baselines/data-lake-analytics-security-baseline

The following sections will help you understand how to secure compute instances and compute clusters.

Securing compute instances

The basis of securing both compute instances and compute clusters lies in the combination of using managed identities and network isolation. Let us follow along with the steps to enable them starting with compute instances.

From the Azure Machine Learning workspace, find the **Compute** menu under **Manage** and open it to view the list of available compute. In the **Compute instances** tab, click **+ New** to create a new compute instance:

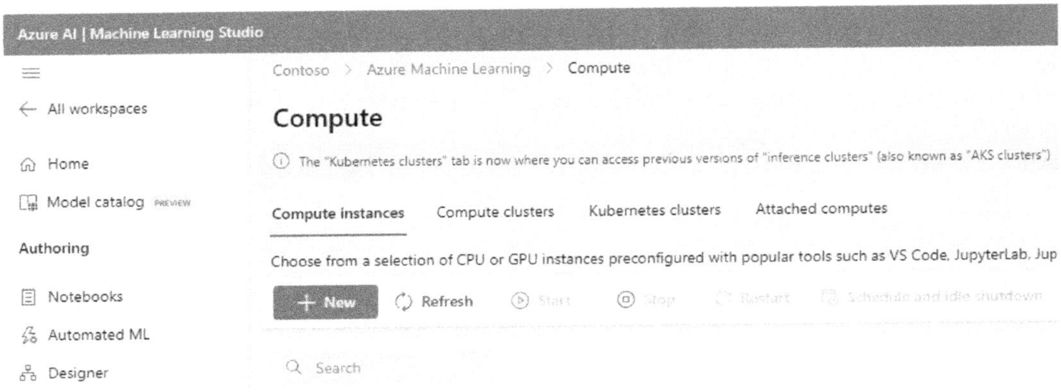

Figure 7.22 – New compute instance

Fill in all tabs as desired until you reach the **Security** tab. Enable the **Assign a managed identity** button and leave the **Identity** type as **System-assigned**. Ensure that the **SSH** button is disabled to prevent public access, as when using a VNet, you can still **Secure Shell (SSH)** within that VNet to the machine. If you have previously restricted access to the workspace and associated resources, **Enable virtual network** will be enabled by default, making it mandatory to choose a **Virtual network** and **Subnet**. Choose the one created previously:

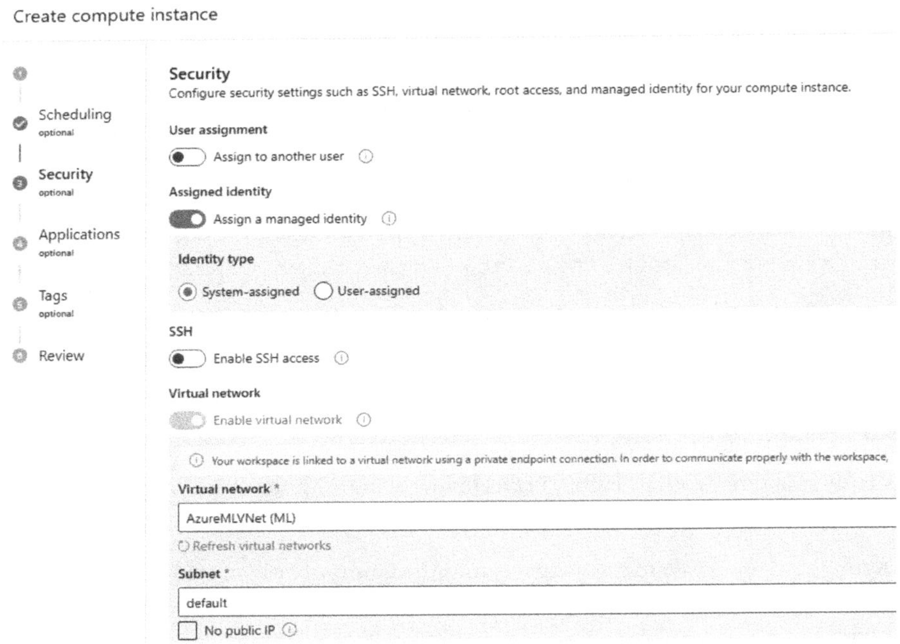

Figure 7.23 – Setting compute instance security

Fill in the rest of the tabs as desired and create the compute. Remember to use the proper credentials in the scripts when using this compute for training.

Let us move on to securing compute clusters.

Securing compute clusters

The process of securing compute clusters is very similar. To initiate the process from the **Compute** menu under **Manage**, choose the **Compute clusters** tab and click **+ New** to create a new compute instance:

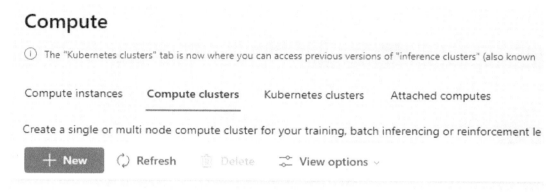

Figure 7.24 – New compute cluster

Fill in the **Virtual machine** tab as desired until you reach the **Advanced settings** tab. Scroll down until you reach the **Advanced settings** drop-down and ensure that **Enable SSH access** is disabled to prevent public access, enable **Assign a managed identity**, and leave the **Identity type** as **System-assigned**.

If you have previously restricted access to the workspace and associated resources, again, the **Enable virtual network** will be enabled by default, making it mandatory to choose a **Virtual network** and **Subnet**. Choose the one created previously, as demonstrated in the following screenshot:

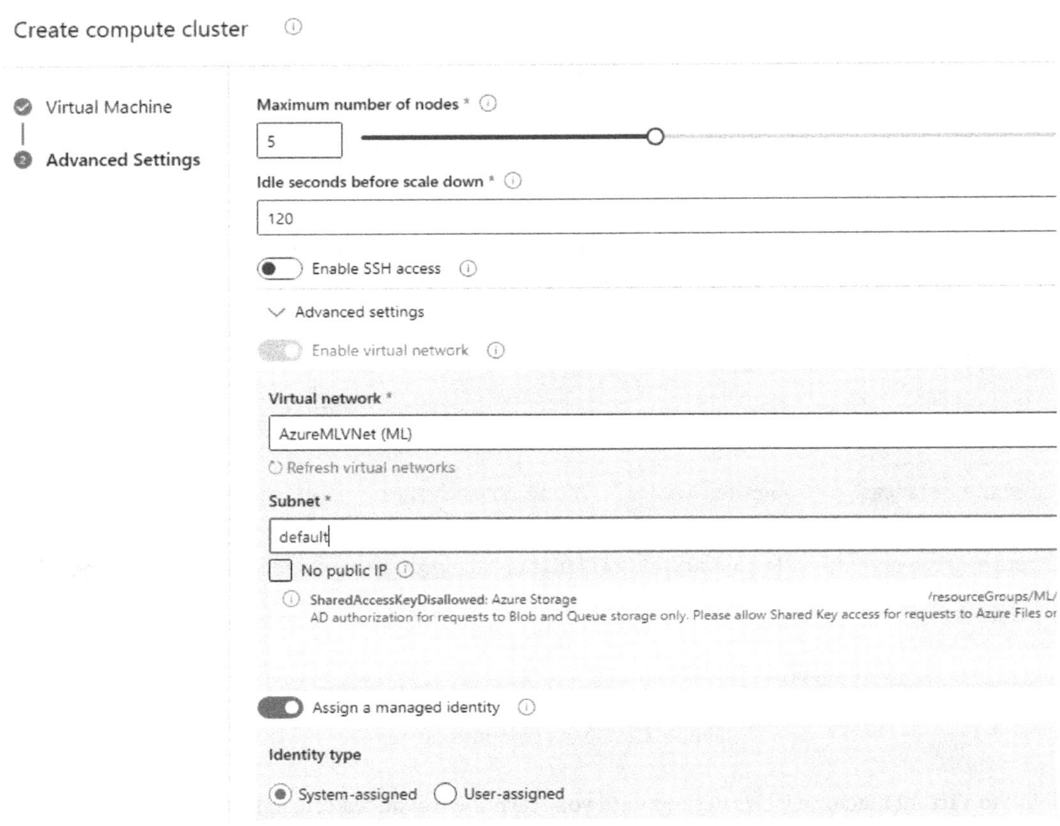

Create compute cluster ⓘ

Figure 7.25 – Setting compute cluster security

The process might be simple, but it is enough to isolate our compute resources from the public internet, preventing further vulnerabilities. Just remember that when running scripts on notebooks through compute, ensure the appropriate credentials are passed in the code. For an example of how to use managed identities, review the *Working with managed identities* section in *Chapter 6*.

Let us review the last resource associated with the workspace and its security features: Azure Container Registry.

Managing container registries and containers

Azure Machine Learning provides an integrated, end-to-end data science workflow, enabling data scientists and developers to prepare data, experiment with models, and then deploy them in a scalable environment. A pivotal aspect of this deployment process involves containerization, which brings us to **Azure Container Registry** (**ACR**). ACR is a managed, private Docker container registry service based on the open source Docker Registry 2.0. ACR allows users to build, store, and manage container images and artifacts in a secure and scalable manner within Azure. ACR integrates well with existing container development and deployment pipelines, and it's especially useful for storing and managing the custom Docker images that can be deployed in various Azure services.

When working with Azure Machine Learning, there's an underlying process that packages models for deployment. This packaging involves creating a Docker image that contains the model, the scoring script, and all the dependencies required to run the model. Once this Docker image is created, it needs to be stored somewhere where it can be fetched and run.

This is where ACR comes into play. When you deploy a model for the first time using Azure Machine Learning, even if you haven't explicitly set up an Azure container registry, the platform will automatically create one for you. This is a seamless experience; however, we need to be aware of the implications for cost and security.

In the next section, we will see how to secure our ACR and deployed containers in **Azure Container Instances (ACI)**. Let us start with ACR.

Securing images with Azure Container Registry

Securing ACR involves a combination of best practices in network security, access control, and image security. Similarly, to the compute, security best practices for ACR involve using managed identities where possible and ensuring that the ACR is behind the same virtual network as the workspace.

To isolate the container registry in a VNet, the steps are similar to other resources. However, before we are able to use the networking features, we need to update the service to use a **Premium** pricing tier.

To update the pricing tier, visit the ACR blade of the resource associated with your workspace and find the **Properties** section. Update the values as shown in the next screenshot and click **Save**:

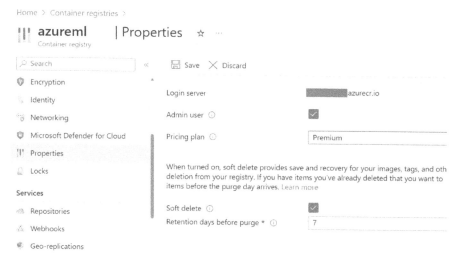

Figure 7.26 – Updating container registry properties

Now we can use the networking features of the ACR. As we have already seen multiple times, go to the **Networking** section and set **Public access** to **Disabled**, as demonstrated in the following screenshot:

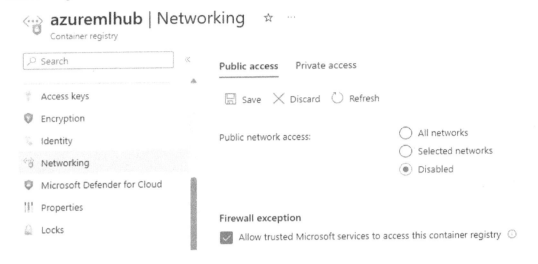

Figure 7.27 – Disable public access

On the **Private access** tab, click on **Create a private endpoint connection**:

Figure 7.28 – Creating a private endpoint for the registry

Follow the steps as usual, ensuring that in the **Resources** tab of the **Private endpoint** form, you fill in the proper **Resource** and **Resource type**:

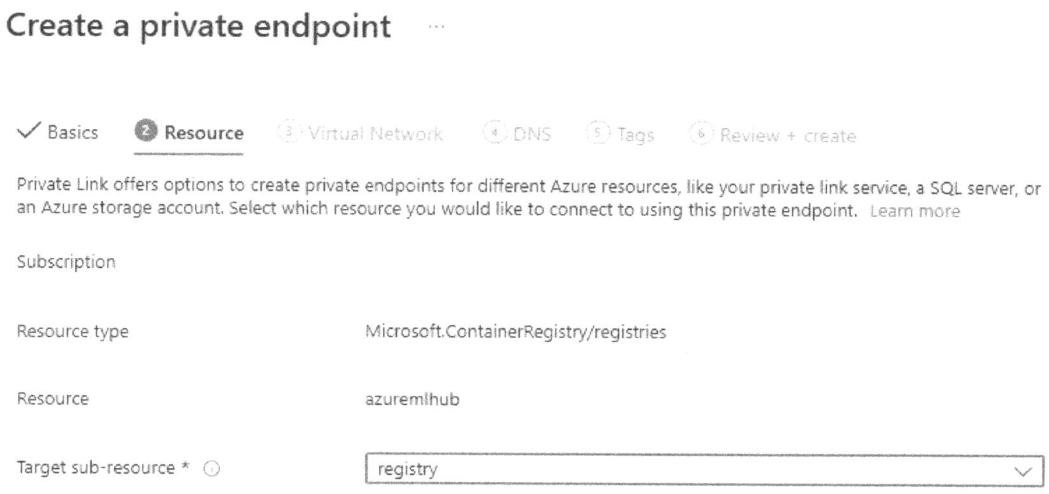

Create a private endpoint   ...

✓ Basics   ② **Resource**   ③ Virtual Network   ④ DNS   ⑤ Tags   ⑥ Review + create

Private Link offers options to create private endpoints for different Azure resources, like your private link service, a SQL server, or an Azure storage account. Select which resource you would like to connect to using this private endpoint. Learn more

Subscription

Resource type   Microsoft.ContainerRegistry/registries

Resource   azuremlhub

Target sub-resource * ⓘ | registry   ⌄ |

Figure 7.29 – Filling in the private endpoint form

Securing ACR is a multi-faceted process. By taking a comprehensive approach that encompasses network security, access control, and constant monitoring, you can ensure that your container images remain safe and are only accessed by authenticated users or applications.

Container registries are only the repositories of the models. They can be exposed in published endpoints so that they can be available to applications. Let us explore how to secure those endpoints when deployed with ACI.

Working with ML endpoints

When we deploy a model via the workspace, the options available are Azure Kubernetes and ACI. The fastest option is to use ACI, as they are deployed quickly via the workspace and there is no further configuration. If you want to be reminded of the process of deploying a model, you can review the *Deploying the model* section of *Chapter 1*.

After deploying an endpoint through the workspace, there is no option to disable public access to the container. In that case, what you can do is still register the model, but redeploy it using the saved container from the repository in a new ACI deployment. This provides the opportunity for network isolation.

To do this, we need to choose the deployed image from the ACR connected with our workspace in the **Basic** tab of the container instance form. Begin to fill out the form as usual like in the next screenshot:

Basics   Networking   Advanced   Tags   Review + create

ᵉˢ Azure Container Instances (ACI) allows you to quickly and easily run containers on Azure without managing servers or having to learn new tools. ACI offers per-second billing to minimize the cost of running containers on the cloud.
Learn more about Azure Container Instances

Project details

Select the subscription to manage deployed resources and costs. Use resource groups like folders to organize and manage all your resources.

Subscription * ⓘ	⌄
Resource group * ⓘ	Containers ⌄
	Create new

Container details

Container name * ⓘ	azuremldemo ⌄
Region * ⓘ	(Europe) West Europe ⌄
Availability zones (Preview) ⓘ	None ⌄
SKU	Standard ⌄

Figure 7.30 – Filling in the basic details

When we reach the part where we need to choose an **Image source**, choose the ACR connected to your workspace. Fill in **Registry**, **Image**, and **Image tag** to correspond to your model and then fill out the rest of the form as desired:

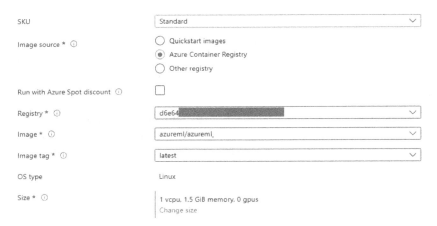

Figure 7.31 – Choosing the correct ACR

Next, you will find the **Networking** tab. From here, you can restrict networking.

Application considerations with VNet isolation

Be careful in this stage. It all depends on where your application is hosted since this endpoint is meant to be consumed by an external application to the service. If it is an application hosted on Azure, you can probably configure the access easily. If it is an internal application hosted on-premises, you would need some of the services mentioned previously, such as a VPN gateway to access the isolated endpoint. If it is a public-facing application, you might need to further configure the network security group or firewall attached to the VNet to allow access properly. As this part of the process is heavily dependent on other factors, ensure that you have explored all options of networking and authentication before proceeding to use that API endpoint for scoring, training, and so on.

To isolate behind a VNet, choose the **Virtual network** and **Subnet**. The subnet must be a different one than the one we have used so far to accommodate endpoints instead of VMs. Refer to the following screenshot:

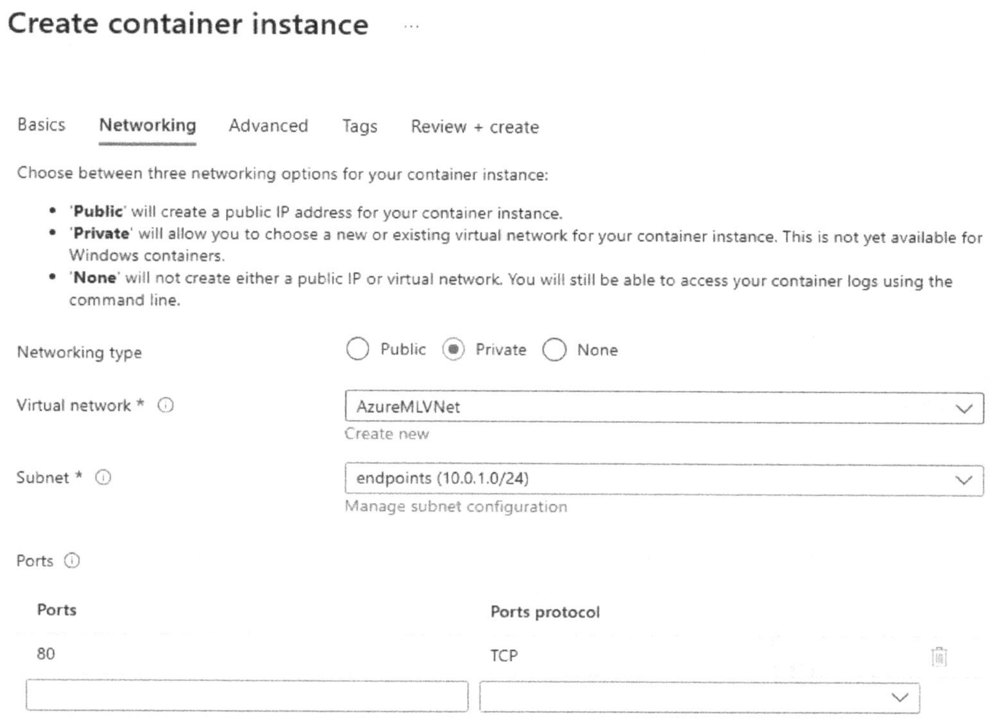

Create container instance   ...

Basics   **Networking**   Advanced   Tags   Review + create

Choose between three networking options for your container instance:

- '**Public**' will create a public IP address for your container instance.
- '**Private**' will allow you to choose a new or existing virtual network for your container instance. This is not yet available for Windows containers.
- '**None**' will not create either a public IP or virtual network. You will still be able to access your container logs using the command line.

Networking type	○ Public ● Private ○ None
Virtual network * ⓘ	AzureMLVNet ⌄
	Create new
Subnet * ⓘ	endpoints (10.0.1.0/24) ⌄
	Manage subnet configuration

Ports ⓘ

Ports	Ports protocol	
80	TCP	🗑
		⌄

Figure 7.32 – Configuring network isolation

Then, you can complete the rest of the settings as desired and create the endpoint. Pay attention to environment variables if any are required. These can be filled in in the **Advanced** tab. Then, you can **Review + Create** the service. You can test the service from a VM deployed in the same VNet to test connectivity. This is just one way of isolating endpoints. Another way is to use workspace-managed network isolation, which is a new feature that is yet to be fully available. It is worth keeping up to date with this feature for the future.

Workspace-managed network isolation

Azure Machine Learning currently offers another option for integrated management for VNet isolation: automating the process with a VNet managed by the workspace. This feature is still in preview at the time of writing and should not be used for production workloads, as the service provides no **Service Level Agreement (SLA)**. If you want to learn more, you can find more information at `https://learn.microsoft.com/en-us/azure/machine-learning/how-to-managed-network?view=azureml-api-2&tabs=azure-cli`.

We have explored multiple ways to leverage Azure infrastructure to secure our Azure Machine Learning workspace and its associated resources. It is easier if we already have cloud infrastructure we can leverage that is used within our organization for other purposes. It is worth exploring even if we do not, as it can help not only with isolating our resources and reducing the attack surface area but also with preventing data exfiltration in the case of a security incident.

Summary

In this chapter, we talked about multiple aspects of leveraging networking to protect our Azure Machine Learning workloads.

The main aim of this chapter was to learn basic networking practices to isolate the workspace and all associated services, specifically storage accounts, key vaults, and Azure Container Registry. Although public access means access from the public internet and not unauthorized access, credentials can be leaked and malicious actors can gain access. By isolating our resources using VNets, we are reducing the attack surface area.

Combining networking and best practices regarding identity, such as configuring managed identities where possible and using proper RBAC with our users and services, we can take one step closer to maintaining a baseline security posture across our cloud services and infrastructure.

In the next chapter, we will see how to automate best practices with **continuous integration and continuous delivery (CI/CD)** for our ML tasks.

8

Managing and Securing the MLOps Life Cycle

As important as data and infrastructure are, their management can create overhead and take away from the actual ML tasks. When different roles collaborate on an ML project, there is a need to automate and standardize things to make the daily tasks more efficient.

In this chapter, we will explore MLOps best practices and how we can implement them using Azure and other tools. We will dive into how to leverage **Infrastructure as Code** (**IaC**) and some applications of DevOps in the ML life cycle for **continuous integration/continuous delivery** (**CI/CD**) using Azure DevOps. These are not the only ways to implement MLOps, though. Azure provides us with comprehensive monitoring and logging capabilities, which we can leverage with services such as Event Grid and others to initiate event-driven workflows. This means we are not limited to tools but we can implement our own workflows and easily tailor them to our own processes.

In this chapter, we're going to cover the following main topics:

- Working with MLOps in Azure Machine Learning

- Leveraging IaC

- Implementing CI/CD

- Exploring event-driven workflows in Azure

By the end of the chapter, we will know what MLOps is, what CI/CD looks like in Azure Machine Learning, and how to combine different services and create our own workflows.

Technical requirements

This chapter delves into several DevOps concepts. Some experience with Git, version control, and DevOps will be useful to understand the concepts described in this chapter. If you lack knowledge of the preceding technologies, the following learning resources will help you understand some basic concepts and functions. Go through them to review the prerequisites needed to understand the content of this chapter:

- **Git and version control**: `https://learn.microsoft.com/en-us/training/modules/intro-to-git/`

- **Building applications with Azure DevOps**: `https://learn.microsoft.com/en-us/training/paths/build-applications-with-azure-devops/`

- **GitHub Actions**: `https://learn.microsoft.com/en-us/training/paths/automate-workflow-github-actions/`

Working with MLOps in Azure Machine Learning

The term **MLOps** is a combination of **Machine Learning** and **Operations** and refers to the practices, tools, and strategies for the life cycle management of ML models in a production environment. Just as DevOps aims to streamline the development and operations processes for software, MLOps aims to do the same for ML systems. Implementing MLOps can improve productivity, reproducibility, and agility in ML projects. MLOps focuses on a specific set of practices.

Let us explore each practice and how we can use Azure Machine Learning features for each one:

- **Collaboration**: Facilitating effective collaboration between various roles such as data scientists, ML engineers, and operations teams is core in ML projects as there are multiple roles involved in the success of the project. By using shared platforms and tools, a data scientist focuses on model prototyping, an ML engineer ensures it's production-ready, and an operations specialist monitors its real-time performance. Azure Machine Learning is already implemented via a dedicated workspace where everyone can collaborate, promoting transparency and teamwork. Additionally, it is based on Azure, and with the help of Microsoft Entra ID and RBAC, we can implement collaboration easily while adhering to security best practices.

- **Versioning**: Version control in MLOps is not restricted to just code. It extends to datasets, model configurations, parameters, and results. The aim is to ensure that any experiment or model training can be deterministically reproduced at any time. Consider a scenario where a model's performance suddenly drops. Using version control, a team can revert to an earlier, better-performing model configuration, identifying which dataset and hyperparameters were used at that time. This involves maintaining a systematic record of model versions, training data, decisions, and changes. It is essential for compliance, especially in regulated industries, and ensures that model decisions are transparent and traceable. Azure Machine Learning allows us to have tracking and versioning in data and models by registering them to the workspace.

- **Model validation**: This practice ensures models meet quality standards before deployment. It involves rigorous testing, including unit tests for code, validation against holdout datasets, and even real-world scenario simulations. For example, before deploying a self-driving car model, it's tested in a virtual environment to ensure it correctly identifies pedestrians, obeys traffic signals, and reacts to various weather conditions. This can be implemented as part of a CI/CD pipeline.

- **CI/CD**: CI/CD for ML automates the model training, validation, and deployment processes. When new data arrives or the code changes, the model is retrained and, if it meets set standards, is automatically deployed. For example, after refining a model's architecture, a data scientist pushes the changes to a repository. The CI/CD pipeline retrains the model, evaluates it, and, if it surpasses a predefined accuracy threshold, updates the model in production without manual intervention. In the next section, we will see some implementations using DevOps.

- **Monitoring and logging**: Continuous monitoring tracks a model's health, performance, and any potential data drift. Logging captures predictions, input data, and anomalies, ensuring there's traceable evidence of the model's behavior in production. An image recognition model in production begins misclassifying certain objects. Monitoring tools detect this performance dip, and by inspecting the logs, engineers can identify the issue. Azure Machine Learning maintains logs about multiple aspects of the workspace, whether it is data drift or an endpoint not responding.

- **Scalability**: MLOps focuses on building ML systems that can scale with increasing data or demand, ensuring that infrastructure and processes can handle growth without degradation in performance. Suppose a start-up's user base grows tenfold in a year. Their recommendation system, designed with scalability in mind, handles this surge without requiring a complete overhaul or causing service interruptions. As Azure Machine Learning leverages the Azure infrastructure, we can scale endpoints and compute to accommodate scaling scenarios such as this one.

- **Reproducibility**: Central to MLOps is the ability to recreate experiments, results, or model deployments. This ensures consistency, aids debugging, and promotes trust in the system. Suppose a team member discovers a groundbreaking model improvement; using MLOps practices, other team members can replicate the exact conditions, data preprocessing steps, and training configuration to verify and further build upon the findings. Model registration handles this within the workspace.

- **Automation**: Many stages of the ML life cycle, from data ingestion to model retraining, are automated to enhance efficiency and reduce manual errors. When monthly sales data is uploaded to cloud storage, an automated pipeline preprocesses the data, retrains a forecasting model, and updates dashboards with new predictions—all without human intervention. Depending on what it is that we want to do, we can leverage services such as DevOps, Azure Functions, or simple Webhooks to automate pipelines and workflows.

Incorporating MLOps practices in Azure Machine Learning creates a comprehensive and efficient ML life cycle management system, ensuring models are reliable and efficient and bring consistent value.

Let us see some of those practices in action, starting with IaC.

Leveraging IaC

IaC is a key practice in DevOps that enables developers and operations to automatically manage, provision, and configure IT infrastructure through code. In Azure, there are a variety of tools and services that facilitate IaC practices. We have already mentioned some of these previously but we will review everything here.

Let us delve into how IaC is implemented in Azure and the services we can use:

- **Azure Resource Manager (ARM) templates**: ARM templates are the native IaC solution in Azure. They are JSON files that define the resources you need to deploy for your solution. By using ARM templates, you can define and deploy your infrastructure declaratively. We can make them more modular by defining parameters for our templates to create reusable deployment scripts and implement conditional logic for resource deployment.

- **Azure Bicep**: Bicep is a language for deploying Azure resources declaratively. It's essentially a transparent abstraction over ARM templates, making it easier to write and manage Azure infrastructure. Bicep offers a more concise and readable syntax compared to ARM's JSON, and there are development environment integrations that provide autocompletion, type safety, and other helpful features.

- **Azure CLI and PowerShell**: Both Azure CLI and Azure PowerShell are command-line tools provided by Azure for managing Azure resources. While they are technically imperative tools (you're telling Azure exactly what to do, step by step), they're often used in scripts to automate provisioning and configuration tasks in an IaC manner.

- **Azure Blueprints**: Azure Blueprints allows organizations to define a repeatable set of Azure resources that adhere to organizational standards and requirements. Blueprints are more comprehensive than ARM templates, as they can define role assignments, policy assignments, and ARM template deployments. Like code, blueprints are versioned, so previous versions can be used when assigning new subscriptions.

- **Terraform on Azure**: Terraform is an open source IaC tool developed by HashiCorp. It uses a language called **HashiCorp Configuration Language** (**HCL**) to define and provision infrastructure. Azure fully supports Terraform, allowing you to use it as an alternative to ARM templates. Other supported third-party platforms are Ansible, Chef, and Pulumi for infrastructure automation in Azure.

Regardless of which service you use, there are multiple benefits to using IaC. We gain consistency by eliminating environmental drift and ensuring that every environment is provisioned the same way. There is reusability because we can use the same scripts or templates across different environments or projects. In services that support it, such as Azure Blueprints, we can have versioning. For others that do not support this out of the box, we can still save the scripts using version control systems, to keep track of changes and roll back when necessary. Additionally, we can integrate IaC into CI/CD pipelines to automatically provision or update infrastructure as part of the deployment process.

Let us discover how IaC integrates with Azure Machine Learning.

Combining IaC with Azure Machine Learning

Combining IaC with Azure Machine Learning means that we are integrating the automated setup, management, and provisioning of ML resources with the broader cloud infrastructure on which they rely. This approach ensures consistency, reproducibility, and efficiency in ML operations.

Here are some examples of combining IaC with Azure Machine Learning:

- **Infrastructure**: Everything starts with setting up the resources needed, including the workspace itself, compute instances such as training clusters (for example, **Azure Kubernetes Service (AKS)** or AML compute), inference clusters, and networking components such as VNets, subnets, and security groups.

- **Datastores and datasets**: Datastores in Azure Machine Learning represent storage backends (for example, Azure Blob Storage). After the provisioning, we can use the Azure Machine Learning SDK to programmatically register datastores and datasets once they are set up via IaC.

- **Model deployment**: The same principle as for the data follows the models. Once models are trained, they can be deployed to endpoints for real-time or batch inferencing. We can use IaC to provision deployment targets such as AKS or **Azure Container Instances (ACI)**. Then, we can use the Azure Machine Learning SDK to deploy models to these targets and integrate features such as autoscaling, logging, and monitoring.

- **Automation and orchestration**: We can store all IaC scripts and ML code in a version control system such as Git. Then, we can use Azure DevOps, GitHub Actions, or other CI/CD tools to automate the deployment of infrastructure and execution of ML workflows. This ensures that infrastructure changes or updates to ML models initiate automated processes.

By integrating IaC with Azure Machine Learning, teams can ensure a consistent environment, streamline ML workflows, and foster collaboration between data scientists, ML engineers, and DevOps teams. As IaC is an integral part of MLOps, this setup ensures that every change—whether it's infrastructure-related or model-related – is versioned, reproducible, and automatically processed. This streamlined process minimizes manual interventions and potential errors, optimizing the ML development life cycle.

Another core part of MLOps is continuous integration and delivery. Let us explore how to use it with Azure DevOps.

Implementing CI/CD

CI/CD is a software engineering practice that promotes frequent code integration and automated deployment. This approach is becoming increasingly popular in ML projects to ensure models are constantly improved, validated, and deployed in a streamlined manner. In Azure Machine Learning, there are multiple tools and services to help you implement CI/CD in your ML life cycle.

Here's an example of CI/CD:

1. By using VS Code with Azure Machine Learning extensions for development, we can develop our scripts.

2. Those scripts can be version-controlled using Git repositories (such as GitHub or Azure Repos).

3. If we have the expertise, we can set up automated testing to validate our models. This might include unit tests, integration tests, and other validation or data checks.

4. We can configure Azure Pipelines to automatically trigger when changes are made to the repository. A CI/CD pipeline could include the following:

   - Training the model

   - Logging metrics

   - Retrieving the registered model

   - Packaging and deploying the model

Let us see an example of Azure DevOps and Pipelines next.

Working with Azure DevOps

Azure DevOps is a set of development tools and services to work and collaborate on code development and build and deploy applications.

Azure DevOps consists of a range of services, such as the following:

- **Azure Boards**: This provides work tracking with Kanban boards, backlogs, team dashboards, and custom reporting. It allows teams to plan, track, and discuss work across the entire development life cycle.

- **Azure Repos**: This is a version control system that provides Git repositories for source control. It supports pull requests, branching, and searching.

- **Azure Pipelines**: This is a CI/CD platform for deploying and testing applications to different platforms both for cloud and on-premises offerings.

- **Azure Test Plans**: This is a platform that includes multiple testing tools for different scenarios such as exploratory or continuous testing.

- **Azure Artifacts**: This allows collaboration between teams to share packages from private or public repositories such as NuGet or Maven into their pipelines.

Signing up for Azure DevOps

To get started with Azure DevOps, follow this quickstart guide: `https://learn.microsoft.com/en-us/azure/devops/user-guide/sign-up-invite-teammates?view=azure-devops`.

For Azure Machine Learning, we can leverage pipelines to trigger ML tasks. Let us see how we can connect the Azure Machine Learning workspace and run our ML pipelines via Azure DevOps.

Creating a connection to the workspace

Before we work with anything that has to do with the Azure Machine Learning workspace, we need to create a service connection with Azure DevOps. For this, we need to create a new project in Azure DevOps. Here are the steps for it:

1. Open your Azure DevOps project and, under **Project Settings**, look for **Service connections**:

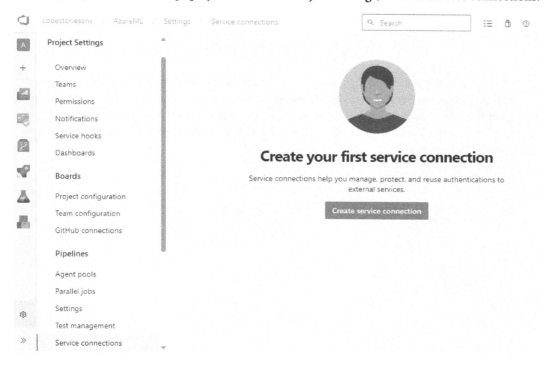

Figure 8.1 – Creating a service connection

2. Click on **Create service connection**, and in the form that follows, choose **Azure Resource Manager**, as shown here:

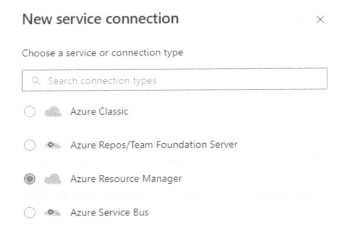

Figure 8.2 – Starting with the Azure Resource Manager option

3. Click **Next** at the bottom of the page, and in the **Authentication method** options, the fastest option is to choose **Service principal (automatic)** because it requires no further configuration from the Azure portal. For better security, you might consider **Managed identity** if you have one created, but if you are not sure, you can just go ahead with the **Service principal (automatic)** option.

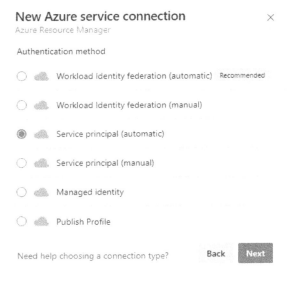

Figure 8.3 – Choosing the Service principal option

4. Then, choose the workspace resource in your **Subscription** level by filling in the details shown in the following screenshot:

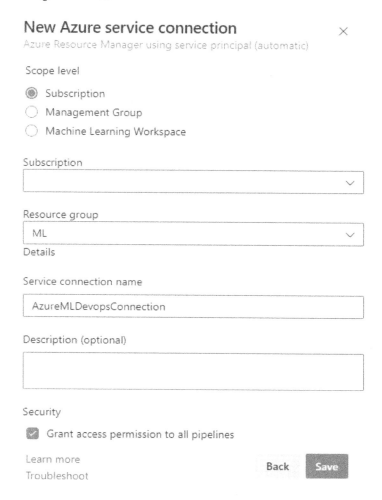

Figure 8.4 – Selecting and connecting to the workspace resource

That is it! Now we have a connection to the workspace, and we can use it to run pipelines. You can still make any updates or see usage data by choosing your connection from the list.

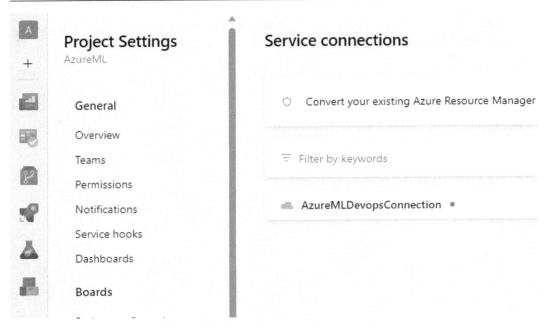

Figure 8.5 – Changing connection properties

Now that we have our connection, we are free to run pipelines. Let us see how in the following section.

Creating a new pipeline

The steps to create a new pipeline are straightforward. The challenge is to have the necessary preparations in place to call the Azure Machine Learning pipeline from Azure DevOps.

If you do not have any examples, you can use the following repository, which includes pipeline examples and code.

> **Azure Machine Learning example repository**
>
> If you don't have a pipeline and would like to explore some ML examples in Azure, you can fork and run code from this repository: `https://github.com/Azure/mlops-v2-ado-demo`.

In Azure DevOps, you will need to build a YAML pipeline to run your tasks. Here are the steps necessary to create a new pipeline:

1.   Start by creating a new pipeline, as shown in the following screenshot:

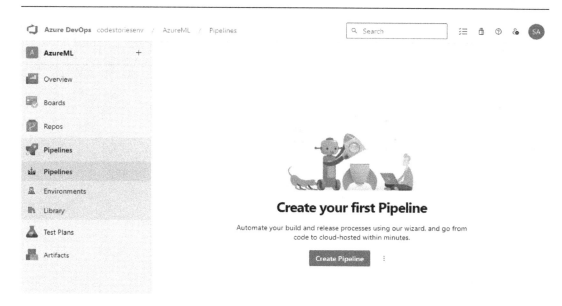

Figure 8.6 – New pipeline

2. You will need to provide the repository where your scripts are stored. You can use the repository from your project or an external one such as Bitbucket or GitHub:

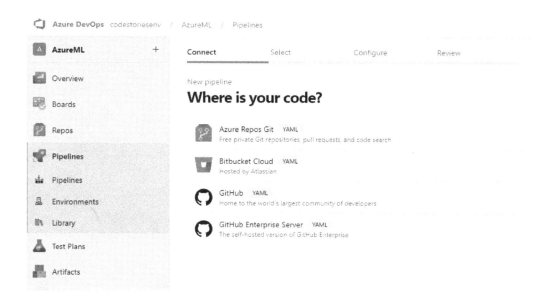

Figure 8.7 – Choosing your code repository

3. I selected the one in the repository in the same project, so all I have to do is select the name of the repository, as shown in the next screenshot:

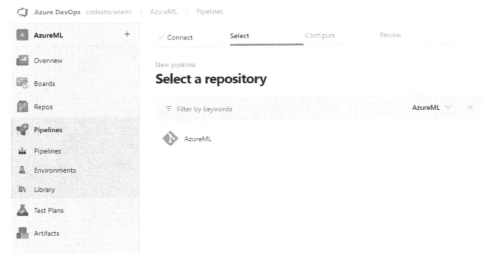

Figure 8.8 – Selecting the repository from the list

4. Here, select the **Starter pipeline** template to load a simple pipeline YAML file:

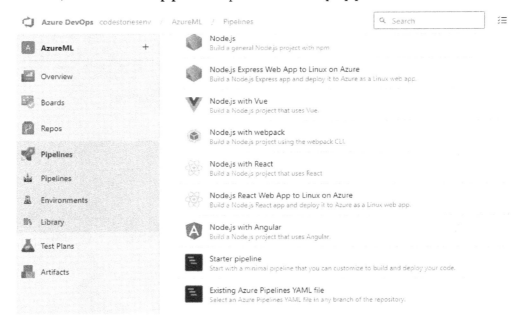

Figure 8.9 – Choosing the Starter pipeline template

Now, here is the big challenge. You need to define the triggers and start up your Azure Machine Learning pipeline from here. An effective way to get started is to use the CLI to submit any ML jobs.

The starter pipeline does provide some sample code, as shown in the next screenshot, to get started and fill in the details. For several things, such as variables, you can also add them via an integrated designer:

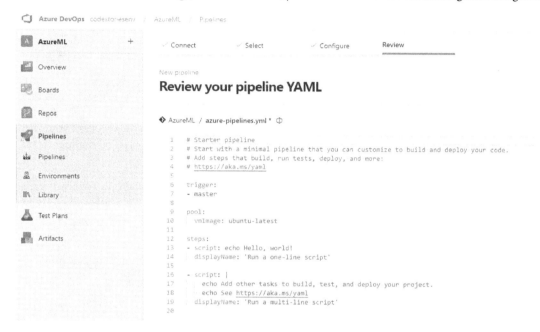

Figure 8.10 – Filling in the code to call your pipeline

If you chose to clone the repository suggested in the previous section, you can find the pipeline YAML code in the `mlops/devops-pipelines` folder. Copy and paste the file of your choice and submit the code.

Once you submit the code, you can run your pipeline. If anything goes wrong, you can see what happened with the associated error messages and you can always go back to fix the pipeline code and resubmit the job.

YAML pipeline editor

For a brief introduction to the YAML editor in Azure DevOps, take a look at the information at this link: `https://learn.microsoft.com/en-us/azure/devops/pipelines/get-started/yaml-pipeline-editor?view=azure-devops`.

Azure DevOps provides logs and output that can help you monitor the run. Additionally, you can also monitor the run directly from the Azure Machine Learning workspace. Consider using *triggers* in Azure DevOps to automate the ML pipeline run – for example, every time there is a change to your training script or dataset.

GitHub Actions

Similar functionality can also be accomplished using GitHub Actions. For a quickstart guide, take a look at this tutorial: `https://learn.microsoft.com/en-us/azure/machine-learning/how-to-github-actions-machine-learning?view=azureml-api-2&tabs=userlevel`.

Remember, the specific steps and tasks you will undertake will depend on the complexity of your ML project and how you wish to structure your CI/CD pipelines. The preceding steps offer a high-level guide, but you might need to delve into specifics depending on your requirements.

Azure DevOps offers a comprehensive and integrated suite of tools that facilitate agile software development, CI/CD, testing, and collaboration among teams. However, it is not the only CI/CD tool that integrates with Azure Machine Learning. We can use GitHub Actions or create our own workflows by using other services altogether.

Let us see how we can use Azure events and logs to drive workflows in Azure Machine Learning.

Exploring event-driven workflows in Azure

In the context of Microsoft Azure, the term *event* can be associated with several services and concepts, but most commonly, it refers to a message or notification that indicates the occurrence of something on the platform. For example, every action we complete in the workspace generates events, such as when the workspace was created or when we changed settings. These events can be leveraged by other services such as Azure Event Grid to create workflows triggered by the event. Let us check it next.

Exploring Event Grid

Azure Event Grid is a fully managed event routing service. It enables you to easily build applications that react to changes or events happening within Azure services or even on-premises. Azure Event Grid is designed to connect different parts of a cloud-based application together through events. Applications can greatly benefit from Azure Event Grid in various scenarios, such as automating workflows in response to events (for example, creating a thumbnail when an image is uploaded to Azure Blob Storage) or monitoring resources in Azure (for example, getting notifications of virtual machine changes).

Event Grid uses a publish-subscribe model to distribute events. The **publish-subscribe** (often abbreviated as **pub-sub**) model is a messaging communication pattern used in distributed systems. It decouples the senders (publishers) from the receivers (subscribers), allowing them to operate independently. This decoupling means that the publisher and subscriber don't need to know about each other's existence.

Here's how the publish-subscribe model works. There are at least three components:

- **Publisher**: This is the entity or component that produces messages or events. It doesn't send them directly to a specific receiver or subscriber. Instead, it publishes the messages to an intermediary known as a topic or channel.

- **Topic or channel**: A topic (sometimes called a channel) is a conduit where messages are published. Subscribers express interest in one or more topics and only receive messages that are of interest, without knowing who the publishers are.

- **Subscribers or handlers**: This is the entity or component interested in receiving certain messages. It subscribes to a specific topic or channel and gets notified when a publisher sends a message to that topic.

Publish-subscribe model

Here is a little more information regarding the publish-subscribe model: `https://learn.microsoft.com/en-us/azure/architecture/patterns/publisher-subscriber`.

Event Grid is an eventing plane that takes care of managing topics, storing messages, and notifying subscribers. Here are some key benefits:

- **Event sources**: Azure Event Grid supports various built-in event sources such as Azure Blob Storage, ARM, and more. It also allows the creation of custom topics for user-defined events.

- **Unified event schema**: Event Grid has a common event model, which makes it easier to handle events across different Azure services.

- **Event filtering**: It enables fine-grained control by allowing subscribers to filter the events they're interested in based on event type or subject.

- **Reliability**: It offers an *at-least-once* delivery guarantee to ensure that events are always delivered to subscribers. It also provides an option called **dead lettering** to save events that were, for whatever reason, *dropped* to a storage blob for further processing.

- **Scalability**: It is built to automatically scale based on demand, ensuring that your application can handle large numbers of events, as provided by most Azure services.

- **Low latency**: It provides consistent low-latency event delivery, which is crucial for real-time applications.

- **Decoupling**: By separating event producers from event consumers, Event Grid allows for greater flexibility and more modular application architectures.

In the next section, we will see an example where the publisher is the Azure Machine Learning workspace, and the handler is the storage queue.

Let us see how to implement this using the Event Grid.

Working with events in Azure Machine Learning

We can start the process directly from the Azure portal. Here are the steps to do it:

1. Open the **Azure Machine Learning Resource** blade and find the **Events** section:

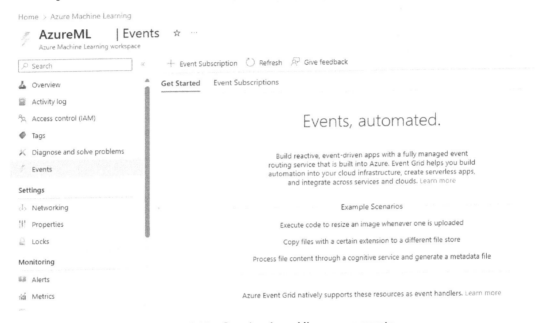

Figure 8.11 – Opening AzureML resource events

2. In the **Get started** tab, if we scroll down, we can see which event handlers are natively supported by Event Grid. Of course, we can always create our own:

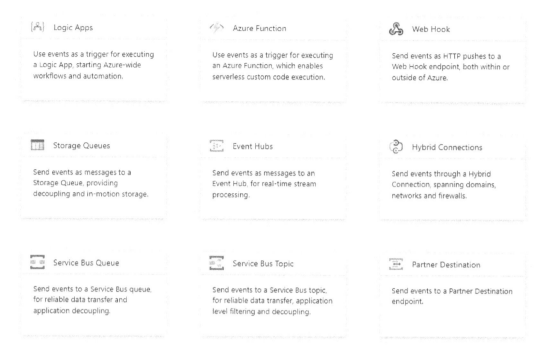

Figure 8.12 – Azure Event Grid handlers

3. At the top of the page, we can click on **+ Event Subscription** to create a new event subscription. Fill in the basic fields, carefully choosing the event we want to monitor, as shown in the following screenshot:

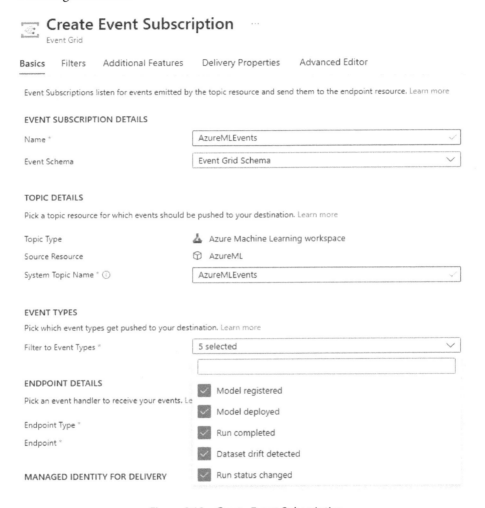

Figure 8.13 – Create Event Subscription

4. Then, we can choose a destination. For this example, we are going to add them to a storage queue for further processing, but always remember that you can trigger simple to complex workflows by using another service such as Azure Functions or Azure Logic Apps. Under **ENDPOINT DETAILS**, select the **Storage Queues** endpoint type and click **Select an endpoint**:

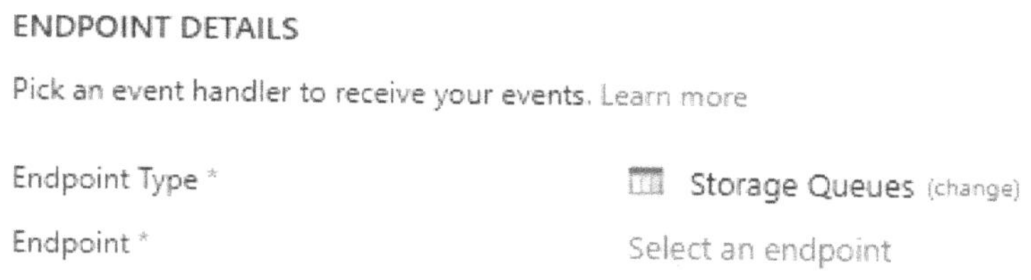

ENDPOINT DETAILS

Pick an event handler to receive your events. Learn more

Endpoint Type *   Storage Queues (change)

Endpoint *   Select an endpoint

Figure 8.14 – Choosing a storage queue

5.   Complete the details and, when prompted, select **Create new queue** and provide a name for it:

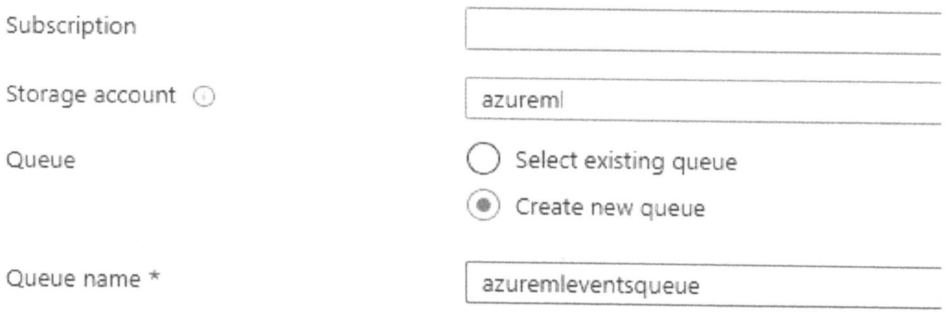

Subscription

Storage account ⓘ   azureml

Queue   ◯ Select existing queue
                                ◉ Create new queue

Queue name *   azuremleventsqueue

Figure 8.15 – Creating a new queue

6.   Under **MANAGED IDENTITY FOR DELIVERY**, select **System Assigned**:

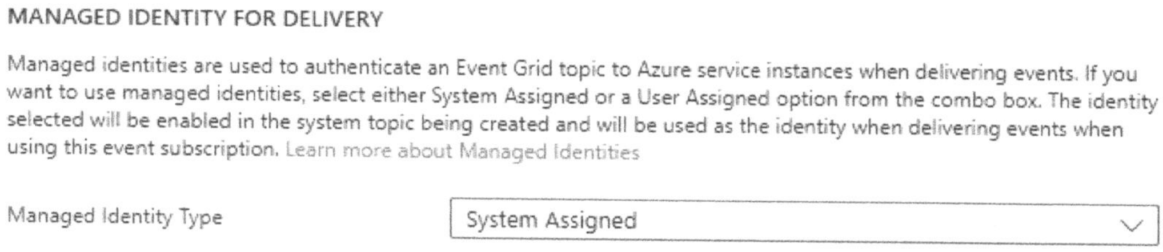

MANAGED IDENTITY FOR DELIVERY

Managed identities are used to authenticate an Event Grid topic to Azure service instances when delivering events. If you want to use managed identities, select either System Assigned or a User Assigned option from the combo box. The identity selected will be enabled in the system topic being created and will be used as the identity when delivering events when using this event subscription. Learn more about Managed Identities

Managed Identity Type   System Assigned   ⌄

Figure 8.16 – Selecting a managed identity

7.   In the **Filters** tab, you can select your desired filters. I will skip this tab for now:

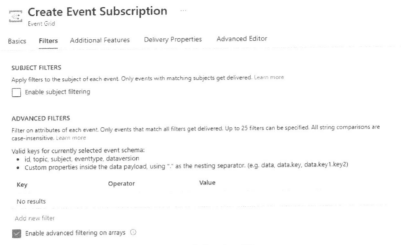

Figure 8.17 – Selecting filters

8.   In the **Additional Features** tab, it is wise to select the **Enable dead-lettering** option, and you can choose your desired **RETRY POLICIES** and **EVENT SUBSCRIPTION EXPIRATION TIME** values:

Figure 8.18 – Enabling additional features

9. In the **Delivery Properties** tab, select an appropriate storage queue message **time to live** (TTL). The default is **7 days**:

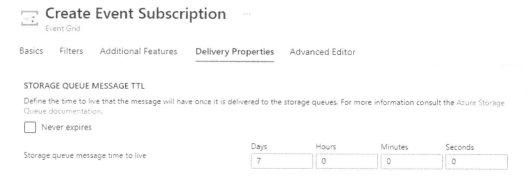

Figure 8.19 – Selecting the message time to live

10. Finally, click on **Create** and that is it. Now, every time an event is logged into the service, it will be saved in the storage queue.

Of course, this is not the only option we have; we can use multiple services as event handlers to capture events from Event Grid. Let us explore those services next.

Discovering event handlers in Azure

When working with Event Grid, there are other options that integrate seamlessly. In **EVENT TYPES** in the previously demonstrated **Event Subscription** form, the following are the options we have to choose from:

TOPIC DETAILS

Pick a topic resource for which events should be pushed to your destination. Learn more

| Topic Types | Machine Learning Workspaces ⌄ |

| Subscription * | ⌄ |

Resource Group *	
Resource *	Azure Function
	Web Hook

EVENT TYPES

Pick which event types get pushed to your dest Storage Queues

Filter to Event Types * Event Hubs

           Hybrid Connections

           Service Bus Queue

ENDPOINT DETAILS

Pick an event handler to receive your events. Le Service Bus Topic

           Partner Destination

Endpoint Type * ⌄

Figure 8.20 – Endpoint options in Azure Event Grid

Let us explore some of those services and how they work with Event Grid:

- **Azure Functions**: Azure Functions is a serverless compute service. It allows developers to run pieces of code (functions) in response to specific events without worrying about the infrastructure. These functions can be written in multiple languages, including C#, Java, JavaScript, Python, and PowerShell. Azure Functions integrates easily with Event Grid as it supports an Event Grid trigger. This means that when an event is published, the Azure Functions function will automatically get triggered and process the event data.

- **Azure Logic Apps**: Azure Logic Apps is a cloud service that enables users to design and execute workflows that integrate different services and systems. These workflows can be both within Azure and outside of it, connecting cloud-based and on-premises systems. The primary focus of Logic Apps is integration, making it easy to connect disparate services, orchestrate data flows, and automate processes. This description is very similar to the Azure Functions service; however, Logic Apps requires no-code scenarios and provides a visual design experience, making it simple to create workflows using drag-and-drop connectors. When an event occurs (for example, a file is added to Azure Blob Storage), Azure Event Grid can notify a Logic Apps app, which, in turn, can start a predefined workflow.

- **Webhooks**: Webhooks are user-defined HTTP callbacks. They provide a mechanism for one system to send real-time data to another system as soon as an event occurs. The receiving system waits for the incoming HTTP POST requests (from the Webhook) to act upon. Webhooks are often used as a lightweight method to integrate different systems or services on the web. Azure Event Grid can use Webhooks to send event data to external systems. Essentially, the external system subscribes to an Event Grid topic via a Webhook, and when events are sent to that topic, Azure Event Grid uses the Webhook to push the event data to the subscriber's endpoint.

- **Event Hubs**: Azure Event Hubs is a big data streaming platform and event ingestion service provided by Microsoft Azure. It can receive and process millions of events per second, making it ideal for telemetry and event stream analysis scenarios, such as real-time analytics, application monitoring, and IoT telemetry. Event Hubs essentially acts as a highly scalable "front door" for your event pipeline, allowing you to ingest vast amounts of event data and then process or store it downstream.

While Azure Event Grid and Azure Event Hubs both deal with events, they serve different purposes. Event Grid is designed for event routing and event-driven architectures across different Azure services. Event Hubs, on the other hand, is designed for high-throughput, large-scale event streaming.

Azure Event Grid can be used in conjunction with Azure Event Hubs in scenarios where you want to respond to specific events related to Event Hubs, such as when a new event stream is created.

These are some of the most common handlers for Event Grid. However, as we can build our own handlers using Webhooks or Azure Functions, we can integrate any business logic based on those events, including triggering pipeline endpoints in the case that we do not want to use external DevOps services such as Azure DevOps or GitHub. In essence, Azure Event Grid simplifies event-based application creation and allows for a more reactive and dynamic cloud application landscape.

Summary

In this chapter, we saw a brief explanation of MLOps and how valuable it is in ML projects. By using MLOps tools and best practices, we can streamline our ML tasks to facilitate efficiency and collaboration.

Although MLOps has tools and practices that range from data, models, deployments, and development, we focused more on how we can use IaC to handle our resources, and how to implement CI/CD using DevOps. Although using established code development tools offers the most common ways of working, when it comes to Azure, they are not the only ones. As Azure collects several logs and events in its services, we can leverage those to automate and create our own custom workflows using other Azure services and tools. The logs that Azure collects about its services can be used for more than telemetry and reporting.

Let us move on to the next chapter now, in which we will see how we can use the Azure Monitor service for logging, monitoring, and threat detection.

Logging, Monitoring, and Threat Detection

Following best practices is not enough. The threat landscape changes every day and adversaries find new ways to gain access to our resources. Monitoring the safeguards we have put in place is vital to maintaining our security posture. In this chapter, we will see how to monitor our resources and see how effective our security measures are in preventing and detecting threats. We will learn how Azure Monitor works and how to configure logging, retention, and notifications. Finally, we will explore some features of Defender for Cloud and Microsoft Sentinel that can further help us protect our resources and mitigate threats even in real time.

In this chapter, we're going to cover the following main topics:

- Enabling logging and configuring data retention for Azure services
- Securing resources with Microsoft Defender
- Exploring threat management with Sentinel

By the end of this chapter, we will be able to set up alerts, create analytics queries, improve our organization's security posture, and see what the next steps are in skilling up to mitigate threats in real time.

Technical requirements

Although this chapter deals mostly with monitoring and logging, knowing the **Kusto Query Language (KQL)** might come in handy when implementing solutions.

KQL is a query language used to query, analyze, and visualize large datasets stored in Azure Data Explorer, Azure Monitor, Microsoft Sentinel, and Application Insights. KQL is a powerful language that allows you to perform various operations on your data, including filtering, aggregating, joining, and visualizing it.

KQL learning resources

Some resources to learn KQL can be found here: `https://learn.microsoft.com/en-us/azure/data-explorer/kql-learning-resources`.

Enabling logging and configuring data retention for Azure services

As soon as we create an Azure subscription, we get full monitoring capabilities with the **Azure Monitor** service. This is a service where we do not need to enable or do any action, it is automatically available for our subscriptions. Although it provides us with full stack monitoring and advanced analytics, there are different things we can do with services that work on top of Azure Monitor. Azure Monitor can monitor and combine data in Azure, on-premises, and other clouds.

You can access the Azure Monitor service by searching for `monitor` on the search bar and clicking on the resource. In this blade, you will see all Monitor has to offer:

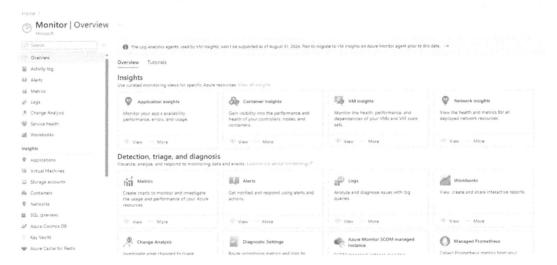

Figure 9.1 – An Azure Monitor overview

Let us see the key components of Azure Monitor.

Working with Azure Monitor

There are two types of data Monitor gathers, **metrics** and **logs**. Metrics are numerical values that represent various aspects of the performance and health of Azure resources at a specific point in time. These metrics provide real-time data about how a resource is functioning and can be used to monitor and troubleshoot applications and infrastructure in Azure. Azure Monitor collects a wide range of metrics, including performance indicators such as CPU usage, memory usage, network traffic, and disk activity. These metrics are specific to different types of resources, such as virtual machines, databases, and web apps.

Metrics in Azure Monitor are collected at different time frames, depending on the type of resource. For example, some metrics might be collected every minute, while others might be collected every hour. Metrics collected by Azure Monitor metrics are also used in Azure autoscale to automatically adjust the number of resources in a resource group, based on demand. Data is retained in the service for 90 days. For longer retention, there are other services such as *Log Analytics* or infinite retention in a *Storage account* using the Azure APIs.

In the following screenshot, we can see how metrics are visualized in graphs:

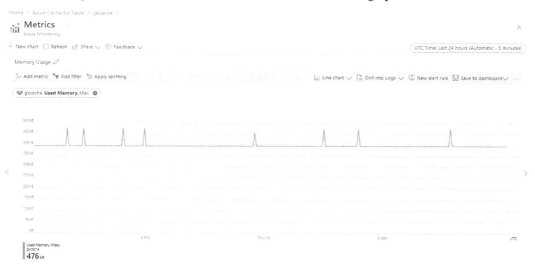

Figure 9.2 – Azure Monitor metrics

These graphs can be filtered and modified to show different metrics, can be used to generate alerts, and can be saved and added to Azure dashboards.

Azure Monitor also collects logs. Logs are records of events from various sources across your Azure subscriptions and tenants. Logs can be collected from a wide variety of sources, including Azure resources, guest operating systems, databases, security events, networking event applications, and custom logs from external sources that use APIs to import data.

Logs and metrics work together in Azure Monitor. You can correlate metrics data with log data to gain a comprehensive view of the health and performance of your resources. We can view individual logs for each resource by going to the **Resource** blade and clicking on **Activity log**, as shown in the following screenshot:

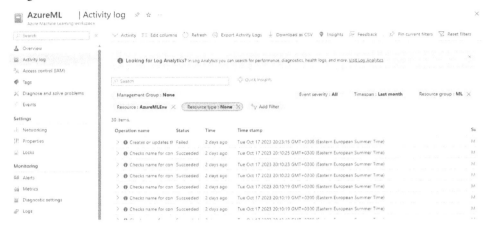

Figure 9.3 – Azure Monitor logs

The activity log is also available from the Monitor main page or the top bar in the Azure portal by clicking the bell icon. You can get metrics and logs via the Rest API and command-line tools.

Monitor also has built-in RBAC roles when interacting with monitoring or **Log Analytics** data. Take a look at the following screenshot of the table to see what these roles can do:

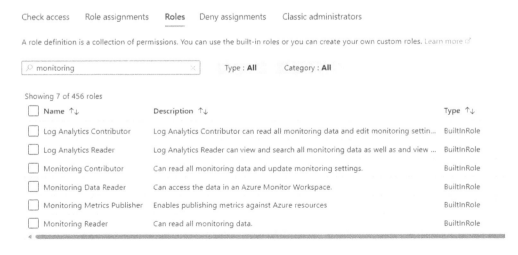

Figure 9.4 – Azure Monitor RBAC

Moving forward, let us see how we can query and gain insights from the logs using Log Analytics.

Setting up Log Analytics

Azure Monitor holds data for 90 days as we saw previously. If we need to hold data for a longer time period, we can use Log Analytics. It is a powerful tool that helps us collect data from multiple sources and save it in one or more workspaces, which act as containers for our logs. They provide a scope for queries, views, and other configurations. We can have multiple workspaces to organize and manage log data from different sources. These queries can be visualized, exported, and saved for continuous monitoring. Azure Monitor Logs uses KQL to query and analyze log data. KQL is a powerful, SQL-like language specifically designed to query large datasets efficiently. It allows us to perform complex searches and analytics on our logs.

To start collecting logs, we need to create a Log Analytics workspace. Search for Log Analytics workspaces and then click on + **Create** to create a new workspace, as shown here:

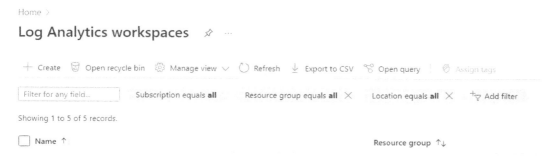

Figure 9.5 – Azure Log Analytics workspaces

On the creation form, fill in the name and the rest of the required information, and then click the **Review + Create** button to deploy the resource.

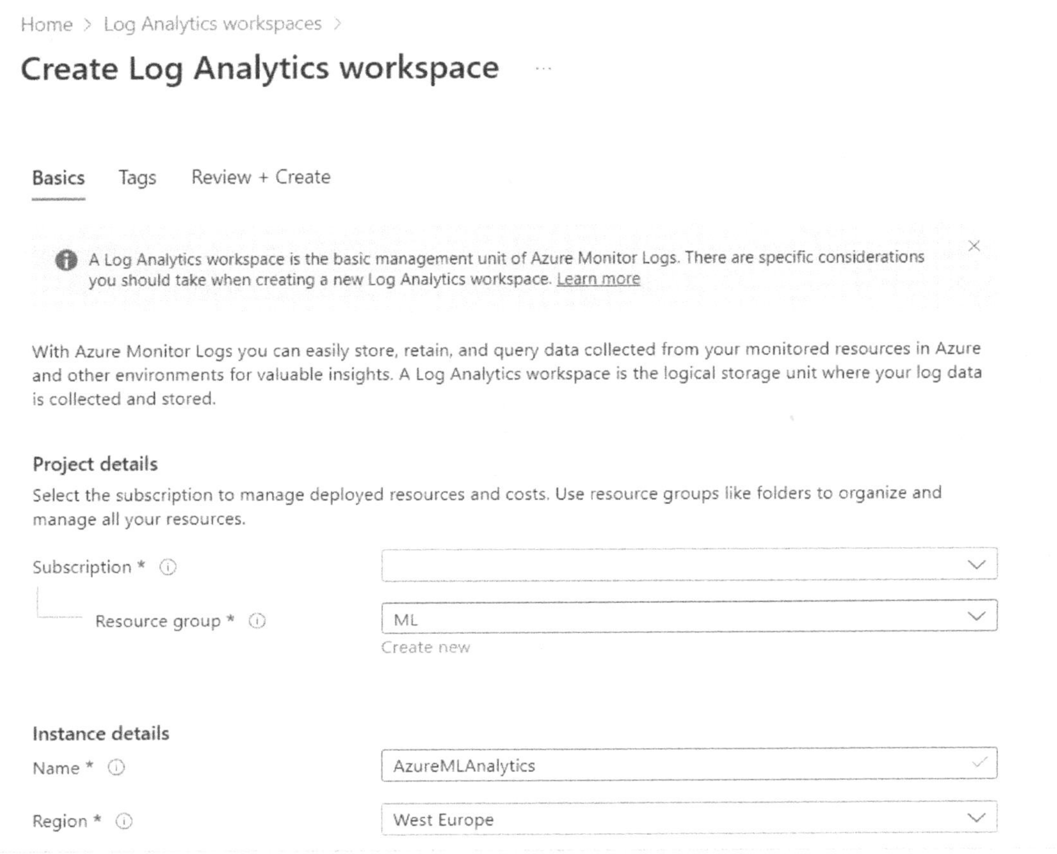

Home > Log Analytics workspaces >

Create Log Analytics workspace   ...

Basics   Tags   Review + Create

ⓘ A Log Analytics workspace is the basic management unit of Azure Monitor Logs. There are specific considerations   ✕
you should take when creating a new Log Analytics workspace. Learn more

With Azure Monitor Logs you can easily store, retain, and query data collected from your monitored resources in Azure
and other environments for valuable insights. A Log Analytics workspace is the logical storage unit where your log data
is collected and stored.

Project details

Select the subscription to manage deployed resources and costs. Use resource groups like folders to organize and
manage all your resources.

Subscription * ⓘ   [⌄]

  └── Resource group * ⓘ   [ML   ⌄]
                                      Create new

Instance details

Name * ⓘ   [AzureMLAnalytics   ✓]

Region * ⓘ   [West Europe   ⌄]

Figure 9.6 – Create Log Analytics workspace

Now that we have a Log Analytics workspace, all we need is some data. In the next section, let us see how to enable diagnostics settings for our Azure Machine Learning resource and send them to the workspace.

Enabling diagnostic settings

Azure diagnostic settings allow us to collect and route diagnostic data from various Azure resources to different destinations for analysis, monitoring, and compliance. This feature helps you gain insights into the performance and operational health of our resources and provides us with filtering and bigger retention, depending on what the destination is. Common destinations include an Azure **Storage account**, **Log Analytics workspace**, and **Event Hubs**. We can send data to multiple destinations simultaneously. For example, we can send data to both, a Log Analytics workspace and an Azure Storage account, for redundancy or different types of analysis.

Let us enable **Diagnostic settings** on our Azure Machine Learning resource.

To start, open your Azure Machine Learning resource, select **Diagnostic settings**, and click on **Add diagnostic setting**, as shown in the following screenshot:

Figure 9.7 – Add diagnostic setting

Select the log categories you are interested in and click to choose the destination details. For this one, we will use the **Log Analytics** resource we created in the previous section. Check the **Send to Log Analytics workspace** checkbox and provide the required details, as shown in the following screenshot. Then, click on **Save**:

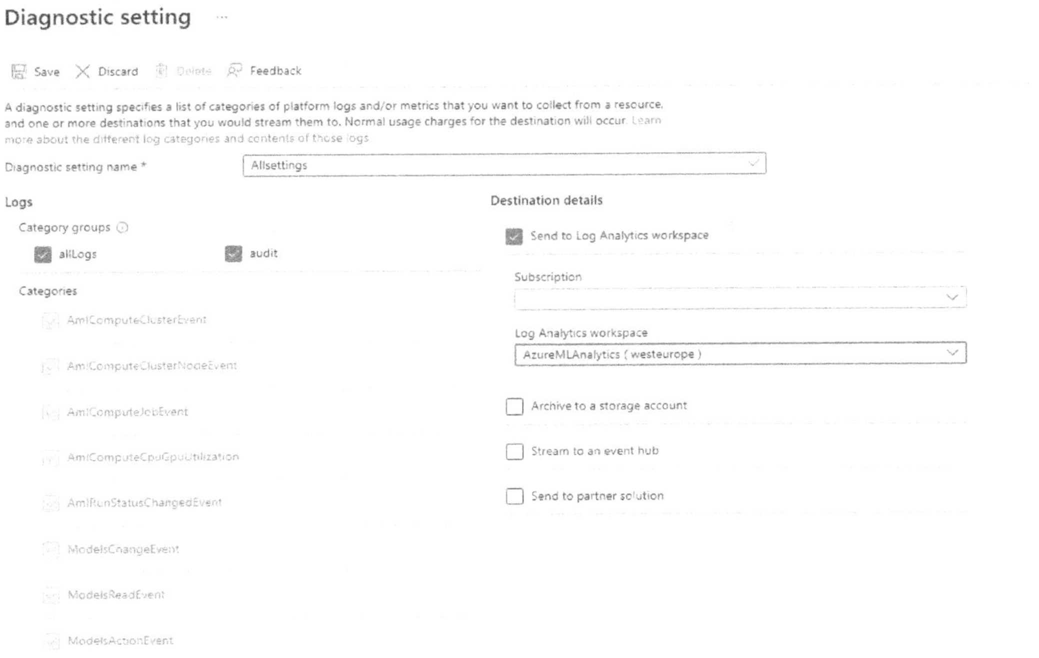

Figure 9.8 – Selecting log categories and a destination

One of the most important reasons we have to enable additional logs and more data is to get notifications when something is happening in our system. Let us review how to set up alerts in Azure Monitor.

Working with alerts

Alerts help us to monitor and manage resources in Azure. We can use alerts and get notifications when certain conditions are met, which can help us proactively respond to issues or changes. There are a lot of components that go into creating and working with alerts, so let us see what they are.

We will start by going to **Alerts** under the **Monitor** blade. Here, we can see **Alerts** that have been fired by priority and create new alerts:

Figure 9.9 – Monitor | Alerts

However, before we dive into **Alerts** creation, let us review action groups.

Creating an action group

It is better to create an action group before we create an alert. Action groups define a set of notifications and actions to be taken when an alert is triggered. This can include sending emails and SMS messages, making HTTP requests, and triggering Azure functions. We can create am action group directly from the alert form, but it makes things simpler if it already exists.

Click on **Create**, and from the dropdown, choose **Action group**. This will take you to the **Create action group** form. Fill in some basic details, as shown in the following screenshot, and click **Next**.

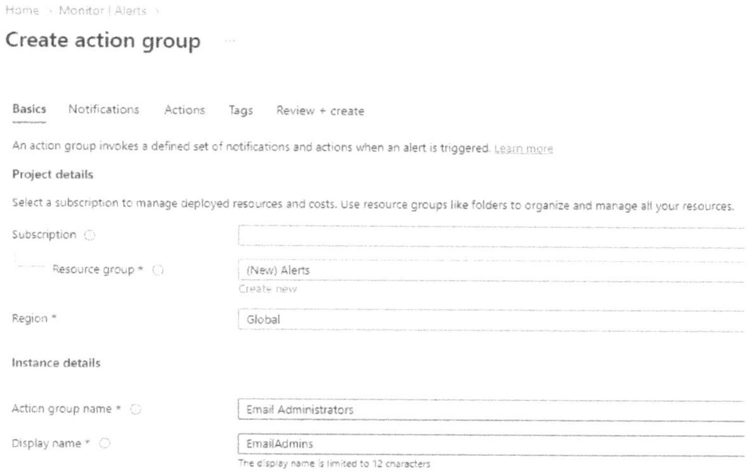

Figure 9.10 – The Create action group basic details

Next, in the **Notifications** tab, there are two types of notifications we can create – email to a specific role or email/send an SMS to a specific account/number. We will configure both options here. Choose **Email Azure Resource Manager Role** on the dropdown to reveal the menu on the right. Choose **Owner** as the role, and click **OK**. There are other options for the role to be notified, including **Contributor** and **Reader**. On this screen, you also need to provide a name:

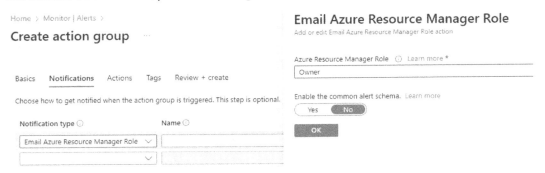

Figure 9.11 – Creating a role notification

On the next row, choose the second option of the **Email/SMS message/Push/Voice** dropdown to reveal the menu on the right. Here, the easiest way to get notifications is to provide an email or send a push notification to the Azure mobile app; however, there are more options available that might incur extra charges, such as **SMS** and **Voice**. Check the desired option and provide the necessary details. For example, in the **Email** section, you have to provide an individual email as shown here:

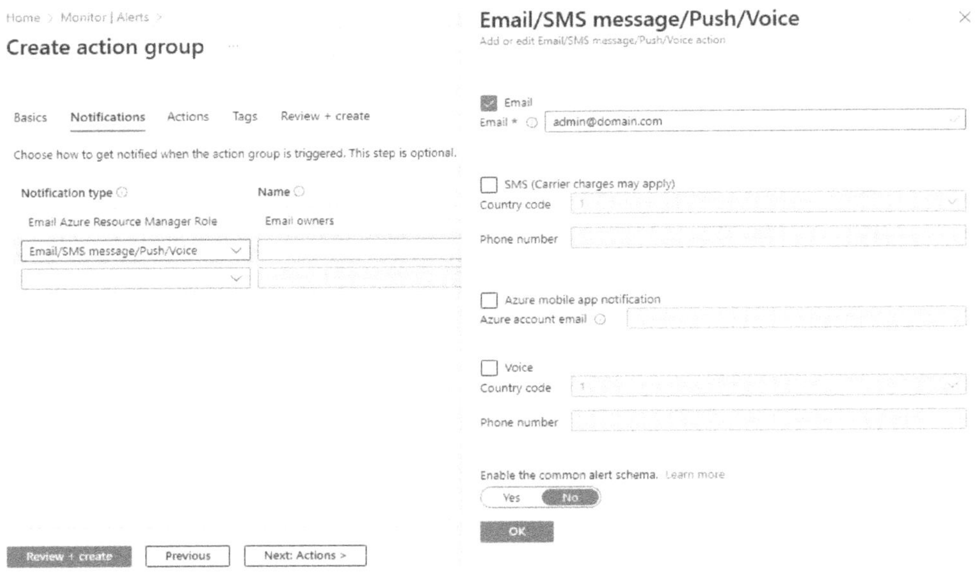

Figure 9.12 – Creating an email notification

If you need more roles or more emails, you can always add more rows and configure them accordingly. This is how it looks:

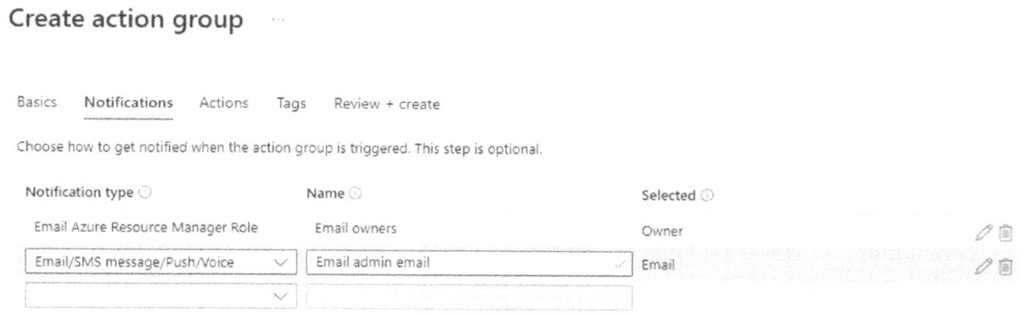

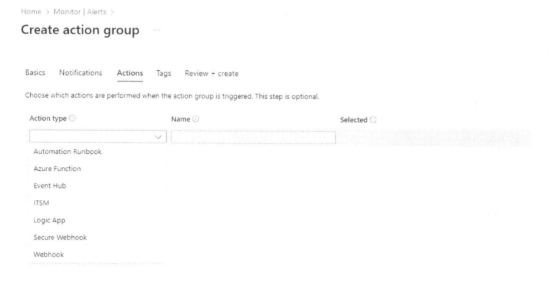

Figure 9.13 – Multiple notifications enabled

As soon as you are done, click **Next** to go to the next tab, **Actions**.

In the **Actions** tab, we can set up actions. Actions are not required; however, it is another way for doing both, sending a notification and triggering some other action in one step. Our options include the following, as shown in the following screenshot:

Figure 9.14 – Action types

We will not set anything, but let us review our options anyway. Some of these we have already seen in *Chapter 8*:

- **Automation Runbook**: Runbooks are a way to automate tasks in Azure. They are built using PowerShell, Python, or a graphical workflow designer. They can perform a wide range of tasks, from simple scripts to complex workflows involving multiple Azure services.

- **Azure Function**: This is a serverless compute service that allows us to run event-triggered code without having to explicitly provision or manage infrastructure.

- **Event Hub**: This is designed to collect, process, and analyze large streams of events or data. An event hub can handle millions of events per second, making it a powerful tool to process high-throughput data streams.

- **ITSM**: This is a way to integrate Azure Monitor alerts with **IT Service Management (ITSM)** tools such as ServiceNow or System Center Service Manager. It allows you to automatically create incidents or tickets in your ITSM system when specific conditions in your alerts are met.

- **Logic App**: This is a cloud-based workflow automation platform that enables you to automate and integrate various tasks and business processes across different applications and services, using a visual designer and connectors.

- **Secure Webhook/Webhook**: Another way for an application to provide other apps with real-time information is by using a webhook.

These are all our options under **Actions**. Depending on the specific case, we might need multiple action groups, and as soon as we have them in place, we are ready to start creating alert rules.

Creating alert rules

To create a new alert rule, click on **Create**, and on the dropdown, choose **Alert rules**. This will take us to the **Create an alert rule** form:

Figure 9.15 – The Alerts blade

The first step is to choose the scope of the rule. This can be a subscription, a resource, or a resource group. Here, we can choose the Azure Machine Learning resource.

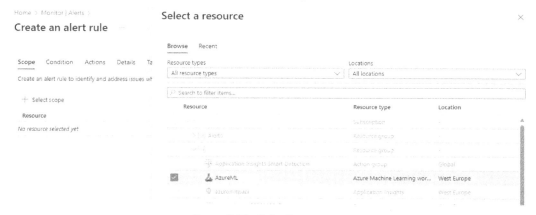

Figure 9.16 – Selecting a scope

On the second tab, we can select **Condition**. There are different types of conditions:

- **Based on metrics emitted by Azure resources**: For example, you can set an alert to trigger when CPU usage exceeds a certain threshold

- **Based on operations performed on resources**: For instance, you can set an alert to trigger when a specific type of operation occurs, such as a virtual machine being deleted

- **Based on log queries against data collected by Azure Monitor Logs**: You can create complex queries to define the conditions for your alert

Here, go to the **Select a signal** dropdown, and select the **All Administrative operations** option. This will send an alert for any administrative change on the Azure Machine Learning resource:

Figure 9.17 – Select a signal

Depending on the signal, you might get more options, such as frequency, but here, we have only a few in terms of **Alert logic**, as shown in the following screenshot. Leave the values as default and click **Next**:

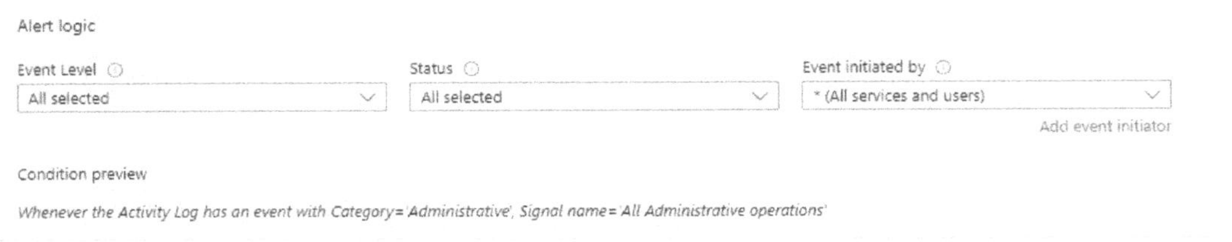

Figure 9.18 – Alert logic

On the **Actions** tab, choose the action group we created previously and click **Next**:

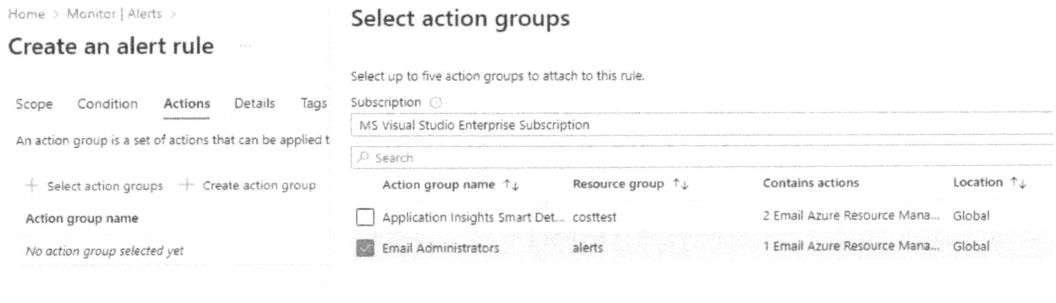

Figure 9.19 – Select action groups

On the **Details** tab, we can fill in some basic details to ensure that we can recognize the alert in the list, as shown in the following screenshot:

Home > Monitor | Alerts >

Create an alert rule ···

Scope   Condition   Actions   **Details**   Tags   Review + create

Project details

Select the subscription and resource group in which to save the alert rule.

Subscription ⓘ

       Resource group * ⓘ

Alerts
Create new

Alert rule details

Alert rule name * ⓘ

Azure ML Administrative operations

Alert rule description ⓘ

∧ Advanced options

Settings

Enable alert rule upon creation   ☑

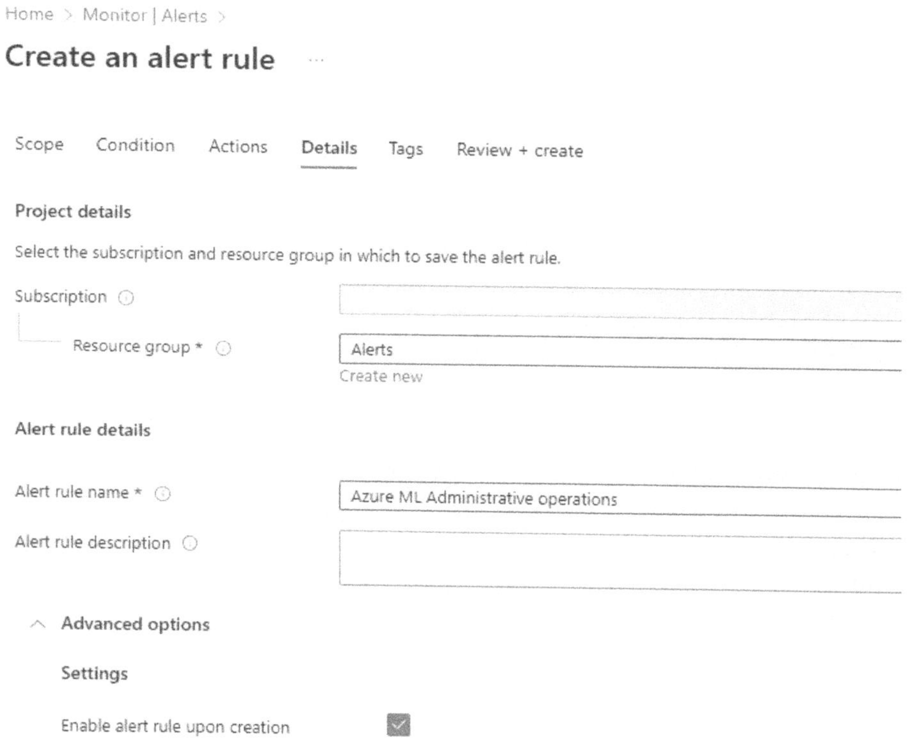

Figure 9.20 – The alert name and description

Now that we have completed the configuration, all we have to do is wait for the alert to fire.

Let us see in the following section how we can manage multiple alerts.

Managing alerts

When events fire, you will get notified depending on how you have set up the action group. Another way to monitor alerts is from the **Alerts** menu in the **Monitor** blade, as shown in the following screenshot, where we can see an event firing. Alerts can be filtered by resource or severity:

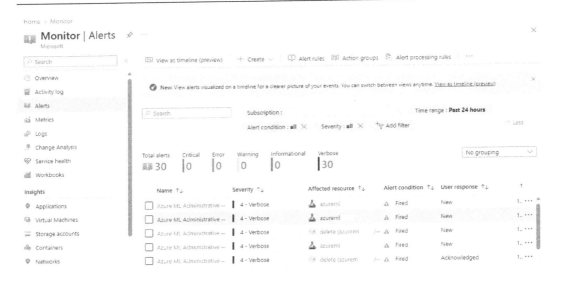

Figure 9.21 – Alerts fired

To ensure that not everyone works on the same alert, we can change the user response on this alert by clicking the three-dot menu on the right, switching from **New** to either **Acknowledged** or even **Closed**, as shown here:

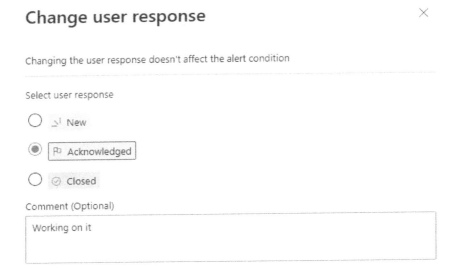

Figure 9.22 – Changing a user response

Remember that Azure Monitor alerts are a critical part of maintaining the health and performance of your Azure resources. Properly configured alerts can help you stay proactive in managing your resources and responding to any issues promptly. Although throughout this chapter we will see more ways to monitor our resources, this is the fastest and simplest way to get started.

Now, let us see how to monitor our models and endpoints using Application Insights.

Working with Application Insights

When we created a workspace, one of the associated resources was **Application Insights**. Application Insights works on top of Monitor and provides real-time monitoring of your applications. It tracks various metrics such as request rates, response times, failure rates, and dependencies. This helps you identify performance bottlenecks, errors, and exceptions. Applications Insights can help us troubleshoot ML endpoints deployed in **Azure Kubernetes Service (AKS)** or **Azure Container Instances (ACI)**. Application Insights collects the following information:

- Exceptions
- Responses
- Output data
- Request rates, response times, and failure rates
- Dependency rates, response times, and failure rates

Let us see how to enable Insights via the Azure Machine Learning Studio or the SDK.

Configuring logging via the Studio and SDK

In *Chapter 1*, we deployed a model to an ACI endpoint. In the model deployment screen, all we have to do to enable Application Insights is to expand the **Advanced** dropdown and check the **Enable Application Insights diagnostics and data collection** checkbox, as shown here:

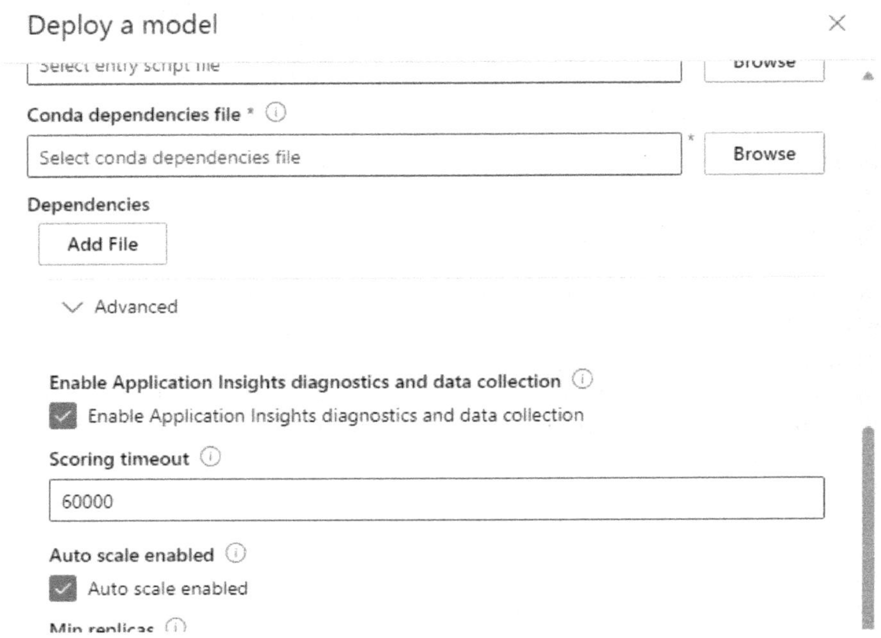

Figure 9.23 – Model deployment advanced settings

Now, after deployment, we will get insights regarding this endpoint. If you are already using the SDK, the process might be simpler. Depending on the service, all you need to do is set the `enable_app_insights` flag to `true` or `false` to enable or disable logging, respectively.

First, we need to get a reference to the web service and then update the flag, as shown in the following code snippet:

```
From azureml.core.webservice import Webservice
# reference the web service
my_web_service= Webservice(workspace, "service-name")
# update the enable_app_insights flag
my_web_service update(enable_app_insights=True)
```

Then, we can see the results in the **Applications Insights** resource blade:

Figure 9.24 – Application Insights

Here, besides the logs and metrics available, we can integrate with DevOps, create a live metrics stream, and track users and sessions along with dependent apps and services. By clicking on **Logs**, we can run log analytics queries.

Here is an example of a simple KQL query:

```
requests
| where timestamp > ago(24h) // Filter for requests in the last 24
hours
| where resultCode !startswith "2" // Filter for non-2xx status codes
| project timestamp, name, url, resultCode, operation_Id, duration,
client_Type
| order by timestamp desc
```

Let's examine the query:

- `requests`: This is the table that contains information about all the HTTP requests made to your application.

- `where timestamp > ago(24h)`: This line filters the requests to only include those that occurred in the last 24 hours. You can adjust the time frame as needed.

- `where resultCode !startswith "2"`: This line filters for requests where `resultCode` does not start with 2. This effectively filters for non-2xx status codes, which usually indicate an error.

- `project`: This selects specific columns to display in the result. You can adjust this to include more or fewer columns, depending on your needs.

- `order by timestamp desc`: This line orders results by timestamp in descending order so that you see the most recent errors first.

This query will provide you with information about recent requests that resulted in errors, including details such as the timestamp, request name, URL, status code, operation ID, duration, and client type. Depending on what we need to monitor, we would need to change the query to the appropriate tables. On top of that, we can add our own custom exceptions to the logs.

The Application Insights API for custom events and metrics

To ingest or send data to the Applications Insight resource, make sure you familiarize yourselves with the available API and SDKs here: `https://learn.microsoft.com/en-us/azure/azure-monitor/app/api-custom-events-metrics`. Application Insights also provides a dashboard to monitor everything.

Figure 9.25 – The Application Insights dashboard

We can access this dashboard from the **Overview** blade of the Application Insights resource. All we need to do is click on **Application Dashboard** to open the dashboard view (as shown in *Figure 9.24*).

Creating Azure dashboards

To learn more about the Application Insights dashboard, read this documentation: `https://learn.microsoft.com/en-us/azure/azure-monitor/app/overview-dashboard`.

> To learn how to work with Azure dashboards in general, see here: `https://learn.microsoft.com/en-us/azure/azure-portal/azure-portal-dashboards`.
>
> Dashboards can also be created programmatically by using templates. Find out more information in this link: `https://learn.microsoft.com/en-us/azure/azure-portal/azure-portal-dashboards-create-programmatically`.

Application Insights is designed to help developers monitor the performance and usage of their applications, identify and diagnose issues, and gain insights into how users interact with our applications. It is very useful in Azure Machine Learning, as it can monitor your endpoints, and by using the connection string, we can also gather logs from our applications.

Logs and metrics can be difficult to read, but in large datasets, it is easier to visualize them. Let us see some ways that we can visualize metrics and logs gathered from Azure Monitor.

Visualizing the data

To visualize data from Azure Monitor, we have various tools and techniques. Let us see some of those here.

- **Dashboards**: Azure dashboards allow us to combine multiple visualizations (such as charts, tables, and other widgets) in a single view. We can pin visualizations from Azure Monitor Logs to a dashboard for easy access and monitoring. Dashboards can also be set as the Azure portal start page so that we can see them right away.

- **Workbooks**: Azure Workbooks provides a flexible and customizable way to visualize data from Azure Monitor logs. It includes a range of pre-built workbook templates for common scenarios, such as virtual machines, that can be customized to suit our specific needs. Workbooks can be shared with team members and scheduled for regular updates.

- **Log Analytics language**: You can write queries in the Azure Log Analytics query language to retrieve specific data from your logs. Once you have the data, you can use visualization functions to display it in a graphical format.

- **PowerBI**: Power BI can connect to Azure Monitor logs and help you create more complex and interactive visualizations.

Azure Monitor is a critical tool to maintain the health and performance of your Azure infrastructure and applications. It's particularly valuable for businesses running mission-critical applications in the cloud, as it helps in identifying and resolving issues quickly, optimizing resource utilization, and ensuring a smooth user experience.

Now, let us see a couple of other tools to help us monitor our resources, which can also provide security recommendations.

Securing resources with Microsoft Defender

Microsoft Defender for Cloud is a **cloud-native application protection platform** (**CNAPP**) designed specifically for cloud environments. It offers a comprehensive set of security measures and best practices, aimed at safeguarding cloud-based applications against a wide range of cyber attacks and vulnerabilities. Microsoft Defender for Cloud combines several functionalities, including a **cloud workload protection platform** (**CWPP**) focusing on infrastructure, storage, and so on, a **cloud security posture management** (**CSPM**) solution to prevent security issues, and a **DevSecOps** solution that helps to secure code across different clouds if needed. Defender includes a basic CSPM without additional cost. There are advanced features that you can enable on top of that, including attack path analysis, the cloud security explorer, advanced threat hunting, security governance, as well as tools to evaluate your security compliance across regulatory standards that apply to specific industries' locations.

> **Microsoft Defender for Cloud pricing**
> You can check out Defender pricing and features here: `https://azure.microsoft.com/en-us/pricing/details/defender-for-cloud/?v=17.23h`.

Let us walk through the service and see how we can leverage it in our Azure Machine Learning resources.

The following is the main blade of **Microsoft Defender for Cloud**. You can open it by typing `Defender for Cloud` in the top search box:

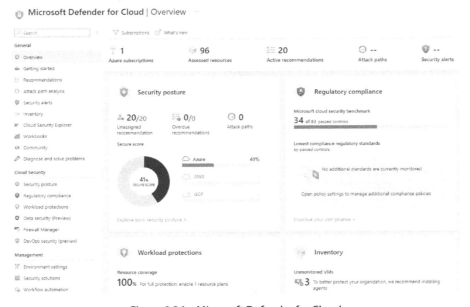

Figure 9.26 – Microsoft Defender for Cloud

At first glance, we can see the **Security posture** secure score of our workloads, which is based on implemented security recommendations in our resources; our **Regulatory compliance** score, which is based on applied policies; our **Workload protections** percentage; and an inventory of monitored assets. There are also other articles available on the rest of the screen and announcements regarding Defender.

Let us see how we can use the information provided to secure our Azure Machine Learning resources.

Improving our security posture

The first thing is to click on **Security posture** to see recommendations to improve our secure score. The secure score is an indicator that evaluates and assigns a score to the security status of your Azure resources and workloads. The lower the score, the less your resources are following security recommendations. To improve our score, we need to implement recommendations for each of our resources.

Note in the following screenshot that the security posture is evaluated for Azure, **Amazon Web Services (AWS)**, and the **Google Cloud Platform (GCP)**. You can connect your analytics and create a unified security blade.

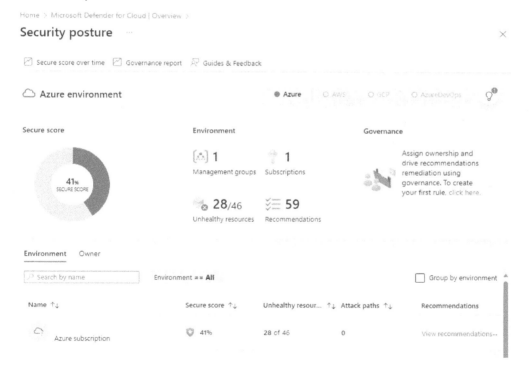

Figure 9.27 – Security posture

To get started with recommendations, click on your subscription on the **View recommendations** link.

Then, we can see the recommendations for all our resources:

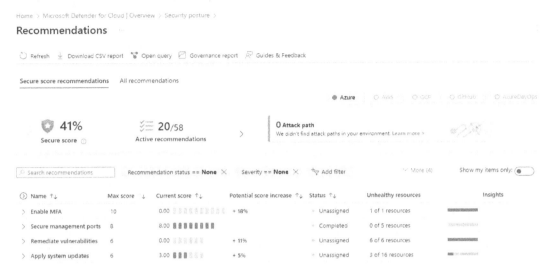

Figure 9.28 – Recommendations

To focus on the Azure Machine Learning recommendations, filter this list appropriately. As my ML resources are in the same resource group, I will filter by **Resource group**, containing my Azure Machine Learning workspace and associated services:

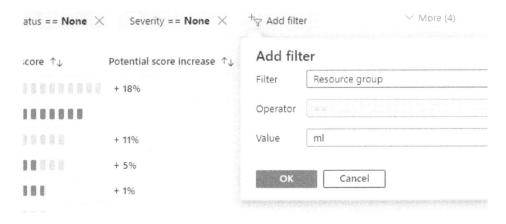

Figure 9.29 – Adding a filter to the resource group

For each recommendation, we can see how the implementation will improve our score. All recommendations under each category must be implemented to get the aforementioned score increase. For example, the **Apply system updates** recommendation only has one action in the following screenshot, but the implementation will improve our score by **5%**. To implement the recommendation, you can click on the link to see more information:

Figure 9.30 – Security posture recommendations

Here, we can see the issue severity, a description, the remediation steps, and the affected resources. We can then manually proceed and update the resources as instructed:

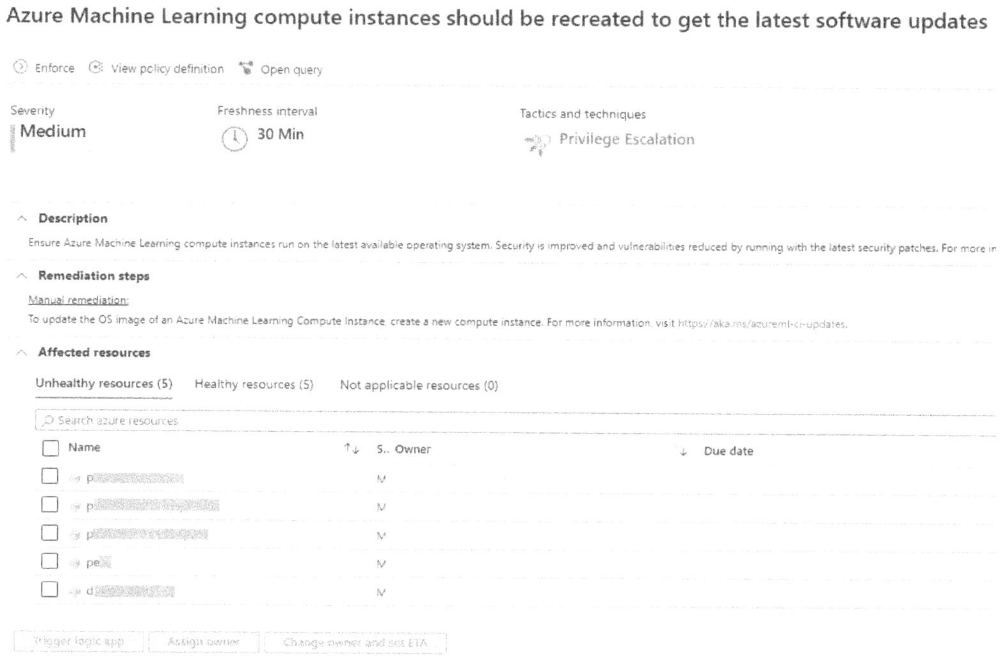

Figure 9.31 – Recommendation remediation

We can even enforce this in the future by clicking the **Enforce** button, as shown in the previous screenshot, which will assign this recommendation as a policy.

Similarly, we can implement security recommendations in our Azure Machine Learning instance and any other resources in our subscriptions. The recommendations are part of the Azure security baseline, which we will analyze in more detail in *Chapter 10*, where we will create a security baseline for our Azure Machine Learning environment by using security best practices.

Now, let us explore Microsoft Sentinel to help us secure and automate our response to security incidents.

Exploring threat management with Sentinel

Microsoft Sentinel is a cloud-native **Security Information and Event Management (SIEM)** and **Security Orchestration, Automation, and Response (SOAR)** solution. It offers intelligent security analytics and threat intelligence centrally for Azure and other clouds. With Sentinel, we have smart alert detection, threat visibility, hunting, and response, all in a single pane. There are several benefits to using Sentinel for the aforementioned tasks:

- As a cloud solution, it scales with our data, and we pay for what we use.

- Microsoft Sentinel gathers data using connectors from a wide range of sources, including Azure services, on-premises environments, and other clouds.

- The service comes with built-in ML models that help to identify suspicious activities and reduce false positives. Over time, these models can be trained to improve their accuracy based on your organization's unique patterns.

- Threat hunting is done using KQL to identify threats, anomalies, and patterns, and there are templates available to get you started.

- Beyond just detection, Microsoft Sentinel also allows you to automate common tasks and responses. This can help organizations respond more quickly to threats.

- We can use workbooks to visualize and help teams drill down into data, find patterns, and understand security postures better.

- Microsoft Sentinel provides tools to handle incidents, from identification to investigation to remediation.

- Default data retention is at 30 days, but it can be increased to 90 days.

To work with Sentinel, we need a Log Analytics workspace to gather logs. Refer to the previous sections of this chapter to create a new Log Analytics workspace. After you have a workspace, you can add Microsoft Sentinel to the workspace. Find `Microsoft Sentinel` from the search bar of the Azure portal, and on the page that loads, click on **Create**.

Home >

Microsoft Sentinel ✧ ...

+ Create   ⚙ Manage view ∨   ↻ Refresh   ↓ Export to CSV   Open query   ⊡ View incidents

| Filter for any field... | Subscription equals **all** | Resource group equals **all** ✕ | Location equals **all** ✕ | Add filter |

Showing 1 to 1 of 1 records.

☐ Name ↑	Resource group ↑↓	Location ↑↓
☐ 🛡 MyWorkspace	logs	West Europe

Figure 9.32 – Microsoft Sentinel

In the next step, **Add Microsoft Sentinel to a workspace**, choose the workspace we created previously, as shown in the next screenshot.

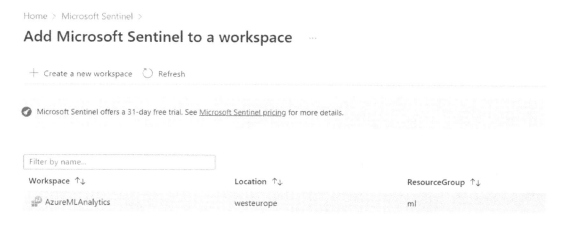

Home > Microsoft Sentinel >

Add Microsoft Sentinel to a workspace   ...

+ Create a new workspace   ↻ Refresh

ℹ Microsoft Sentinel offers a 31-day free trial. See Microsoft Sentinel pricing for more details.

| Filter by name... |

Workspace ↑↓	Location ↑↓	ResourceGroup ↑↓
AzureMLAnalytics	westeurope	ml

Figure 9.33 – Adding Sentinel to a workspace

As soon as you add a workspace, you can leverage the Sentinel threat management capabilities. This is the main page of Sentinel. Everything you need to work with threat management can be found on the left menu.

Let us explore the most useful features of Microsoft Sentinel:

- **Incidents**: In Microsoft Sentinel, incidents are compilations of related alerts, representing potentially harmful activities or patterns within a system. They provide a consolidated view to help security analysts estimate the scope and sequence of a potential attack. Incidents in Microsoft Sentinel are equipped with information such as the entities involved, a timeline of related alerts, and other relevant details. Incidents allow security teams to focus on broader events rather than individual alerts, helping prioritize responses based on the combined severity of related alerts.

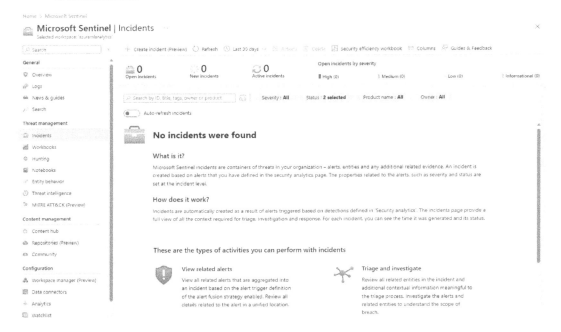

Figure 9.34 – Incidents

- **Hunting**: Hunting in Microsoft Sentinel refers to proactive queries and exploration of data to identify signs of malicious or suspicious activities that haven't necessarily raised automatic alerts. We can run predefined or custom KQL queries to filter through collected data, searching for anomalies or patterns of interest. The goal is to discover hidden threats, identify previously unnoticed patterns, and strengthen detection capabilities.

  To access hunting queries, click on **Hunting**. The process of creating a hunt is easy. From the main page, click on **New hunt**.

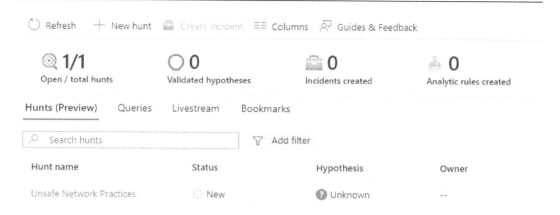

Figure 9.35 – Hunting queries

Provide a *name* and more information if necessary, and then click **Create**.

Create hunt   ✕

Hunt name *

Unsafe Network Practices

Description

B *I* U̲ S̶ 🔗 *T*ₓ

Owner

Search users and groups

Status

New   ⌄

Hypothesis

Unknown   ⌄

Figure 9.36 – A new hunt

A hunt is composed of one or more queries. To add your query, click on the hunt name you just created, and under **Query actions**, you can select **New query** or **Add queries to hunt** to choose from existing queries. Queries are written in KQL.

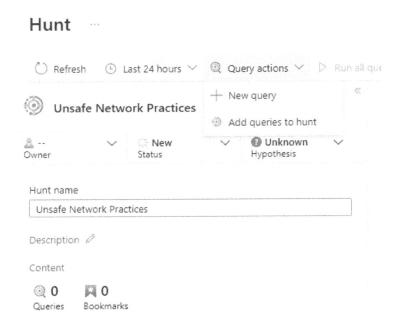

Figure 9.37 – Adding queries

I chose the latter and selected these two queries from the list, as shown in the next screenshot.

Add existing queries to hunt   ✕

Adding queries to the current hunt.

Queries will be cloned when adding to a hunt. Updates to queries will not impact the copied instance after it is cloned to a hunt.

	Query	Results	Results delta	Results delta p...	Data sources	Tactics	Techniques
☑	Azure Network Security Group NSG Administrative...	--	--	--	AzureActivity	Impact	T1496
☐	Port opened for an Azure Resource	--	--	--	AzureActivity		T1071 +2 ⓘ
☐	Microsoft Sentinel Analytics Rules Administrative ...	--	--	--	AzureActivity	Impact	T1496
☐	Anomalous Azure Operation Hunting Model	--	--	--			T1570 +1 ⓘ
☐	Rare Custom Script Extension	--	--	--	AzureActivity	Execution	T1059
☑	Azure Virtual Network Subnets Administrative Ope...	--	--	--	AzureActivity	Impact	T1496
☐	Azure VM Run Command executed from Azure IP ...	--	--	--			T1570 +1 ⓘ
☐	Granting permissions to account	--	--	--	AzureActivity		T1098

Figure 9.38 – Adding existing queries

Now, you can run these queries to confirm your hypothesis and discover suspected threats. Upon discovery, we can create an incident directly from the hunting page.

- **Threat intelligence**: Threat intelligence in Microsoft Sentinel involves leveraging information about existing and emerging threats and vulnerabilities. Microsoft Sentinel integrates with Microsoft Defender's Threat Intelligence, which provides data about known malicious IP addresses, URLs, file hashes, and so on. When this data matches activity in your environment, Sentinel can raise alerts. The integration of threat intelligence allows organizations to cross-reference their real-time data with known threat indicators, improving the detection of potential security breaches and understanding the broader threat landscape.

These are just the basics. Sentinel has a lot of capabilities, as it integrates with multiple Microsoft services such as Defender for Cloud and Microsoft 365. To skill up in Sentinel, take a look at the following resources, ranging from learning paths to certifications.

Get started with Microsoft Sentinel

To get started with Microsoft Sentinel, check out the following learning paths: `https://learn.microsoft.com/en-us/azure/sentinel/skill-up-resources`.

Summary

In this chapter, we learned to utilize multiple services, ensuring we can monitor our resources effectively by enabling different services and learning how we can start to use the logs we gather to prevent security incidents. The first one we worked with was Azure Monitor, using Monitor alerts to make sure we can be notified about any issues. By combining the capabilities of Monitor Log Analytics and Application Insights, we can have end-to-end monitoring of our resources and our model endpoints. Additionally, by using Microsoft Defender for Cloud, we can get recommendations to implement best practices, and we can use Microsoft Sentinel for advanced threat management. Now that we have a comprehensive view of the best practices across different surface areas included in a ML project, we can combine them and see how we can build a security baseline for our Azure resources in the next chapter.

Part 4: Best Practices for Enterprise Security in Azure Machine Learning

In this part, you will review the best practices outlined in this book and explore more services that could be used to further secure your cloud resources. You will also see a sample solution architecture that incorporates all those practices. Finally, you will learn how to work with threat modeling, developing a strategy to maintain the same level of security and stay protected in the future.

This part has the following chapter:

- *Chapter 10, Setting a Security Baseline for Your Azure Machine Learning Workloads*

10
Setting a Security Baseline for Your Azure Machine Learning Workloads

In this chapter, we will summarize all the best practices outlined in this book for creating a security baseline for your machine learning workloads from start to finish to help you create a security strategy. We will mostly focus on Azure services, as we have in the rest of the book. Of course, there are always more things to consider, such as code or application security, but these are not the focus of this book.

We will review a couple of other services that, although not directly related to Azure Machine Learning, are useful to consider so that we can increase security in our Azure services overall. When it comes to security, we can use threat modeling to ensure that any practices we have identified and mitigated are continuously maintained and updated with any past and new security recommendations for as long as those services are up and running. Finally, we will review the cloud responsibility model so that we always remember that certain tasks are our responsibility to implement correctly. Although Azure has many tools and security controls available, it is up to us to configure them correctly.

In this chapter, we're going to cover the following main topics:

- Setting a baseline for Azure Machine Learning
- Theat modeling for Azure Machine Learning
- Reviewing the share responsibility model for cloud security

By the end of this chapter, we will have learned how to create a baseline for our ML project and develop a threat modeling strategy based on popular frameworks.

Setting a baseline for Azure Machine Learning

Throughout this book, we have seen multiple services and explored several ways to secure the Azure Machine Learning workspace and its associated services in Azure. All those best practices are part of the suggested best practices. As we focus on securing our workloads, it's essential to establish a security foundation to guide our efforts. A security baseline is a set of the minimum security controls we need to implement for a system. Let us again review what the minimum requirements are to protect workloads running in Azure Machine Learning, which we have already outlined previously in this book, and learn how to extend this functionality further by using other services.

Let us review the baseline Azure Machine Learning best practices organized by the Zero Trust model we reviewed in this book:

- Securing identity (*Chapter 6*):
    - Use Microsoft Entra ID best practices:
        - Enable **multi-factor authentication** (**MFA**) in user accounts
        - Use more than one admin on services
    - Plan for **role-based access control** (**RBAC**) and use the least privilege principle
    - Work with application identities and managed identities when possible
    - Enable conditional access
    - Enable privilege identity management for RBAC
    - Prevent the exposure of keys and secrets by utilizing Azure Key Vault

- Securing data (*Chapters 3, 4, and 5*):
    - Discover, classify, and label sensitive data
    - Create a company-wide data governance strategy
    - Encrypt data at rest
    - Encrypt data in transit
    - User customer-managed keys for encryption when available
    - Secure key management in Azure Key Vault
    - Use certificates when possible
    - Use only approved and secure datasets from reputable sources
    - Stay compliant by using policies

- Securing infrastructure and endpoints (*Chapter 7*):

  - Keep up to date and disable public access in compute instances

  - Disable public access in compute clusters

  - Disable public/anonymous access in container registries and containers

  - Follow best security practices for external compute (AKS, ACI)

- Securing network (*Chapter 7*):

  - Disable public network access

  - Use Service or Private Endpoints

Outside the Zero Trust categories, we also talked about the following best practices:

- Planning for backup and recovery (*Chapter 4*):

  - Ensure regular backups for each service

  - Test the restore process

  - Utilize resource locks to avoid accidental deletions

  - Enable soft-delete and point-in-time restore where applicable

- Improving the security posture and vulnerability management (*Chapter 9*):

  - Enable Azure Defender and implement recommendations

  - Enable Microsoft Sentinel

- Logging and monitoring (*Chapter 9*):

  - Enable logging and alerts

  - Use log analytics workspaces to get insights

Azure Machine Learning security baseline mapping file

To develop our strategy, we applied guidance from the Microsoft cloud security benchmark at `https://learn.microsoft.com/en-us/security/benchmark/azure/overview` to the services associated with Azure Machine Learning.

To see the complete mapping of the Machine Learning service to the Microsoft cloud security benchmark, see the following document:

`https://github.com/MicrosoftDocs/SecurityBenchmarks/tree/master/Azure%20Offer%20Security%20Baselines/3.0/machine-learning-service-azure-security-benchmark-v3-latest-security-baseline.xlsx`

Setting a baseline is organization-specific, and although the preceding recommendations might read as a checklist, they are only recommendations. You can pick and choose which ones to implement according to your scenario and way of working. How should you decide which ones to apply to your ML project? Let us review in the next sections how to develop your own threat modeling strategy and what else you need to consider when working with security in the cloud.

We will start by exploring some services that although not directly connected to Azure Machine Learning, are important to consider when it comes to cloud security. We will then move on to an example of the solution architecture.

Discovering services for added security

In this book, we focused more on securing services directly associated with Azure Machine Learning. However, all the services we discussed have their own best practices and connected services. When we are working with big data there are a lot of things that we can further consider, such as the network or the application. Here are some services to consider when further exploring how to secure our Azure Services. Some we might have mentioned, others not, so let us review them all together here:

- **Network security groups** (**NSGs**): NSGs are a vital component of network security in cloud computing environments. NSGs are used to control and secure network traffic to and from resources deployed within a **virtual network** (**VNet**) or subnet. They act like a stateless firewall, allowing you to define and enforce rules for controlling inbound and outbound traffic at the network level.

- **VPN gateways**: A **virtual private network** (**VPN**) gateway is a network device or service that provides secure and encrypted communication between two or more separate networks or devices over an untrusted network, such as the internet. VPN gateways play a crucial role in ensuring the privacy, integrity, and security of data transmitted over public or untrusted networks. It is a way to connect our on-premises data center to the cloud.

- **ExpressRoute**: ExpressRoute is a service that provides a dedicated, private, and highly reliable network connection between an organization's on-premises data center or network and Microsoft Azure's cloud services. It is designed to enable secure, high-throughput, low-latency connections that offer a superior alternative to using the public internet for accessing Azure resources.

- **Azure Firewall**: Azure Firewall is a cloud-based network security service that acts as a protective barrier for resources and applications deployed within the Azure VNet by filtering and inspecting incoming and outgoing network traffic. Azure Firewall provides features for network security, threat protection, and traffic monitoring.

- **Azure Virtual wide area network** (**VWAN**): Azure VWAN is a networking service provided by Microsoft Azure that simplifies and optimizes connectivity between various Azure regions, on-premises locations, and branch offices. It's designed to streamline the management of **wide area networking** (**WAN**) infrastructure and improve the performance and security of network connections.

- **Web application firewall (WAF)**: Azure WAF is a cloud-based web application firewall service. It offers advanced security and protection for web applications and websites hosted on the Azure platform. Azure WAF is designed to defend against a wide range of web application threats and vulnerabilities. You can enable it on the Front Door and Application Gateway services.

- **Distributed Denial of Service (DDoS) Protection**: Azure provides DDoS protection services to safeguard your applications and resources from DDoS attacks. DDoS attacks can overwhelm your network and services, making them unavailable to users. Azure DDoS Protection helps detect and mitigate these attacks, ensuring the availability and performance of your applications.

- **Azure Front Door**: Azure Front Door is a global, scalable, and highly available content delivery and application acceleration service. It is designed to improve the availability, security, and performance of web applications and content by optimizing and routing traffic through a global network of Microsoft-managed **points of presence (PoPs)**. It can be used with the WAF and NSGs for better security.

- **Azure Application Gateway**: The Azure Application Gateway is a Layer 7 (application layer) load balancer and web traffic manager service. It is designed to improve the availability, scalability, and security of web applications by distributing incoming traffic, performing SSL termination, and providing advanced application-level routing and security features.

- **Microsoft Defender for Cloud**: Enable the Defender for Cloud advanced features. These are **cloud security posture management (CSPM)** and **cloud workload protections (CWP)**, and they will help to improve Azure threat and vulnerability management.

- **Azure Site Recovery**: Azure Site Recovery is designed to ensure business continuity by providing a comprehensive disaster recovery solution. It helps organizations replicate and recover their virtualized workloads and data from one location to another, whether it's from on-premises to Azure, Azure to Azure, or between on-premises data centers.

End-to-end security in Azure

This article outlines all security services and the security capabilities of each of the available tools:

```
https://learn.microsoft.com/en-us/azure/security/fundamentals/
end-to-end
```

Exploring an example solution architecture

If we were to use some of the previously mentioned services together with the best practices outlined in the book to create a secure Azure Machine Learning solution architecture, the next figure demonstrates what it might look like:

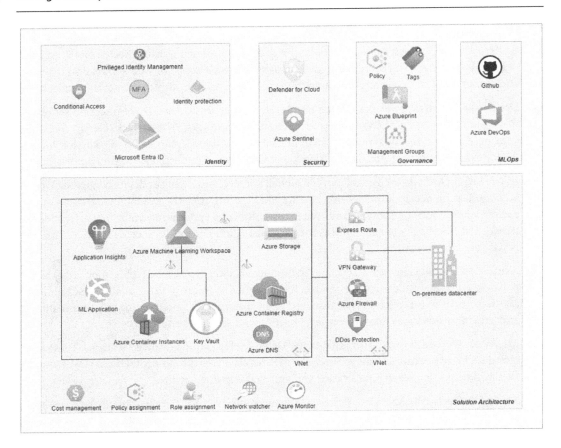

Figure 10.1 – Azure solution architecture

In this example, we have secured and isolated all resources associated with Azure Machine Learning within a VNet by using private links. Public access is disabled at this point. This VNet is paired to another VNet, which has several services that can be shared across multiple peered VNets. This networking architecture is called a **hub-spoke topology** where the hub is a central virtual network in Azure that hosts services that are shared by multiple spokes, such as Azure Firewall and VPN Gateway. The spokes are virtual networks that peer with the hub. Each spoke can be used to isolate workloads, environments, applications, or departments. Spokes allow for dedicated resources per workload or application, improving security and organization. In this architecture, the spoke is used to isolate the Azure Machine Learning resources. This can also be used to isolate different environments such as development and production. We can even take it a step further and host these VNets through different subscriptions. We can then have private connectivity with the on-premises systems by using Express Route or VPN Gateway. The Azure Firewall can be used to protect the cloud and on-premises resources in this example scenario and allow access from specific IPs or external networks.

On top of those services, we can leverage the Microsoft Entra ID management features depicted, Defender for Cloud and Sentinel for security and incident management, GitHub or Azure DevOps for MLOps, and other services such as Policy and management groups for governance. Each subscription also comes with cost management, the Azure Monitor service, and more.

This is just one example of course. Depending on different organizations and needs, we might utilize more or fewer services. To browse different solution architectures about ML, AI, and more, you can browse through the Azure Architecture Center shown in the next callout.

> **Browse Azure architectures**
>
> If you want to get inspired on how to organize your Azure resources, you can find multiple solution architectures similar to the one presented here in the Azure Architecture Center:
>
> `https://learn.microsoft.com/en-us/azure/architecture/`

This is not enough though. Depending on the programming language used, we will need to leverage secure coding practices to ensure that the code cannot be compromised and provide access to the underlying secure infrastructure, especially for public-facing services.

> **Secure code best practices with Azure Machine Learning**
>
> In this documentation, you will find some coding security best practices when working with Azure Machine Learning and notebooks:
>
> `https://learn.microsoft.com/en-us/azure/machine-learning/concept-secure-code-best-practice?view=azureml-api-2#next-steps`

Now that we have a good grasp of the available services and possible architectures, let us review how to decide and prioritize which services we need by developing our own threat modeling strategy.

Threat modeling for Azure Machine Learning

Threat modeling is a structured methodology for detecting and ranking potential threats to a system and evaluating the impact that potential mitigations might have in decreasing or eliminating those threats. It is commonly used in the field of information security and cybersecurity, and we can apply this process to Azure Machine Learning as well to proactively protect our systems. What we are trying to determine when working with threat modeling are answers to the following questions:

- What are we working on?
- What can go wrong with the system?
- How are we going to deal with the issue?
- Is that enough? Did we miss anything else?

The process often follows these general steps, and it is an iterative process:

Figure 10.2 – The threat modeling process

Let us review each one:

1. **Define objectives and review the architecture**: Here, we need to clarify what we are trying to protect by understanding the value of our data and the system's components. This sets the stage for the threat modeling exercise by focusing on what is important. As soon as we have the components, we should understand the system's architecture. This can include data flow diagrams to show how data moves through the system and trust boundaries to indicate where data changes trust levels, such as crossing a network or moving between processes. The following is a simple Azure Machine Learning architecture:

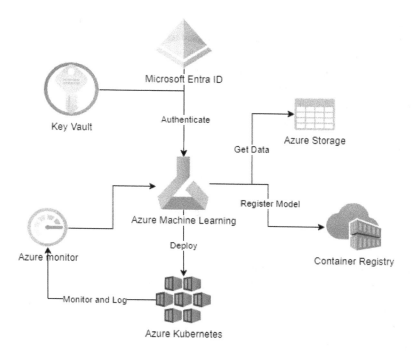

Figure 10.3 – Azure Machine Learning architecture

2. **Decompose the architecture**: Break down the system into its core components and functionalities. This can include understanding the technologies being used, the entry points into the system, and the assets that you are trying to protect. For Azure Machine Learning, this includes workspaces, compute, data storage, pipelines, models, and all associated services.

3. **Identify threats and vulnerabilities**: Utilize frameworks such as MITRE ATLAS, as we discussed in *Chapter 2*, to identify specific threats or vulnerabilities for each component of our ML workflow. Prioritize the threats based on their potential impact and the likelihood of occurrence. This will help focus efforts on the most critical security issues.

4. **Define mitigation strategies**: For each threat, we need to determine the most appropriate way to mitigate the risk. This could involve changes in the architecture, adopting new security controls, applying patches, or changing operational practices.

5. **Validate and review**: After mitigation strategies have been implemented, they should be tested to ensure they are effective. This can involve code review, tests, and compliance checks. Keep thorough documentation of the threat model and mitigation strategies. Azure Policy and Azure Blueprints can help enforce and track compliance with your security requirements.

Threat modeling is not a one-time process but should be an ongoing activity throughout the system's lifecycle. As new features are added or changes are made to the system, the threat model should be updated to reflect the new state of the system. Accordingly, we need to continuously review and update the threat model for our Azure Machine Learning workloads. New features, data, or integration with other Azure services can introduce new threats or vulnerabilities. By applying these principles, you can create a robust threat model for your Azure Machine Learning workloads, helping to ensure that our ML solutions are secure and reliable.

Various tools and resources are available to assist with threat modeling, from Microsoft's Threat Modeling Tool to OWASP's resources, such as the Application Threat Modeling framework. It is also important to stay up to date with the latest threat intelligence and industry best practices to keep the threat models relevant and effective by using the MITRE framework, for example, which we highlighted in *Chapter 2*. No matter where we base our strategy, we must ensure that it enables us to periodically validate and review the results.

> **The Application Threat Modeling framework**
>
> Learn more about the OWASP's Application Threat Modeling framework here:
>
> `https://owasp.org/www-community/Threat_Modeling`

We have already seen the MITRE ATLAS framework, which is a great knowledge base to get started with and base our strategy on, and the OWASP framework we mentioned is more geared towards applications. Of course, we don't have to use all those frameworks and methodologies at once. We can choose which one suits our needs best and can be used in the long term. Let us briefly explore the STRIDE methodology as well because the Microsoft Threat Modeling Tool we will use later on in this chapter is based on it.

Exploring the STRIDE methodology

The **STRIDE** methodology is a security framework used to analyze and categorize security threats and risks in computer systems, software, and applications. STRIDE was primarily created as part of the procedure of threat modeling. STRIDE is an acronym that stands for the six categories of security threats: *spoofing, tampering, repudiation, information disclosure, denial of service (DoS)*, and *elevation of privilege*.

Let us review each category:

- **Spoofing**: Spoofing threats involve impersonating someone or something to gain unauthorized access or deceive a user. This can include identity spoofing, where an attacker pretends to be a legitimate user or system, or website spoofing, where a fake website is created to deceive users.

- **Tampering**: Tampering threats refer to the unauthorized modification of data or code. This can include data tampering, where an attacker changes data to disrupt operations or steal information, or code tampering, where an attacker modifies the code to introduce vulnerabilities or malicious functionality.

- **Repudiation**: Repudiation threats involve the denial of actions or events. For example, a user may claim that they did not perform a particular action or a system may not log actions in a way that can be used to prove what happened. Non-repudiation mechanisms are used to prevent and detect these threats.

- **Information disclosure**: Information disclosure threats involve the unauthorized exposure of sensitive data. This can include data leaks, where sensitive information is exposed to unauthorized users, or data theft, where attackers steal sensitive data for malicious purposes.

- **DoS**: DoS attacks aim to disrupt the availability of a system or service. Attackers may overload a system with traffic, crash it, or use other means to make it unavailable to legitimate users. DDoS attacks are a common example.

- **Elevation of privilege**: Elevation of privilege threats involve attackers gaining higher levels of access or privileges than they are supposed to have. This can lead to unauthorized access, control, or manipulation of a system or data.

To address security threats using the STRIDE methodology, we typically perform the steps outlined in the previous sections to identify the assets of the systems that are at risk, find the corresponding threats and their mitigations, and then validate and review the processes after implementation.

This methodology is often used together with Microsoft's Threat Modeling Tool and is designed to help identify and address security vulnerabilities early in the software development process. We can also use it independently.

Let us review how to work with the Microsoft Threat Modeling Tool.

Getting started with the Microsoft Threat Modeling Tool

The Microsoft Threat Modeling Tool helps us identify threats and plan mitigations. This tool uses the STRIDE methodology and provides us with basic reporting.

To get started with the tool, you can download it here:

```
https://aka.ms/threatmodelingtool
```

After downloading and installing the tool, this is the main screen that opens up:

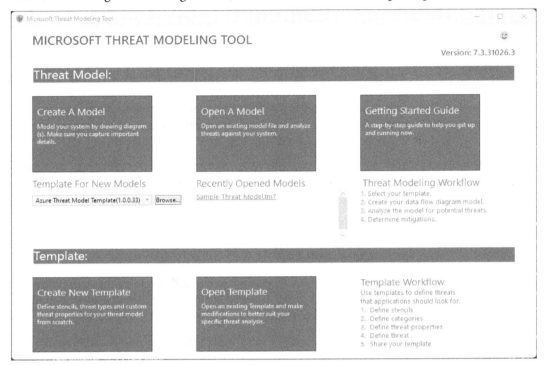

Figure 10.4 – Microsoft Threat Modeling Tool

In this screenshot, we can see several options, from using templates to starting from scratch. We will begin by clicking the **Create A Model** button.

The tool provides a graphical interface for creating threat models called the **Design View**. Users can diagram the components and data flows of their application or system to visualize potential attack vectors and security boundaries.

In our example, we will simply drag and drop from the **Stencils** toolbar to the right of the **Azure AD** component (currently rebranded as Microsoft Entra ID), as this is where our users are managed and the **Azure ML** component that represents our workspace is. By right-clicking on the canvas, we can create connections between components. For this example, you can click on **Bi-Directional Connect** as shown in the following screenshot:

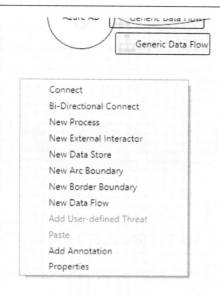

Figure 10.5 – Making a connection

By clicking on each component, we can also change or define properties. For example, in the Azure Storage component, you can specify if it is a blob or a file, and so on. For the components we have here, it is not necessary. The final result is depicted in the next screenshot:

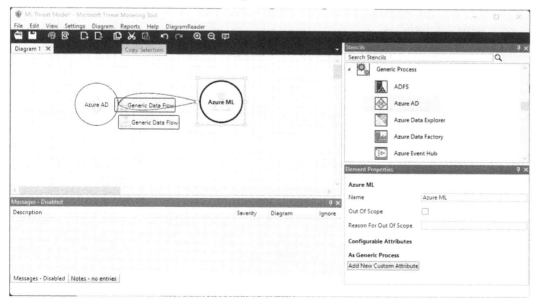

Figure 10.6 – Creating a diagram

As soon as we are done, we can click on the **Analysis View** button on the top bar to get the analysis. We can switch between the **Analysis View** and the **Design View** by using those two side-by-side buttons as shown here:

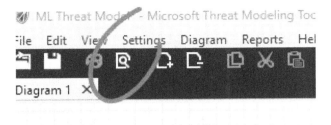

Figure 10.7 – Opening the Analysis View

In the Analysis View, we can see **Threat List**, and by clicking on each threat, we can see **Threat Properties**:

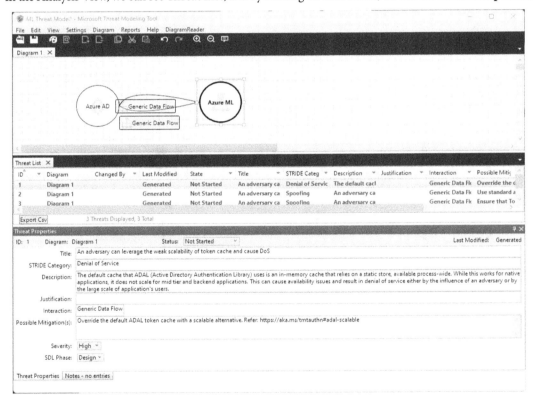

Figure 10.8 – Getting the analysis result

The fields in **Threat Properties** are editable, and we can change the **Status** to **Not Started**, **Needs investigation**, **Not applicable** or **Mitigated**, the **Severity** to **Low**, **Medium**, or **High**, and **SDL phase** to **Design** or **Implementation** along with the descriptions. An example is shown here:

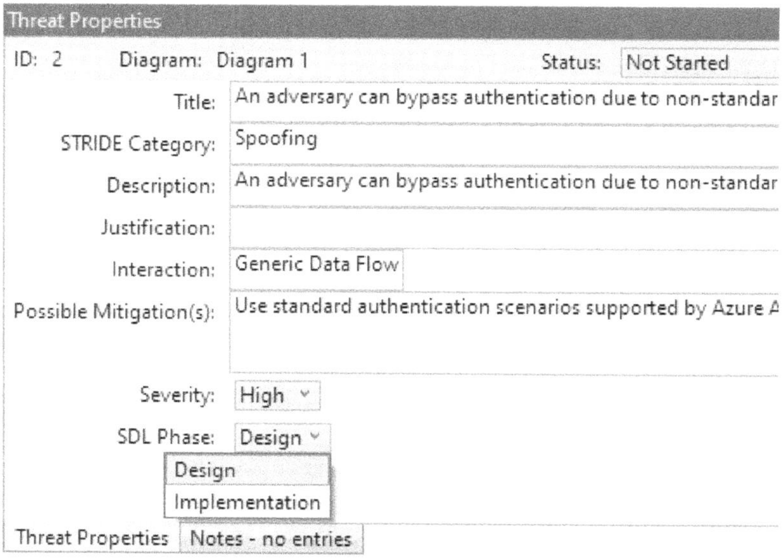

Threat Properties

ID: 2   Diagram: Diagram 1   Status: Not Started

Title: An adversary can bypass authentication due to non-standar

STRIDE Category: Spoofing

Description: An adversary can bypass authentication due to non-standar

Justification:

Interaction: Generic Data Flow

Possible Mitigation(s): Use standard authentication scenarios supported by Azure A

Severity: High ˅

SDL Phase: Design ˅

Design

Implementation

Threat Properties | Notes - no entries

Figure 10.9 – Editing properties

At any point in this process, we can save the document, share it, or generate reports summarizing the identified threats, their associated risks, and recommended mitigation strategies. These reports can be shared with stakeholders and development teams to prioritize and address security concerns.

To extract a report, click **Reports** and then **Create Full Report...** as shown here:

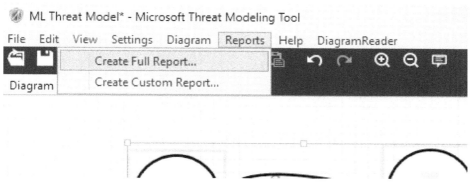

ML Threat Model* - Microsoft Threat Modeling Tool

File   Edit   View   Settings   Diagram   Reports   Help   DiagramReader

Create Full Report...

Diagram   Create Custom Report...

Figure 10.10 – Generating the report

Choose which additional properties to include in the report and click **Generate Report**; this is what we get:

Figure 10.11 – Choosing the report items

The report gets saved into an HTML file that contains the diagram and all recorded information within the tool. The report from the previous example is depicted in the following screenshot:

Figure 10.12 – Saving the report as HTML

> **Microsoft Threat Modeling Tool documentation**
>
> Find the complete documentation for this tool here:
>
> `https://learn.microsoft.com/en-us/azure/security/develop/threat-modeling-tool`

Overall, the Microsoft Threat Modeling Tool is a valuable resource for organizations and software development teams looking to enhance the security of their applications and systems. By using this tool, we can systematically identify and address security threats and vulnerabilities, leading to more robust and secure software products. It's important to keep in mind that while the tool provides valuable assistance, it does not replace the need for security expertise and best practices throughout the development process and it is not the only one we can use.

> **Threat modeling AI/ML systems and dependencies**
>
> Here is a documented example of threat modeling for AI/ML systems:
>
> `https://learn.microsoft.com/en-us/security/engineering/threat-modeling-aiml`

However, although this tool provides us with suggestions, if we have a specific suspicion that is not conceptual or is not part of the baseline, we can create a hypothesis and use threat hunts in Sentinel to dive into the data and confirm before we come up with any mitigations. A quick demonstration of how to work with threat hunts in Sentinel is in *Chapter 9*.

Let us wrap up this book by reviewing our responsibilities when it comes to securing our services.

Reviewing the shared responsibility model for cloud security

When it comes to migrating to the cloud, some of our responsibilities transfer to the cloud provider, such as the responsibility to purchase and maintain hardware. This concept is vital for understanding who is responsible for what when it comes to securing data, applications, and infrastructure in the cloud. The exact division of responsibilities can vary depending on the type of cloud service model being used, including **infrastructure as a service (IaaS)**, **platform as a service (PaaS)**, **software as a service (SaaS)**, and the specific cloud service provider.

The responsibility model according to Microsoft is as follows for each category of services:

Responsibility	SaaS	PaaS	IaaS	On-Premises
Information and data	Customer	Customer	Customer	Customer
Devices (Mobile and PCs)	Customer	Customer	Customer	Customer
Accounts and identities	Customer	Customer	Customer	Customer
Identity and directory infrastructure	Shared	Shared	Shared	Customer
Applications	Provider	Shared	Shared	Customer
Network controls	Provider	Shared	Shared	Customer
Operating system	Provider	Provider	Shared	Customer
Physical hosts	Provider	Provider	Provider	Customer
Physical network	Provider	Provider	Provider	Customer
Physical datacenter	Provider	Provider	Provider	Customer

Table 10.1 – Shared responsibility model

The same division of responsibilities applies to security. It's essential to clearly understand the shared responsibility model with Azure and take the necessary steps to fulfill our part of the responsibility. Failure to do so can result in security vulnerabilities and compliance issues.

Let us review a general breakdown of the shared responsibility model for cloud security.

Exploring the cloud provider responsibilities

We will start with the cloud service provider responsibilities:

- **Physical security**: Cloud providers are responsible for securing the physical infrastructure, including data centers, servers, networking equipment, and physical access controls

- **Network infrastructure**: The cloud provider manages and secures the underlying network infrastructure, including firewalls, load balancers, and the virtualization layer

- **Hypervisor security**: In IaaS environments, cloud providers are responsible for securing the hypervisor layer that manages virtual machines

- **Data center security**: The physical security of data centers, including surveillance, access control, and environmental controls, falls under the cloud provider's responsibility

- **Core cloud services**: The core cloud services themselves, such as compute, storage, and networking, are maintained and secured by the cloud provider

It is also worth noting that this division of responsibilities can vary between different providers, and as services change or as changes are added, those responsibilities may change over time. Therefore, we must stay up to date with the latest security updates and practices to bridge any gaps and prevent future issues.

Let us review our own responsibilities.

Reviewing customers' responsibilities

Everything else is the customer's responsibility, which means us! More specifically, let us review the categories we need to keep in mind when securing our workloads:

- **Data**: Customers are responsible for securing their data and ensuring appropriate encryption, access controls, and data management practices. If data applies to a specific industry or local law, the customer is responsible for tracking all those regulations and taking appropriate action if necessary.

- **Operating systems**: For IaaS environments, customers are responsible for securing and patching the operating systems of virtual machines they deploy. That includes complete machine management, including licensing.

- **Applications**: Customers are responsible for securing and maintaining the security of the applications they build and deploy on cloud platforms at the code level. Although we might enable all security controls for the service hosting the application, any security vulnerabilities in the code might still provide unintended access to other services.

- **Identity and access management (IAM)**: Customers are responsible for managing user access, permissions, and authentication mechanisms, typically through identity and access management tools provided by the cloud provider.

- **Configuration management**: Configuring and maintaining security settings and configurations for cloud resources, such as firewall rules and security groups, is the customer's responsibility.

- **Compliance and data governance**: Ensuring compliance with industry regulations and data governance policies is the responsibility of the customer.

- **Security monitoring and incident response**: Customers are responsible for monitoring their cloud environments for security incidents and responding to any security breaches.

- **Backup and disaster recovery**: While cloud providers often provide some level of redundancy and availability, customers are responsible for their specific backup and disaster recovery plans.

It is important to remember that Azure and any cloud provider give us all the tools necessary to protect our resources, but we must do our part in securing and monitoring them. This is why we must always keep in mind the shared responsibility model. Each system is as strong as its weakest user, so let us make sure that we have done our best to prevent or at least detect and mitigate any issues as soon as possible.

Summary

Securing our resources is an iterative process. Although we may have completed all necessary steps to protect our resources, every update or new addition to our project might affect the overall security of the system. The first step is to maintain a security baseline for the resources we are using and the second is to develop a strategy to stay up to date using threat modeling frameworks to be proactive in mitigating possible threats. We saw the STRIDE methodology and the Microsoft Threat Modeling Tool, but there are more frameworks available. For example, we can base the strategy on the MITRE framework and tailor the steps for our organization.

Remember, security in the cloud is a shared responsibility. While Azure provides the tools and infrastructure to secure the cloud environment, it's up to us to secure our configurations and data.

Cybersecurity has a multi-faceted nature and adversaries are becoming more creative every day. As our cloud ecosystem evolves, attacks evolve with it, and we need to be vigilant to stay secure. I hope this book and the tools and services outlined here have equipped you with the knowledge to secure your existing Azure Machine Learning services and provided you with the insight to develop a strategy and stay one step ahead of any possible ML and non-ML attacks in the future.

Index

Packtpub.com

Subscribe to our online digital library for full access to over 7,000 books and videos, as well as industry leading tools to help you plan your personal development and advance your career. For more information, please visit our website.

Why subscribe?

- Spend less time learning and more time coding with practical eBooks and Videos from over 4,000 industry professionals
- Improve your learning with Skill Plans built especially for you
- Get a free eBook or video every month
- Fully searchable for easy access to vital information
- Copy and paste, print, and bookmark content

Did you know that Packt offers eBook versions of every book published, with PDF and ePub files available? You can upgrade to the eBook version at packtpub.com and as a print book customer, you are entitled to a discount on the eBook copy. Get in touch with us at customercare@packtpub.com for more details.

At www.packtpub.com, you can also read a collection of free technical articles, sign up for a range of free newsletters, and receive exclusive discounts and offers on Packt books and eBooks.

Other Books You May Enjoy

If you enjoyed this book, you may be interested in these other books by Packt:

Machine Learning with LightGBM and Python

Andrich van Wyk

ISBN: 978-1-80056-474-9

- Get an overview of ML and working with data and models in Python using scikit-learn
- Explore decision trees, ensemble learning, gradient boosting, DART, and GOSS
- Master LightGBM and apply it to classification and regression problems
- Tune and train your models using AutoML with FLAML and Optuna
- Build ML pipelines in Python to train and deploy models with secure and performant APIs
- Scale your solutions to production readiness with AWS Sagemaker, PostgresML, and Dask

Machine Learning for Emotion Analysis in Python

Allan Ramsay, Tariq Ahmad

ISBN: 978-1-80324-068-8

- Distinguish between sentiment analysis and emotion analysis
- Master data preprocessing and ensure high-quality input
- Expand the use of data sources through data transformation
- Design models that employ cutting-edge deep learning techniques
- Discover how to tune your models' hyperparameters
- Explore the use of naive Bayes, SVMs, DNNs, and transformers for advanced use cases
- Practice your newly acquired skills by working on real-world scenarios

Packt is searching for authors like you

If you're interested in becoming an author for Packt, please visit `authors.packtpub.com` and apply today. We have worked with thousands of developers and tech professionals, just like you, to help them share their insight with the global tech community. You can make a general application, apply for a specific hot topic that we are recruiting an author for, or submit your own idea.

Share Your Thoughts

Now you've finished *Machine Learning Security with Azure*, we'd love to hear your thoughts! Scan the QR code below to go straight to the Amazon review page for this book and share your feedback or leave a review on the site that you purchased it from.

`https://packt.link/r/1-805-12048-4`

Your review is important to us and the tech community and will help us make sure we're delivering excellent quality content.

Download a free PDF copy of this book

Thanks for purchasing this book!

Do you like to read on the go but are unable to carry your print books everywhere?

Is your eBook purchase not compatible with the device of your choice?

Don't worry, now with every Packt book you get a DRM-free PDF version of that book at no cost.

Read anywhere, any place, on any device. Search, copy, and paste code from your favorite technical books directly into your application.

The perks don't stop there, you can get exclusive access to discounts, newsletters, and great free content in your inbox daily

Follow these simple steps to get the benefits:

1. Scan the QR code or visit the link below

https://packt.link/free-ebook/9781805120483

2. Submit your proof of purchase
3. That's it! We'll send your free PDF and other benefits to your email directly

www.ingramcontent.com/pod-product-compliance
Lightning Source LLC
Chambersburg PA
CBHW080626060326
40690CB00021B/4827